THE SACRED COMPLEX OF KASHI

(A Microcosm of Indian Civilization)

About the Author

Lalita Prasad Vidyarthi, Professor and Head of the Department of Anthropology, Ranchi University is an internationally known authority on Anthropological and Ethnological Sciences. Widely travelled around the world, he has been closely associated with several institutions and professional bodies in India and the world-over. In adition to writing books, he supervises and conducts research projects.

Prof. Vidyarthi has presided over the International Union of Anthropological and Ethnological Science since 1973. The Xth International Congress of Anthropological and Ethnological Sciences is to be held in India this year.

Prof. Vidyarthi's books, *The Tribal Culture of India and Rise of Anthropology in India* have been received very well in India and abroad.

THE SACRED COMPLEX OF KASHI

(A Microcosm of Indian Civilization)

L.P. VIDYARTHI
MAKHAN JHA
B.N. SARASWATI

CONCEPT PUBLISHING COMPANY PVT. LTD.
NEW DELHI-110059

ISBN: 978-93-5594-633-1

Edition 2025

Published and Printed by

Concept
Since 1974

Concept Publishing Company Pvt. Ltd.
A/15-16, Commercial Block, Mohan Garden,
New Delhi-110059 (India)
T : 91-11-41101460
E : publishing@conceptpub.com, *W*: www.conceptpub.com

CONTENTS

LIST OF PLATES

LIST OF MAPS

LIST OF FIGURES

LIST OF TABLES

PREFACE

THE release of this report on the 'Sacred Complex of Kashi' marks another milestone in the current history of Indian Anthropology. It was in 1961 when my book on the *Sacred Complex of Hindu Gaya* was released. Though the book was of specialized nature dealing with a Hindu place of pilgrimage, it attracted the attention of scholars of civilization and complex societies. Written under the influence of Redfieldian approach to the study of civilization, this study was found useful in understanding the cultural role of the traditional town in context with the complexity of Indian Civilization. The descriptive terms and concepts used in this study proved of use to other researchers in this little-explored field, and their researches mentioned elsewhere further established the wider applicability of the terms and concepts proposed in this book.

Along with confirming similar phenomena elsewhere, the researches brought to light certain facts which needed to be examined in greater depth in Gaya as well as elsewhere. It was pointed out that the institution of pilgrimage, for example, deserved to be studied carefully from different angles and in all its ramifications (S. Narayan 1974, P. Chakravarti 1974)[1]. The various types of Holy Circuits[2] (B.N. Saraswati 1965), the social composition of the pilgrims, who wander from one part of India to another, their spiritual preparedness, inspirations and objectives, their sacred and secular experiences during the journey as well as the varied involvement to the sacred complex, and centres of pilgrimage, and then, their status, roles and spiritual involvement after their return to the villages, etc., deserved to be carefully studied. Current researches also brought to light varied types of 'secular incentives' linked with the Sacred Complexes[3] (Saraswati 1975). The use of the places of pilgrimage as trade and manufacturing centres, and use of the network of pilgrimage organisations and *mathas* by the *Gosains* for promoting trade evidently opened up new area of research to explore sacred-secular continuum in context with centres of civilization as well as regional and all India network provided by the institution of pilgrimage.[4] (Cohn, Bernard 1974).

In order to attempt a broader frame for describing a centre of Indian Civilization, and to make up a wider coverage, not attempted in the study of Gaya, I took up a 'group research' of this great traditional city of Kashi which is described as 'microcosm of Indian Civilization'. Methodologically, thus, if the study of Gaya provided the first basic structure for such an appraisal of civilization, the present study of Kashi provides the complete superstructure in all its details. In other words, several questions engaging the minds of the students of Indian Civilization find answers in this book to a great extent.

This study could be possible only because of initial encouragements and a generous grant made by the efforts of the Late Prof. D.R. Gadgil, the then Chairman of the Indian Council of Social Science Research. Shri J.P. Naik, the Member-Secretary of the Council also deserves my special thanks for helping me at all stages, and for his keen interest in the successful completion of this project.

In order to conduct field researches our field camp was established in Kashi for about two years. During this period, Dr. B.N. Saraswati, the Senior Deputy Director supervised the field operations, guided the field investigators and gave them the benefit of his long experiences in this field of research. The other members of team of researchers included Dr. M. Jha, Deputy Director, Dr. S. Narayan, Research Supervisor and four Research Officers (Shri M.N. Jha, Shri A.K. Sinha, Shri B.N. Sahay and Shri Onkar Prasad). The Research Supervisor and the Research Officers stayed in Varanasi for more than 20 months and carried on field work with considerable rigour, sincerity and caution. It was because of their meticulous painstaking and continued efforts that rich data could be collected, on the basis of which this brief report is being published. It is also our intention, given time and resources, we will release a few volumes of data volumes under their names.

During this prolonged spell of field work, we came in contact with large number of institutions and individuals who placed at our disposal their resources, their wisdom and insights, which enabled us to have adequate appraisal of the Sacred Complex of Kashi, in particular, and Indian Civilization in general. I am specially grateful to the sacred intellectuals and knowledgeable informants who participated in our weekly *goshthis* which we used to organise at our camp office. Some of the Newspapers, specially *Aaj* and *Janavani*, gave wide coverage about our plans of research and, thus, helped in creating helpful atmosphere for our research work.

At the level of the analysis of data we had the occasion of receiving feed back from several distinguished scholars engaged in the study of Sacred Complexes and Indian Civilization. I am particularly grateful to Dr. Basudeo Upadhyay, Dr. K.N. Sahay, Dr. V.S. Upadhyay, Dr. Manmohan Mahapatra, Dr. Prafulla Chakraborty, Mr. B.N. Goswami, Mr. S.C. Morab, Dr. B.K. Roy Burman and Dr. B.C. Agrawal who provided supplementary data, and critical appraisals during the symposium on Sacred Complex in India organized in Ranchi in the last week of September 1973.

The discussions in another seminar on the Social and Cultural Life of Kashi held at Varanasi in January 1973 under the auspices of Manab Vigyan Mandir also helped us in reviewing our materials on Kashi from different and more critical angles. For this I am grateful to the sponsors and participants of the seminar.

At different points of time we received secretarial assistance from several persons in Varanasi, Simla and Ranchi, and we are thankful for their help. I am specially thankful to Shri Ram Autar Prasad for typing the final draft and Shri Raj Kumar for preparing the illustrations.

REFERENCES

[1] For detail see Dr. S. Narayan's "Pilgrimage to Kashi" in L.P. Vidyarthi and M. Jha (eds.), Symposium on the Sacred Complex in India, Ranchi, Council of Social and Cultural Research, Bihar, pp. 20-22, 1974 and Dr. P. Chakravarti's "Some Observances on the Pilgrims and their Pilgrimage : A Case Study at Tarakeshwar", in L.P. Vidyarthi and M. Jha (eds.) Symposium on the Sacred Complex in India, Ranchi, Council of Social and Cultural Research, Bihar, pp. 104-115, 1974.

[2] For detail see Dr. B.N. Saraswati's "The Holy Circuit of Nimsar", Journal of Social Research, Vol. VIII, No. 2, 1965.

[3] For detail see Dr. B.N. Saraswati's "Studying Sacred Complex in Kashi", in L.P. Vidyarthi and M. Jha (eds.) Symposium on the Sacred Complex in India, Ranchi, Council of Social and Cultural Research, Bihar, pp. 6-13.

[4] Refer to Dr. Bernard S. Cohn's paper on "The Role of the Gosains in the Economy of Eighteenth and Nineteenth Century of Upper India" in L.P. Vidyarthi and M. Jha's (eds.) Symposium on the Sacred Complex in India, Ranchi, Council of Social and Cultural Research, Bihar, pp. 88-95.

INTRODUCTION

Works So Far :

ALTHOUGH there was some historical description of Hindu places of pilgrimage by Indologists, orientalists and travellers, before the middle of this century, it was not until the early 'fifties that the cultural analysis of these places began to appear. Gaya was perhaps the first to attract the attention of an anthropologist (L.P. Vidyarthi 1953-54). Bhubaneswar, another sacred centre of ancient origin, was also taken up (Bose 1955-56) in the first phase of the anthropological study of holy places in India. Both these studies were inspired in many ways by the late Prof. Robert Redfield. The work on Gaya, which began with the study of the community of sacred specialists called Gayawals, gradually developed into a total study of the sacred complex (Vidyarthi 1961). Although Redfield's (1955) concept of civilization as a complex structure of great and little traditions, and his collaborator Milton Singer's (1955) definition of 'cultural centre', 'cultural specialists', 'cultural performance', etc., (which he attempted in his study of the city of Madras), and McKim Marriott and B.S. Cohn's (1958) concept of 'networks and centres' in integration of Indian civilization offered useful guidelines to this study, the field situation in Gaya was such that it necessitated certain modifications in their concepts. In Gaya an attempt was also made, for the first time, to approach a Hindu place of pilgrimage as a dimension of Indian civilization; and for this the following hypotheses were specially examined:

1. That the sacred complex—the sacred centres, the sacred performances, and the sacred specialists—of a Hindu place of pilgrimage reflected a level of continuity, compromise, combination between great and little traditions.

2. That the sacred specialists of a place of pilgrimage maintain a distinct style of life and transmit certain elements of the great traditions to the rural population of India by popularizing certain texts, by organizing pilgrimage and by officiating as the ritual temple priests.

3. That the sacred complex in general and the sacred specialists in particular have been in the process of modification and transformation as a result of general development in the larger universe of Hindu civilization of which they are a part.

The main finding of this study was that the sacred complex in Hindu Gaya is based on a trichotomic inter-relation of the phenomena described as the sacred geography, the sacred performances, and the sacred specialists. The complex network of relationship which connects Hindu Gaya with other centres and regions of India was also brought into light.

Following the publication of the *Sacred Complex in Hindu Gaya* (Vidyarthi 1961) some Indian anthropologists, particularly those associated with the Department of Anthropology : Ranchi University, got interested in the study of sacred centres. Shortly after the publication of this monograph, two articles—one dealing with the institution of pilgrimage in Nimsar, a *Pauranic Tirtha*, and another describing the temple organization in Goa—appeared in quick succession (B.N. Saraswati 1962 a, b). Later in 1967, the Anthropological Survey of India launched a programme to study the complex religious institutions at a number of sacred centres, such as Kamakhya in Assam (also independently by M.C. Goswami) and Kalighat in Calcutta (S.C. Sinha 1970), Chamundesvari temple in Mysore (B.B. Goswami and S.G. Morab 1968, 1970, 1975), and Kashi (Sinha and Saraswati 1969). Two more sacred centres, Bhubaneswar (M. Mahapatra 1971) and Puri (N. Patnaik 1964) were studied under the guidance of Cora DuBois with a view to describing the structure and change in the organization of holy places. The sacred geography of Gupta Kashi was also studied (Mahapatra 1974). Tarakeshwar temple in West Bengal (Chakravarti 1974) and many temples in the South and elsewhere in India attracted the attention of anthropologists and non-anthropologists.[1]

But none of these studies has attempted a holistic view of the sacred complex; these studies were primarily concerned with the description and analysis of some specific religious institutions, such as the institution of pilgrimage, the organization of ascetics, and the organization of temple functionaries. Two students of the department of anthropology, Ranchi University came forward to study Janakpur in Nepal (M. Jha 1969) and Deoghar (S. Narayan 1972) for their doctoral dissertations. The preliminary observation of the sacred complex in Rajgir (Narayan 1967), Ayodhya (V.S. Upadhyay 1974), Puri (Jha 1974) has also been made by these students and teachers of the Department. One more student (Sreshtha) has been assigned to study the sacred complex in Pasupatinath in Nepal. In all these studies the Gaya model has been followed. They have shown that the findings of the study of the sacred complex in Gaya have a wider applicability, although certain regional variations in the sacred performance as well as in the organization of sacred specialists have been observed. This model was further applied to the civilizational study of Ratanpur, a Pauranic town of an ancient Hindu kingdom in Madhya Pradesh (Jha 1970). Thus, the study of sacred complex has become over the last two decades one of the major activities of Indian anthropologists.

Gleaning through the works on different aspects of Indian civilization that have made some progress in the last two decades, one becomes aware of the necessity of re-examining the concept of sacred complex not only in terms of its applicability in cross regional situations but also in the nature of the things that have been presented in respect of its textual categories and contextual transformations. The reappraisal of the concept is most desirable for understanding the dimension of Indian civilization. For such a study Kashi which is called the microcosm of Indian civilization is the most appropriate place. Accordingly, in 1972, a comprehensive study of the Sacred Complex in Kashi was taken up under the auspices of the Indian Council of Social Science Research.

PERSPECTIVE

There have been numerous recorded observations on Kashi[2] by Indologists and travellers, and recently by geographers and modern historians. The Anthropological Survey of India was the first to undertake a systematic study of the sacred complex in Kashi—as reflected in the organizations of temples, ascetics and pundits (Sinha and Saraswati 1970); but for some unspecified reasons it subsequently abandoned the project after studying the organization of ascetics (Sinha and Saraswati 1969). Saraswati, however, continued his work in Kashi and completed fieldwork on the pundits under the auspices of the Indian Institute of Advanced Study; but, later, he switched on to the study of the total system view and the self-identifiable cultural traditions of Kashi (Saraswati 1975). Thus in the series of study of the sacred complex which the Survey had planned to bring out the important one, namely the study of temples and shrines, was left unattempted. Thanks to the Indian Council of Social Science Research that it has now been possible for us to examine that untouched aspect of Kashi's sacred traditions.

Four nodal points in Sacred

With a view to exploring the various facets of Kashi's sacred traditions we decided to take up four nodal points from where the pageant of the sacred complex in Kashi can be viewed at a glance:

(*1*) The cult of the *Tirthas;*
(*2*) The cult of Vishwanath;
(*3*) The cult of the Ganges; and
(*4*) The cult of the *Shmashan.*

The main areas of research and some of the questions which were taken up in this study may be briefly mentioned as follows:

(1) The Cult of the Tirthas

The sacred myth about Kashi has been described in the *Matsya Purana*, the *Vayu Purana*, the *Skanda Purana* and various other *Puranas* and *upa-Puranas*. The fourth chapter of the *Skanda Purana*, known as 'Kashi-Khanda', gives the full description of Kashi-kshetra indicating the names and locations of all the *tirthas*. It is also claimed by the knowledgeable sacred intellectuals that the present Kashi is the one described in the *Puranas* and that all the *tirthas* in Kashi are today located exactly in the manner described in the ancient scriptures. The archaeologists, on the other hand, claim that modern Kashi is of recent development and that ancient Kashi lies buried in the mounds scattered near Rajghat, at some distance. To what extent these claims stand anthropological test ? To what extent the oral tradition has been truly supported by textual tradition ? How do the people hold this tradition? Is there a continuity in the Pauranic geography of Kashi? If so, how this continuity has been maintained?

According to the 'Kashi-Khanda', the Kashi-kshetra is divided into three *khandas* (segments) : (*1*) Viseshwara khanda, (*2*) Omkar khanda, and (*3*) Kedar khanda. How the boundaries of these segments have been marked or maintained ? What are the myths associated with these Khandas ?

The various *tirthas* in Kashi are connected with one another by sacred Pauranic myths. Can these *tirthas* be linked up today—organizationally or attributionally—as a single entity ? What are the functions of the sacred myths in organizing pilgrimage to Kashi ? Could these *tirthas* be arranged in a hierarchy of importance (as reflected in sacred Pauranic myths and/or popularly exhibited in terms of pilgrims' visit to the shrines) ?

A number of *tirthas* in Kashi has been abandoned/occupied by the householders for seculaı use. Who are these householders ? How have they responded to their conscience ? How have the religious minded people of Kashi reacted to it ?

Social ecology of the *tirthas* provided heterogeneous contents, so far as local linguistic and caste groups are concerned. Whether these *tirthas* are managed on local patronage ? To what extent are they relevant to the all-India pilgrims visiting Kashi ? Could these be regarded as centres of local worship ? Or, could we arrange them in various orders of worship (*tirthas* of local importance, *tirthas* worshipped by devotees from various *Mohallas* in Kashi, and *tirthas* worshipped by pilgrims from U.P. villages, by all-India pilgrims) ?

(2) The Cult of Vishwanath

Vishwanath is the presiding god of Kashi. But there are four Vishwanath temples in the city: (*1*) Adi Vishwanath, (*2*) Golden temple of Vishwanath, (*3*) Naya Vishwanath, and (*4*) Vishwanath temple in the Banaras Hindu University. Of these the first two are related to the *Joytirlinga* (self-created effulgent lingam) complex. The first temple, Adi Vishwanath, claims to be the original place of *Jyotirlinga* whose temple was demolished by the Muslim rulers. The second temple claims to have enshrined the original *Jyotirlinga* which was reinstalled by Maharani Ahilyabai of Indore in 1777 and whose temple was gilded by Maharaja Ranjit Singh in 1839. The third temple of Vishwanath was constructed with a view to preserving the prestine purity of god Vishwanath whose *linga* was supposedly polluted by the entry of Harijans in 1956. The fourth temple at the Banaras Hindu University is famous for its collosal structure open to all regardless of caste, sect and religion of the visitor.

That the place where the *Jyotirlinga* of Vishwanath was once enshrined continues to be a place of worship, although the present *linga* does not claim to be the *Jyotirlinga*. Why is this place still worshipped in the name of Adi Vishwanath ? What does this signify ? That the golden temple of Vishwanath has acquired popularity as the one enshrining the original piece of *Jyotirlinga*. It is hard to establish historically that the present *linga* is the one that has survived Muslim invasion. What is that which has led the people to uphold such belief ? The origin of Naya Vishwanath temple indicates that the orthodox Brahmins have devalued the god in the golden Vishwanath temple, but the latter continues to enjoy popularity. Why ? Does it show that the concept of sacred has changed ? That the fourth Vishwanath temple presents entirely a new situation; it is open to Muslims and Christians as well. Its popularity seems to be based largely on its architectural magnificence. But is this all for which the pilgrims go there ? From these questions it arises : Whether the Hindu concept of sacred is *sthanapradhan* (importance of place) or *vastupradhan* (importance of object) ? What sustains the sacred myth of *Jyotirlinga* ? Whether the temple of Vishwanath presents a case of hierarchy in the sacred ? Whether and how the concept of sacred is changing in Hindu society ?

The first two temples claim the merit of *Jyotirlinga* Vishwanath in a way which should naturally divide people on the question of treating sacred as manifest in a place (*sthan*) or in an object (*vastu*). The third temple demolishes their claim by presenting an orthodox view of treating a sacred object. The fourth overruns the claims put forth by all the three and presents a new concept of sacred which is all-embracing. Under the circumstances when each of these four temples presents four different concepts of sacred the pilgrims visiting Kashi are apparently led to a situation of cultural conflict, taking them in four directions. But will this lead them to utter confusion and total loss of faith ? Is this a case of Hindu society being led towards a fatal crash or an internal crisis of faith in transcendentalism which has all along been a source of its vitality ? Or is this a case of resilient Hindu society ? To what extent all the four Vishwanath temples differ among themselves on the processes of elaboration, idealization and perpetuation of Hindu sacred tradition in depth and spread ?

(3) The Cult of the Ganges

The uniqueness of the Ganges in Kashi, as common Hindus believe, lies in its physical form—its being *uttaravahini* and *ardhachandrakar*. That in other places its natural course is from north to south, in Kashi it flows from south to north. That its crescent form symbolises the moon brightening the *jata* (matted hair) of the Lord Siva. That it clings to the city of Vishwanath throughout the year. That dirt and filth of the city are drained into the river Ganges and yet the holy water remains unpolluted, healthy and holy. That Kashi without the Ganges is like a body without life, without soul.

That such feelings for the Ganges are verily reflected in the ritual behaviour pattern of the pilgrims. That most of the important rituals are performed on the *ghats* of the Ganges. What are these rituals and to what aspect of life it covers ? Whether the rituals performed at the *ghats* are largely purificatory ? To what extent these rituals are endowed with supreme religious merits, such as *punya* (religious merits) and *moksha* (salvation) ? Whether or not the river Ganges in Kashi forms a sacred complex independent of the cult of Vishwanath ?

That the sacred intellectuals—ascetics and pundits—as also priests and common Hindus live close to the Ganges. That the sacred territory of Kashi is formed along the course of the Ganges, and that the sacredness of a place in Kashi is dependent on its proximity to the river Ganges. That almost all important shrines of Kashi are located within this sacred territory. That the Princely Hindu States from all over India have built here *ghats* and magnificent buildings along the Ganges. What is that which attracts people to settle closer to the Ganges ? To what extent this concept of sacred territory has integrated the people from diverse linguistic regions, sects and professions ? What are the secular networks of integration that have developed mainly on account of sacred requirements ? How far the cultural landscape along the Ganges is an art of the sacred ? To what extent it exhibits the sense of aesthetics in the cultivation of the sacred ?

That the people who earn their livelihood by performing rituals at the *ghats* call themselves Gangaputra (sons of the

Ganges). That the boatmen who ply boats in the Ganges also regard themselves as the sons of the Ganges. To what extent this sacred mother has been able to keep her two sons together as sacerdotalists ? Whether the boatmen who are socially inferior to the Brahmin priests have been able to raise their position in the sacred territory of the Ganges ? Whether or not they have been given a role in the Brahmanic ritual complex ? If so, whether they are allowed to act as priests ritually on a par with the Brahmin Gangaputra ?

Who are the people perpetuating myth about the Ganges ? What modes do they adopt ? Whether the sacred myth about the Ganges finds its support from the cult of Vishwanath ?

(4) The Cult of the Shmashan

Kashi has been referred to in the *Puranas* as Mahashmashana —the 'great cremation place', the city of Siva, the *Mahakal* (the great destroyer). But the 'great destroyer' in this city of Anandavana is also *kalyankari* (auspicious). For, those, who leave their mortal bodies here, at once attain *moksha*. The belief is so deep-rooted that even when a person dies outside Kashi—in some cases, thousands of miles away—his dead body is brought for cremation at the Manikarnika or Harishchandra ghat.

There are several ways to attain *moksha*. While the other *tirthas* are the bestower of *punya* which finally leads the pilgrims to the path of *moksha*, Kashi straightway assures *moksha* to everyone dying within its precincts How far has this belief added importance to Kashi as a *tirtha*, excelling all the other *tirthas* in India ? When did this concept of 'Kashi—the Mokshadayini' appear in the scriptures ? The Buddha for the first time preached the concept of *Nirvana* at Sarnath, 20 kms north of Kashi. The Brahmanic concept of 'Mokshadayini Kashi' might have developed as a challenge thrown to the Buddhist doctrine of *Nirvana*, and hence it is likely to be a post-Buddha concept. But at any rate this has to be ascertained. One must also examine the concept of death as the most 'auspicious one'. How has it come into Indian scriptural traditions ?

If the sacred death at Kashi is the bestower of *moksha*, how have the Hindu scriptures accounted for *pap* (sin) and *punya* as the deciding factors in man's liberation ? How do people explain the theory of *karma* contextually ? To what extent this has affected social behaviour of an individual ? How do people of Kashi conceptualize death ? Whether the concept of 'sacred death' has brought about any change in the usual Hindu mortuary rites ?

There are two burning *ghats* in Kashi : one is the most celebrated Manikarnika which is believed to be the permanent abode of Siva and his consort Parvati, and another one is named after the Pauranic King, the *satyavadi* (one who ever tells the truth) Harishchandra who is known to have sold himself to King of Kashi to serve him as a chandal the lowliest of untouchables in the Hindu society. Why has been Harishchandra, for serving as a chandal here, given such an important and crucial role in man's achievement of *moksha* ? How and when did these Doms (chandals) become the custodian of the 'sacred fire' ? Is this belief held by all sections of the Hindus ? Is this a local custom ? Has it got scriptural sanction ? How does Hindu society rationalize this paradox in its value system ?

Cremation *ghats* are visited by *yogis* and ascetics of various orders for acquiring 'power' and gaining transcendental knowledge. How does Hindu society treat the concepts of 'sacred' and 'profane' ?

CONSUMERS OF SACRED : CITIZENS AND PILGRIMS

The foregoing description relates to the organization of sacred and to some extent it also provides a ground for understanding the nature of the sacred. But unless the consumers of the sacred—the citizens of Kashi and the pilgrims—are examined in the context of their participation in sacred complex the treatment of this subject will remain incomplete and inconclusive. The levels of their participation have to be carefully examined, particularly on caste and regional basis. This can be done by recording (*a*) their daily routine, specifying their activities related to sacred performances, and the distribution of time devoted to sacred/secular activities, and (*b*) their cultural bio-data.

To record the cultural bio-data of the citizens the following points may be covered : What are the places of pilgrimage the informant has visited ? Does he/she follow any pilgrimage cycle ? Where is the level of his/her existing knowledge of the sacred geography of Kashi—the beliefs related to the *tirthas* of Kashi ? What are the sources of such cultural knowledge ? Whether he/

she is a member of some religious or academic institutions, or of political parties ? Whether he/she has the requisite knowledge of the sacred performances ? Whether or not the informant's sacred performance is confined to the sacred centres of his/her locality ? Whether his/her association with sacred centres is governed by linguistic, locational, or purely religious considerations ? In addition to some of these questions, a few more specific questions are relevant to the pilgrims from outside : How was he/she motivated to make a pilgrimage to Kashi ? Whether he/she had read/heard the *mahatmya* (glory) of Kashi before undertaking this pilgrimage ? In the present visit, what new things about the *mahatmya* of Kashi have been added to his/her knowledge ? What are the sources of such knowledge, and how was it acquired ? What is the level of the informant's existing knowledge of the sacred geography of Kashi and the required sacred performances ? How much money the informant has actually spent on the performance of rituals, feeding Brahmins and beggars, and on buying ritual articles, sacred literature and articles of secular use ?

While some work has been done on pilgrims and pilgrimage, practically nothing has been said so far on the participation of the common citizens in the sacred complex in a *tirtha*. Jha (1971) has given an interesting account of the *kutis* (abode of ascetics) and the participation of ascetics as a special group of people; there is a need to examine both specialists and generals. There has also been a tendency to generalize the behaviour of the pilgrims. The implicit assumption is that all those who visit a place of pilgrimage interact fully and equally with the sacred phenomena operating at the sacred centre. While this can be true with Mecca and Jerusalem, one can hardly find it in a Hindu place of pilgrimage. What is important in the study of Hindu sacred complex is to find out how the *tirthas* integrate diverse cultural traditions into a common bond of civilization. This can be done most fruitfully by comparing the culturally patterned behaviour of both citizens and pilgrims in Kashi.

HYPOTHESES

Some of the hypotheses which have been tested in the study of sacred complex in Kashi are the following

1. That the sacred complex developed in the study of Gaya

(Vidyarthi, 1961) is widely applicable to the *Pauranic Tirthas* of India;

2. That each of the three elements of sacred complex, namely, the sacred geography, the sacred specialists, and the sacred performances is formed on the scriptural canons upheld by a long and continuous tradition of sacred myth;

3. That in the process of its transmission the scriptural sacred myth has acquired omnivorous character—guiding varieties of textual and oral traditions;

4. That there is a continuity in the Pauranic sacred tradition in *tirthas*;

5. That the *tirthas* of India are culturally distinguishable from one another as local, regional and all-India centres of sacred complex;

6. That such a spatial distinction may be located even in a single *tirtha* of all-India importance, such as in Kashi.

OPERATION OF THE PROJECT

Field work

The project on the sacred complex in Kashi was initiated on February 1, 1972 under the overall guidance of Professor L.P. Vidyarthi. The organization of the research personnel consisted of anthropologists, as follows

Hon. Director. . . . . Professor L.P. Vidyarthi
Hon. Dy. Directors. . . . . . B.N. Saraswati
and
M. Jha
Supervisor . . . . S. Narayan
Research Assistants . . . . M.N. Jha
Omkar Prasad
B.N. Sahay
Arbind Kumar Sinha

The field investigation continued for nearly 20 months at a stretch when all the four Research Assistants, the Supervisor, and the Deputy Director, Saraswati, stayed in the field. In course of the field-work, the Director made several trips to Varanasi to discuss the problems with the field staff at various levels of investigation. M. Jha, Deputy Director of the Project, also joined the discussions on the problems of field-work on two such occasions.

By the end of February 1972, schedules and questionnaires were prepared. A modified form of open-ended questionnaire (see appendix I) for interviewing the pilgrims and the citizens, and also for according the details of the *Tirthas* was used. Each of the Research Assistants was assigned to study one of the four nodal points in sacred, namely, the cult of the *tirthas*, the cult of Viswanath, the cult of the Ganges, and the cult of Shmashan; and on each of these topics detailed schedules (see appendix I) were prepared. The special feature of our schedule was that it not only enlisted the items to be covered but also highlighted the contextual problems and theoretical questions (as raised in the earlier section) that engaged our mind on the problems of sacred complex. The idea was to help the researcher clarify his conception of the subject and to institute right kind of enquiries on the items specified in the schedule.

Some of the methods of field-work which were specially employed for this study may be briefly recorded as follows:

(1) Participant observation—For making participant observations the field research personnel went on pilgrimage to the shrines, bathed in the Ganges frequently, and participated in the functions of the temples. On two occasions they also accompanied the pilgrims on the Panchakosi holy circumambulation.

(2) Establishing rapport—The Research Assistants made best use of their talents in establishing rapport with their informants. For instance, one of them, Sinha, who had considerable experience of social work under the guidance of Sarvodaya leaders, continued to participate in the activities of the local *Shantisena*, as and when time permitted, and thus gained popularity all over the city. Another person, M.N. Jha who happened to be a Brahmin, sometimes acted as domestic priest of his informants. Prasad and Sahay, who were good singers, participated in the music and drama programme organized by their informants. Thus, they were able to establish close friendly relationship with their informants in a very short time.

(3) Assemblies of informants—The *goshthis* or the assemblies of informants were organized periodically for group interview as well as for making the informants feel that they have a say in the programmes of the project. Two kinds of *goshthis* were organized--one which was organized in the office of the Project when specific topics were discussed and the informants contributed

their opinion; the general theme of the Project was discussed in another kind of *goshthis* which were organized in different *mohallas* of the city. The details of these *goshthis* were covered by the local newspapers; that provided wider publicity. Saraswati who was working in Kashi on ascetics and pandits for the last five years had already established contacts with learned informants, and that made the job of the research personnel of this project comparatively easy.

On the various sacred shrines, 375 were surveyed. The selection was made on the basis of their *Pauranic* reference and contemporary significance. Among the pilgrims and citizens, a sample of five hundred each, was drawn up by purposive method. Detailed participant observations were made of the holy circumambulation of Kashi *Kshetra* on two occasions. Besides empirical work, data were collected also from scriptural sources, historical records, and reports by missionaries and travellers. Life histories of the sacred specialists, citizens and pilgrims were collected, and their geneological tables were also prepared.

Data were collected on field notebooks, and subsequently on 6″ X 9″ cards. The supervisor examined the data before they were finally written out on the cards. For each item of the schedule and for each informant separate card was used, so that at the time of analysis all the answers on a particular item could be put together. Thus, all the data on cards were classified at the first screening itself.

Processing of data

In the last phase of the Project, the field staff was brought back to Ranchi for processing their data. In order to bring out a comparable view of Kashi's sacred complex, each of them was asked to arrange and analyse their data under the following heads: the sacred geography, the sacred performances, the sacred specialists, and pilgrims and pilgrimage.

A workshop on the Sacred Complex in India was organized in Ranchi in September 1973, when the field staff presented summaries of their findings. This workshop provided them with an opportunity to exchange notes and views with those who had first-hand knowledge of the sacred complex in other parts of the country. After this intellectual exercise the Research Assistants submitted their final reports according to their respective assignments.

Report writing

The reports submitted by the Research Assistants were largely descriptive in nature and replete with unwarranted details. They were rewritten and recasted in the format used for writing up the *Sacred Complex in Hindu Gaya.* This onerous job was performed single handed by M. Jha; Saraswati joined him only later to work on the second and the final drafts. The Director and both the Deputy Directors sat together periodically for preparing the three draft reports. The present report is thus an outcome of a joint venture.

REFERENCES

1 For details, see Goswami and Morab (1970).
2 For details, see Upadhyay, B. (1974).

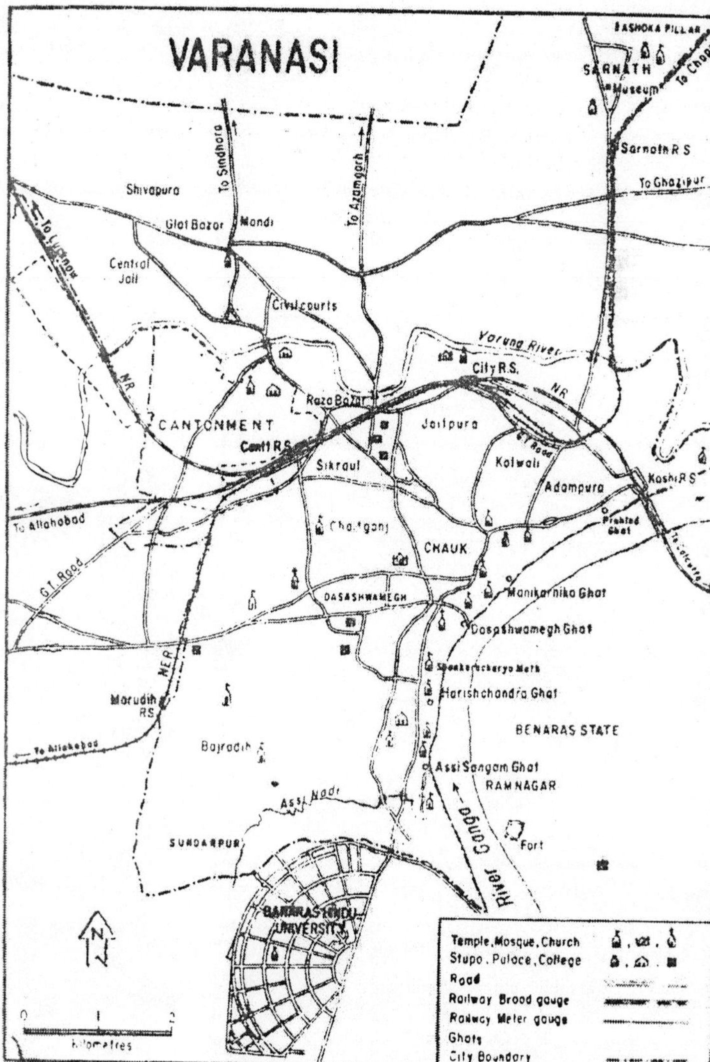

(*Facing Page 24*)

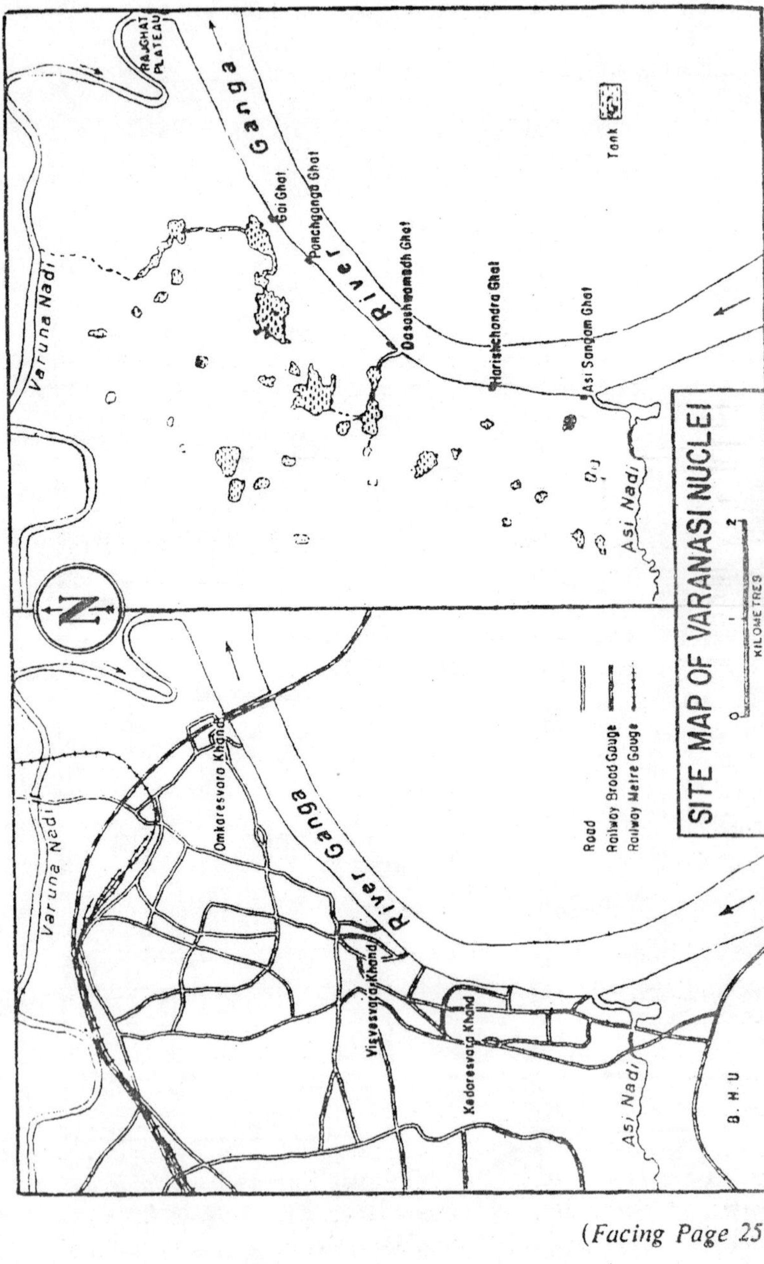

(*Facing Page 25*)

Chapter I

THE SACRED GEOGRAPHY

PAURANIC AND HISTORIC KASHI

KASHI finds prominent mention in various sacred scriptures, such as the *Puranas*, the *Smritis*, the *Nibandhas*, the epics, and the Buddhist and the Jain literature.

Of the *Puranas*, which have described Kashi at some length, mention may be made of the *Agni Purana* (112), the *Padma Purana* (14.191), the *Kurma Purana* (1, 31, 35), the *Matsya Purana* (191), the *Linga Purana* (92), the *Skanda Purana* (4) etc. The fourth chapter of the *Skanda Purana*, known as the '*Kashi khanda*', is exclusively devoted to the *Mahatmya* of Kashi, giving a very detailed description of all the sacred shrines located in Kashi-kshetra (area of Kashi).

Of the *Nibandhas* or the digests describing Kashi as the *tirthasthali*, mention may be made of the *Tirthakalpataru* (particularly the *Tirthavivechankhanda*) written by Lakshmidhar; the *Tirthalisetu* of Narayan Bhatta; the *Chaturvarga Chintamani* of Vachaspati; the *Tirthayatra Vidhi Tattva* of Raghunandan; the *Tirtha-Prakash* by Mitra and Mishra, etc. In all these *Nibandhas* the authors have described the Kashi *tirthas* as the place where both this worldly and the other worldly desires are fulfilled. The modes of performing a pilgrimage have also been indicated in these digests.

Kashi finds mention both in the *Mahabharata* and the *Ramayana*. The 'Anushasana Parva' (108) and the 'Vinaya Parva' (82) of the *Mahabharata* specially record the importance of the *tirtha yatra*, placing it even above the sacrifice. The *Mahabharata* ('Anushasana' chapter XIII) mentions Varanasi as the *tirtha* situated at the confluence of the Ganges and the Gomati. The *Ramayana* (chapter LVIII) describes Varanasi as the capital of Kashi.

In the *Jataka* stories (third century B.C.) Brahmadatta frequently figures as the king of Kashi. The *Udalak Jataka* and the *Somanda Jataka* (532) refer to Kashi Raj in connection with territorial disputes.

Of the Jain works, special reference may be made of the *Kalpasutra* which records that Kashi is the birth place of the *Tirthankaras*.

Kashi's historical reference may be shifted from epigraphic data. Kashi has been described as the Pauranic sacred centre in the Saranath Inscriptions of Kanishka (A.D. 81). Large number of copper plates have been discovered at the Kamouli, which are popularly known as the Kamouli records belonging to the Gahadwal rulers (tenth and eleventh centuries A.D.). The Gahadwal rulers attached great importance to Kashi, made very generous donations of land and other properties, the details of which are mentioned in the Kamouli copper plates. In his famous drama the *Prabodha Chandrodaya* (particularly in Act IV), Pandit Kishan Mishra (eleventh century A.D.) mentions the temple of Adikeshava constructed by the Gahadwals at the confluence of the Varuna and the Ganges. The South Indian records from Karnataka (eleventh century A.D.), also mention Kashi as one of the famous *tirthas* of India.

In addition to these historical records there are a large number of travelogues, of which mention may be made of two by J. Eween, both on Kashi (1886), M.A Shering's Report on *The Sacred City of Hindus* (1868), E.B. Havell's short book on Benaras (1905) and also a very important work on *Benaras* and *Saranath* by A.S. Altekar (1937).

KASHI : THE CULTURAL CITY

Location

Kashi, also known as Benaras or Varanasi is situated at 25.18 degrees N (latitude) and 83.1 degrees E (longitude).

The city is broadly divided into two unequal *mahals* (portions) known as *pucca mahal* and *kachcha mahal.* The *pucca mahal* is that old portion of the city in which the houses are of masonry—a perfect labyrinth of lofty buildings separated from one another by the narrow stone-paved alleys. The *kachcha mahal* consists of the interior and the lower areas of the city. These *mahals* are further sub-divided into 11 municipal wards: Chowk, Dasashwamedh, Adampura, Kotwali, Bhelpura, Jaitpura, Chetganj, Sikraul, Sheopur, Saranath and Nagawa.

The road which connects the Banaras Hindu University and the Raj Ghat bridge, through Godolia, Chowk, Maidagin, Visessarganj and Machchaodari, marks the city into two parts. The area between this silvery road and the Ganges forms the heart of Kashi's cultural complex.

Population

The city of Kashi has witnessed extension both in terms of area and population. The total area of the city is about 28.5 square miles. It is one of the most crowded cities of India with an average density of 72 persons per acre (1951 Census). In 1971 the total population of the city was 5,88,608. In 1951 there were about 43,865 houses within the municipal limits of the city; today the number of houses has gone up to over 45,000.

Cultural Area

The major concentration of the population, both Hindus and Muslims, is in the *pucca mahal.* Even within this area the maximum concentration is in two wards, namely the Dashashwamedh and the Chowk. The *pucca mahal,* particularly these two wards, is a place for varieties of sacred and secular activities. The famous Vishwanath shrine is located in this area. The narrow *gali* which leads to the Vishwanath temple is the main fancy shopping centre of the city. Visessarganj, which is named after the original shrine of Visheshwara, is the main *mandī* (wholesale grain trade) of Varanasi. Between Vishwanath *gali* and Visessarganj there is the wholesale market for Banarsi *sarees*, and there are also several shops of varieties of arts and crafts for which Benaras has been famous through the history. It is also in this area that important Sanskrit *pathashalas* and *mathas*, and all the sacred bathing ghats are located. This is also the home of learned pandits, priests, ascetics, men of literature and artists as well as of *thugs*, *gundas* and prostitutes. In brief this area represents the core of Kashi's sacred and secular life, in other words, the total personality of this great city.

The *pucca mahal* is organized into a number of cultural pockets, each dominated by a particular linguistic group of

Brahmins. Thus, there are the *mohallas* of the Tamilians, the Kannadas, the Andhraites, the Bengalis, the Maithils, the Nepalis, the Gujaratis, and the Maharashtrians. Brahmins from Kashmir, Punjab, Sindh, Rajasthan and various other places are also sporadically found in this culturally heterogeneous region. Of course, the local Brahmins and Brahmins from different parts of Uttar Pradesh are met with everywhere in the city. Khatris, Agarwals, Ahirs, Domes, and various other castes are sporadically distributed in the city. Buddhists, Jains and Sikhs are important element in Kashi's population. A few Christians are also there; but Muslims are numerically significant.

KASHI : THE CITY OF SHRINES

Spatial Classification of Shrines

Sacred Centres

In a Hindu place of pilgrimage the structure of the sacred centres may be single or multiple.

In Kashi, there is a popular saying: '*Kankar kankar main Shankar*', which means that each and every pebble of Kashi is god Shankar; hence the entire Kashi is sacred. Yet, there are almost innumerable numbers of sacred shrines located all over the Kashi-kshetra.

The number of single sacred centre, as recorded in the present study, is 40. Most of these shrines are located in the villages along the Panchakosi route, making holy circumambulation of the Kashi-kshetra. Important among these are Chamunda devi, Veerabhadreshwar, Unmattabhairava, etc.

The multiple sacred centres are those where more than one sacred structures are built up within the precinct of a shrine dedicated to a specific deity. The number of such shrines is very large. Most important in this category of shrines is the famous Vishwanath temple where in addition to the main Shivalinga of Vishwanath, there are a number of deities and godlings, such as Abhimukteshwar, Sringaragauri, Vishnu, Lakshmi, Kali, Annapurna, Hanuman, about 100 Shiva *lingas* of various shapes and sizes. In the Annapurna temple, besides the presiding deity Annapurna, there are the icons of Shiva, Surya, Ganesh, Vishnu, Lakshmi, Hanuman, Kubereshwar, etc.

There are in Kashi both Brahmanic and non-Brahmanic

sacred centres, though in the association of Chatpatimata, which is a known non-Brahmanic deity, many Brahmanic deities, such as Shiva, Parvati, Durga, etc., are also found. In such multiple sacred centres, the sacred performances are, however, made as per the Brahmanic traditions.

In the predominantly Brahmanic multiple sacred centres sometimes a non-Brahmanic deity also finds a place. An interesting example of this comes from Kapileshwara temple where the idol of Pattuguru—a deified hero of the Ahirs—has been recently installed.

It may be made clear at this point that although the sacred centres may thus be designated according to the dominance of Brahmanic or non-Brahmanic deities; in actual practice the pilgrims visiting these shrines make no discrimination between the two classes of deities.

It has also been noticed that the dominance of a deity may change from time to time; this may also change the character of the sacred centre considerably. For instance, the famous Shitala temple, located on the banks of the Ganges, was once, not very long ago, dominated by the Shiva *linga* called Dasashwamedheshwar. The present position is that the Shiva occupies an insignificant place in this centre whereas Shitala has become the presiding deity. A change in the object of performances may also sometimes change the character of the shrine conspicuously. For instance, earlier, goats were sacrificed in the Durga temple. But now with the incorporation of such deities as Saraswati, Lakshmi, Shiva, etc., goats are no more offered now in the precinct of this temple; its offering to Durga is still made but on the threshold of the temple, near the western gate.

Clusters and Segments

When a more than one multiple sacred centres are located in congregation they are called a 'sacred cluster'. In each such cluster there is, of course, a principal centre. For instance, in the Viswanath cluster, the multiple shrines of the Annapurna, Sakshi Vinayaka, Dhundhiraj, Pancha Pandava, Gyanvapi, Kashikarvat, and Tripurabhairavi are included. A pilgrim visiting Vishwanath temple generally pays visit to all these shrines in continuation.

When one or more sacred clusters form a continuous

segment the term 'sacred segment' is used: Kashi may be broadly divided into at least eleven such sacred segments. The clustering of the sacred shrines and the segmentation of the sacred geography of Kashi may be shown in a tabular form as follows:

TABLE 1

Showing the sacred clusters and sacred segments of the Kashi-kshetra

Segment No.	*Name of the segment (wardwise)*	*Cluster No.*	*Name of the dominating sacred cluster*
One	Dasashwamedh ghat east and chowk (Ward No. 2)		Golden Vishwanath, Annapurna, Dhundhiraj, Sakshi Vinayak, Pancha Pandav, Gyanvapi, Kashi-karvat, Tripurabhairavi.
		2	Manikarnika, Sankathaji, Vireshwar, Dharmeshwar, Bare Hanuman, Varahi Devi
		3	Dasashwamedheshwar, Sheetala
Two	Adampura-Kotwali and Jaitpura (Ward No. 2)		Varuna Sangam, Prahaldeshwar, Trilochan, Kameshwar
		2	Kalbhairab, Pancha Ganga, Bindu Madhar
		3	Bare Ganesh, Jaistheshwar
Three	Bhelpura east	1	Skandawata, Tilbhandeshwara
		2	Tulsimanas, Sankatmochan, Durga temple
	Bhelpura	3	Kedar temple, Neelkanth temple
Four	Dasashwamedh west and Bhelpura west		Kamachha, Baidyanatha, Jagannath (of Rathayatra chowk)
Five	Chaitganj		Pisachmochan and others
Six	Sarnath		Saranganath and others
Seven	From Assi Sangam to Kardameshwar		Assi Sangam B H U Vishwanath Kardameshwar
Eight	From Kardameshwar to Bhimchandi		Bhimchandi and others
Nine	Bhimchandi to Rameshwar		Rameshwar and others
Ten	Rameshwar to Panch Pandeshwar (Sheopur)	1	Panch Pandeshwar and others
Eleven	Panch Pandeshwar to Kapildhara		Kapildhara and others

Structural Classification of Shrines

All the shrines located in the Kashi-kshetra may be classified in a number of ways on the basis of : (*1*) physical appearance;

(*2*) sacred performances; (*3*) sects with which the shrine is mainly associated; (*4*) management; (*5*) priests; (*6*) offerings; (*7*) access to the sanctum sanctorum; (*8*) spread (local, regional, universal); (*9*) spiritual significance; and (*10*) hierarchy of importance.

Physical appearance

The physical appearance of the shrines is complex, and it is indeed difficult to define what a shrine is like. The deities are installed in such odd places as footpath, wall niches, and even trees and plants, wells, tanks and tombs. However, these shrines may be placed under six main categories: (*1*) amorphous; (*2*) temples; (*3*) *kunda*; (*4*) *koop*; (*5*) *ghats*; and (*6*) trees and plants.

By an amorphous shrine we mean those sacred centres which consist of certain symbols, paintings, engravings, and even idols without having any structure thereon. Such sacred centres are found all over Kashi-kshetra sporadically. Of the total sacred centres surveyed (375), 13.2 per cent belong to this category of shrine.

The temples are of two kinds: temples on the ground and temples underground. About 2.1 per cent of the temples are constructed underground. Of these Kashikarvat, Manikarnikeshwara and Pitamaheshwara are the most visited ones.

The temples built on the ground may have one or more than one room where the idols of the deities are enshrined.

The temples are generally built with a spire on the top, fitted with *kalasha*, *trishul*, or flags. In some cases where the number of spires is more than two, the middle spire is the highest one. In certain temples instead of spires there are dome-shaped structures; the temple of Varaganesh is an example of this kind. The Annapurna temple has both the spire and the dome. The main Vishwanath temple has several domes plated with gold. About 75.2 per cent of the temples of Kashi have either the spire or the dome, and the rest are built with a flat roof.

The height of the temple is also a distinguishing mark in its structure. The Vishwanath temple located in the campus of the Banaras Hindu University is the highest (85 feet). The approximate height of the temples of Kashi has been recorded as follows:

TABLE 2

Showing the approximate height of the temples and their percentage

Height of the temple in feet	*Percentage*
1-5	5.8
6-10	15.4
11-15	29.4
16-20	9.5
21-25	4.8
26-30	1.6
31-35	2.4
36-40	1.6
41-45	2.6
46-50	1.3
51-55	0.0
56-60	0.2
61-65	0.0
66-70	0.2
71-75	0.0
76-80	0.2
81-85	0.2

Thus most of the temples of Kashi are 11 to 15 feet high.

The sacred *kunda* or tanks are either *kachcha* or *pucca*. The *kachcha kunds* have muddy enclosures; *pucca kunds* have stone-paved bathing places. Of the *pucca kunds*, the Sona kund, also known as Sona talab, located on the Panchkosi route, is the most beautiful. It has many bathing places made of bricks and stones. Among the other important *kunds* there are Haritirtha, Lakshmi kund,· Tara kund, and Suraj kund. It appears that in olden days there were large number of *kunds*, for many of the kunds have been recently filled in and houses have been built in such places. The Agastya kund, which is now a *mohalla* of Varanasi, no longer exists. Going round the city one can see many *kundas* in a dilapidated condition, and under the process of filling up. Yet, of the total sacred shrines of Kashi-kshetra seven per cent belong to the category of the *kunda*.

The *koopas* are sacred wells. Some of these are very deep, storing sufficient water throughout the year. For instance, the Vridhvakal koop and the Gyanvapi koop are very deep, and these are well visited. It is believed that the Gyanvapi koop has underground links which can take one to Badrinath and Kedarnath in the Himalayas. The percentage of such sacred *koops* in the total sacred shrines of Kashi is about 2.7 per cent.

There are about 70 *ghats*[1] or sacred bathing places on the western banks of the Ganges. Some of these *ghats* are exceptionally holy and well visited, namely, tne Manikarnika ghat, largely used for cremation; the Dasashwamedh ghat, the most visited sacred bathing places, the Panchaganga ghat, etc. Most of these *ghats* are paved with stones.

Trees and plants are worshipped all over India, and Kashi is no exception to it. Some of the trees located in particular places have, however, assumed greater importance in Kashi than elsewhere. For instance, the *pipal* trees (*Ficus religiosa*) located near the Dasashwamedh ghat has attracted both local devotees and pilgrims from outside. The *vatavriksha* (*Ficus Bengalensis*) located on the west of the main Vishwanath temple is considered to be ageless. *Tulsi* plants are found in almost all the shrines dedicated to Vishnu.

Sacred performances

The sacred geography of Kashi may be marked into two broad but distinct zones; namely, the sacred river zone and the temple zone. Within the temple zone, however, there are a few *koopas* and *kundas* which fall into the broader category of river zones.

The river zone is conspicuous by certain special forms of performances such as *Gangasnan*, *Gangapujan*, *tarpan*, *pindadan*, *shradha*, and cremation.

Similarly, the temple zone is especially the centre of such performances as *abhishek* of the various deities and also the *darshan* of the gods enshrined in the temple.

The river zone in Kashi is spread along the banks of the Ganges, where the *ghats* are the principal centres of sacred performances. Of the various *ghats*, the five ghats, namely, the Assisangam, the Dasashwamedh, the Manikarnika, the Panchaganga, and Varunasangam are the most important ones. These are called *panchtirthi ghats*. Manikarnika and Harishchandra ghats are used for cremation where dead bodies from various parts of India are cremated round the clock.

Sects

The sacred centres of Kashi can be classified also on the

basis of the sectarian nature of their deities. The sacred centres belonging to Shaiva, Ganapatya, Sakta, Vaishnava and Saurya are easily distinguishable from one another. Shaivism seems to be a dominant and widely spread sect in Kashi; but that does not mean that there is cleavages or conflicts between sects. Indeed it is hard to make a clearcut boundary between the Shaiva and the Vaishnava sects at geographical level. The shrines of the Vaishnava and the Shaiva details are located side by side; and even in the same precinct the idols of the Shaiva and the Vaishnava deities are installed.

But it seems that in the olden days at some stage the people did make a distinction between the Vaishnava[2] and the Shaiva shrines. As the old tradition has it, Kashi is divided into two large zones, named as Shiva Kashi and Vishnu Kashi. While Shiva Kashi is believed to be extended from Assisangam ghat to the Manikarnika ghat; Vishnu Kashi is spread from the Manikarnika ghat to the Varunasangam. In actual situation these zones are not homogeneous; the shrines of Vishnu are located in Shiva Kashi and that of Shiva are found abundantly in Vishnu Kashi.

Management

The sacred shrines of Kashi may be classified also on the basis of their management.

It may be mentioned here that 35 per cent of the 375 sacred shrines studied had no regular priests; and these may be placed under the category of the neglected shrines. Most of these are located on the Panchkosi route.

Of the total shrines studied, 4.5 per cent are managed by caste members; 2.2 per cent are run by formal institutions; and 58.3 per cent are owned by individuals called the *mahantas.*

Some of the shrines are managed by more than one caste; for instance, the shrine of Varadavinayak (located in house No. A 13/18, Ghasiarie Tola) is looked after by the Lohars, Sonars and the Mullahs of the locality.

Shrines are managed by the institution of the ascetics, voluntary organizations of the householders, and even by the universities. The Banaras Hindu University, for instance, has built up one of the most gorgeous temples of Kashi within its campus.

Some more shrines on the Panchkosi route are also looked after by the Banaras Hindu University.

The maximum number of shrines, i.e. practically all the important shrines of Kashi—Vishwanath, Annapurna, Varaganesh, Kalabhairava, Kashikarvat, Sankatamochan and a number of others are owned by the *mahantas*.

Priests

The sacred shrines of Kashi may be distinguished from one another also on the basis of the types of priests associated with them. Priests may be classified on the basis of the nature of their appointment in connections with the temple. Thus, their are self-appointed priests, priests appointed by the management, and priests who own the temple.

As has been noted earlier, 35 per cent of the sacred shrines of Kashi-kshetra are neglected and have no priest at all. Of the remaining shrines the various types of priests find place in the following proportions:

TABLE 3

Showing the types of priests associated with the shrines

Traditional priests who own the temple	*Self-appointed*	*Priests appointed by management*
19.8%	21.2%	24.0%

The priests of the shrines belong to different castes namely, Brahmin, Rajput, Kayastha, Kurmi, Khatri, Baniya, Koeri, Khar, Halwai, Ahir, Teli, Mali, Lohar, etc. That the non-Brahmins particularly the non-Dwijas act as priests is significant even though their percentage is very small. There are also *sanyasis* or ascetics officiating as the priests of the sacred centres. Table 4 on the next page will indicate the distribution of the various castes employed as priests in the shrines of Kashi-kshetra.

Offerings

Offerings are of two kinds: vegetarian, and non-vegetarian.

In about six per cent of the shrines, non-vegetarian offerings are made to the deities. The deities whom non-vegetarian offering is made are either of the Shakta or of the non-Brahmanic Veera order. Sometimes the goat brought for sacrifice is not actually

TABLE 4

Showing the distribution of various Castes employed as priests in shrines

Caste	*Percentage*
Brahmin	56.2
Sanyasi[3]	2.4
Rajput	1.06
Kayastha	0.53
Kurmi	0.53
Bania	0.8
Koeri	1.6
Kahar	0.26
Halwai	0.53
Ahir	0 53
Teli	0 26
Mali	0.26
Lohar	0 52

killed. A small part of its ear is usually cut and offered to the deity and then it is left free. In some cases this sacrificial goat is killed after several months of this ritual, and before it is killed it moves freely in the city and people do not dare harm it. In a Durga temple located on the Panchakosi route when a sacrificial goat is set free in this manner, the villagers would not kill it on their own.

However, in about 94 per cent of the shrines, only vegetarian food is offered to the deities. The vegetarian offerings include sweets, fruits, milk, etc. All the shrines belonging to Shaiva, Vaishnava and Surya sects fall into this category.

Sanctum Sanctorum

In some of the shrines the devotees are allowed to enter the sanctum sanctorum or what is known as the *garbhagriha*; where he can also touch the deity. According to the orthodox Brahmanic tradition, the so-called untouchables, are not permitted to enter into the temple precincts. There are also some temples where even the Brahmin devotees cannot enter into the sanctum sanctorum; it is only the priest who can have a direct access to the deity. The percentage of such sacred centres is about 12.3. Of the temples where entry is thus restricted, mention may be made of the Vishwanath temple, the Vara Ganesh temple, the Sankatamochan, the Annapurna and the Durga temple, to name a few of the most important ones. The Vishwanath temple was built by

Swami Karapatri, as a protest against the Harijan entry into the original Golden Vishwanath temple on 17th February 1954. Today, in the Golden Vishwanath temple there is no restriction for the Hindus to enter inside the precincts or the *garbhagriha*; the non-Hindus (Muslims, Christians and Parsis) are however not yet permitted there to have an access to the god Vishwanath. But another Vishwanath temple located in the Banaras Hindu University campus is open to all, regardless of caste, creed and nationality.

Spread

Sacred shrines may further be classified on the basis of their clientele and the extent of importance, according as the shrines are of local, regional, or of national importance. The importance of a shrine is judged by the number of (*1*) pilgrims, (*2*) patrons[4] (builders and donors of the shrine), and (*3*) the myths or the extent of popularity.

The sacred shrines of all-India importance are those where pilgrims from all over the country and also from across the nation visit. About 6.4 per cent of the shrines in Kashi fall into this category; mention may be made of the original Golden Vishwanath temple, the Annapurna temple, the Gyanvapi koop,[5] the Dasashwamedha ghat, the Panchaganga ghat, the Assisangam, the Varunasangam, the Sankatamochan, the Tulsimanas, the Kalabhairava, and the temple of Vishwanath located in the campus of the Banaras Hindu University.

Some of the shrines have acquired all-India importance mainly because of their location within the cluster of the shrines of all-India importance. For instance, the Shanidev, the Dhundhiraj Ganesh, the Gyanvapi koop, the Sakshi Vinayak, the Kashi karvat, etc., though only of local importance, have acquired an all-India importance because of their location in the sacred cluster of the original Golden Viswanath and Annapurna. Similarly, the Shitala temple situated on the Dasashwamedha ghat, which is visited by large number of pilgrims and tourists from different parts of the world, has become a sacred centre of all-India importance.

The criterion of patronage of the sacred shrine, particularly its builders and donors plays a very important role in ascertaining a spatial importance to the sacred shrine. For instance, the importance of the temple of Vishwanath is perhaps added by the fact that Rani Ahilya Bai Holker of Indore built it in 1777, and Maharaja Ranjit Singh of the Punjab gilded it in 1839. The Vishwanath temple located in the campus of the Banaras Hindu University has similarly acquired importance because of its grandeur which was possible only with donations from the Hindu princes all over India.

The Dasashwamedha ghat has however assumed importance not because of the patronage but simply because of its location in a convenient place.

The myth[6] of a deity also plays a very important role in its popularity. Of the temples which have acquired all-India importance, the Golden Viswanath temple is attributed as the one providing *moksha*; the Annapurna, as the giver of wealth and prosperity; the Kalabhairava, as the *Kotwal* (Guard of the sacred *kshetra* of Kashi); and the Dasashwamedha ghat, as the one where a dip in the Ganges is believed to have the merit of performing several hundreds of *ashwamedha yajna*.

There are some shrines which have regional importance in the sense that only pilgrims from Benaras region frequently visit them. Among the shrines of the regional category there are also a few which are looked after by some specific linguistic groups. For instance, the Kedar temple is maintained by the Tamilians. The performances in these temples are also of regional nature. There are 4.5 per cent shrines of regional importance. Among these mention may be made of the following: Kedar temple, Kedar ghat, Tilabhandeshwar, and Vishalakshi managed by the South Indians; the Amba and the Gopal temples, looked after by the Gujaratis; the Balaji and the temples at Brahma ghat, owned by the Maharashtrians; the Shyama and the Tara temples, owned by the Maithils; the Pishachamochan and the Lakshmi kund, managed by the Bhojpuris; and the Kali temple near the Dasashwamedha and the Shiva temple of Manasarover, owned by the Bengalis. Since the management of regional shrine is generally in the hands of the people belonging to a specific region, pilgrims visiting these shrines also come from the same locality or region.

The temples of local importance are in overwhelming majority (74 per cent). Among these, mention may be made of the Suraj kund, the Bhootabhairava, the Agasteswar, etc. All the shrines of the *Satis* and the *Birs* are local. They are looked after by the inhabitants of the locality where they stand. Some individual members of castes are voluntarily involved in the management of the shrine.

Spiritual power

Several shrines in Kashi are specialized in the treatment of ailments, and are the bestowers of various kinds of human desires. On the basis of their specialization or the nature of their spiritual power these shrines may be categorised briefly as follows:

TABLE 5

Showing the spiritual power of the deities

Sl. No.	*Name of the deity*	*Specialization in spiritual power and bestower of*:
1.	Vishwanath	*Moksha*
2.	Annapurna	wealth
3.	Lakshmi	wealth
4.	Bare-Ganesh	*Vidya* and *Buddhi*
5.	Mrityunjay	Longevity, off-spring etc.
6.	Shitala	Curing small pox
7.	Khokhi Devi	Curing cough and cold
8.	Jwarharneshwar Mahadeo	Curing fever
9.	Chatpati Devi	Giving quick relief from any ailment
10.	Sankatamochan	Remover of *sankat* (obstacles), and gives offsprings.
11.	Sankata Mai	Remover of *sankat*, giving offspring
12.	Kal-Bhairab	Warding off *bhoota* and *preta* (devlish spirits)
13.	Pishachamochan	Warding of evil spirits.

In addition to these shrines there are almost innumerable gods and goddesses with whom Kashi abounds and who fulfil different kinds of human desires. Indeed the popularity of a god or a shrine depends largely upon its specialization and effectiveness in fulfilling the human desires.

Besides the Pauranic sacred shrines many new temples have come up into existence and of these a few have acquired popularity. For instance, the Tulsimanas Mandir, one of the most gorgeous temples of Kashi, is today attracting visitors in large numbers. In the month of Sravan in 1972 nearly fourteen lakhs of people have been reported as the visitors of the Tulsimanas

Mandir. In the following year the number of visitors increased to twenty lakhs.

Hierarchy

Depending upon the capability of the deities, of their effectiveness in fulfilling the human desires, the shrines in Kashi may be arranged in a hierarchical order as follows:

TABLE 6

Showing the names of the presidin deities

Sl. No.	Name of the presiding deity of the shrine
1.	Golden Vishwanath temple
2.	Annapurna temple
3.	Gyanvapi temple
4.	Kashikarvat temple
5.	Dhundhiraj Ganesh temple
6.	Sakshi Vinayak Ganesh temple
7.	Tulsimanas temple
8.	Sankatamochan temple
9.	Sankatamai temple
10.	Kalabhairava temple
11.	Mrityunjay temple
12.	Durga temple
13.	all others

Table 6 shows the general hierarchy of the shrines, as perceived by the pilgrims and the devotees. It has been worked out on the basis of depth interviews of hundred pilgrims selected by purposive sampling. It may be mentioned that the hierarchy of the shrines can be easily worked out on the number of pilgrims visiting them.

The local devotees, however, have a different opinion about the hierarchy of shrines. In most cases, they have rated Sankatamochan higher than the Golden Vishwanath temple. The reasons which they generally assign for giving Sankatamochan a place higher than the Vishwanath, are threefold; firstly, god Vishwanath has been polluted several times by various invasions made by the Muslims; secondly, the untouchables are allowed to enter into the sanctum sanctorum of the Vishwanath temple since 1954, and hence the god in this temple is polluted; and lastly, the suffocating narrow street in the Vishwanath temple has become a perfect nuisance, a dance for the *gundas* and *pandas*.

Physiognomy of the Deities

The deities are given symbolic expressions through images, rivers, tanks, sacred wells, stones, engravings, etc. Shiva's popular phallis is represented mostly by black stone or of white marble. In some places he is represented in his anthropomorphic form—seen in a sitting position meditating, a snake surrounding his neck and frequently with his consort Parvati sitting over his left thigh. Parvati is also seen at various places independently, sitting with folded hands. Annapurna, the goddess of wealth, is seen sitting on a *singhasan* giving alms to Shiva who stands before her with a begging bowl (*khappar*) in one hand, and a *trishul* (trident) in another. Some of the anthropomorphic forms of god Shiva in a meditating posture resembles with the Buddha, although the people worship it as the form of Shiva.

The gods shown in their anthropomorphic form have vehicles. For instance, the Bhairava rides on a dog, Garuda or the vulture is the *vahana* of god Vishnu, the Kartikeya sits on a peacock, the Shiva on the Nandi or ox, and the elephant headed god Ganesh rides on a rat.

Numerically, after the Shiva *linga* come Ganesh--frequently seen standing, sitting, having either four or two hands holding a book and *laddus*.

God Vishnu is seen mostly in a standing posture with *gada*, *shankh*, *chakra* and *padma*. He is seen either with four hands or with two. Usually he stands in *abhaya mudra* (in a benedictory pose) with his wife Lakshmi, and also sometimes in the company of other deities such as Ganga and Saraswati. Vishnu in the form of Rama is seen with a bow and arrow, and in the company of Hanuman, Sita and Lakshman. The Hanuman in the form of ape-god is popular all over Kashi. The statues of the monkey gods Bali and Sugriva are found near Omkareshwar shrine. They are very uncommon. The idol of Bali and Sugriva are about seven feet high standing and holding big *gada*.

The anthropomorphic features of Durga, Kali, Shitala and Surya are represented in various shrines; the Durga riding on a lion with various weapons, like *chakra*, bow and arrow, *dhal*, *trishul*, sword, etc. Goddess Kali, with one of her legs placed on prostrate Shiva, her long and red tongue hanging out and a garland of human heads around her neck, sometimes also seen holding a chopped human head in one of her hands and holds *khappar* in another hand. Goddess Shitala is a deity of small-pox sitting on an ass and holding broomstick in one of her hands. Sun god is represented through various circles carved out around human-like face and rays coming from its periphery. In another form, it appears as a charioteer driving a chariot drawn by two or more horses.

Of the non-Brahmin gods, Birs are shown in fighting postures, holding various weapons like sword, dagger, etc. The deities like Khokhidevi, and the *Sati* are represented in anthropomorphic form either standing or in a sitting form. A few images of ascetics are also worshipped.

PAURANIC GEOGRAPHY OF KASHI[7]

It is said that all the *tirthas* of India are located in Kashi. The sacred intellectuals claim that present Kashi is the one which has been described in the *puranas* and that today all the *tirthas* are located were exactly in the manner described in the ancient scriptures. However, the archaeologists claim that modern Kashi is of recent development and the ancient Kashi lies buried in the mounds, scattered near the Raj ghat. While we may not go into the details of the controversies between the archaeologists and the sacred intellectuals, a comparison between the existing sacred geography and Pauranic geography of Kashi may be attempted in the following section.

Continuity in Pauranic Geography

According to the 'Kashi khand' of the *Skanda Purana*, the Khashi-kshetra is divided into three *khandas* or segments: (*1*) Visheshwar khanda, (*2*) Onkar khanda, and (*3*) Kedar khanda. The details of the boundaries of these *khandus* have also been given in this important scripture; these are recognized by the *antargrahi parikrama* performed periodically by the pilgrims. With Madhyameshwar Mahadev (near Maidagin) as centre, Kashi extends in a radius marking Dehali Vinayaka or Soda a Vinakaya as a point.

The boundaries and the description of the Kashi-kshetra have been described differently in various *Puranas*, and it is said that the physical appearance of Kashi has been changing in different *yugas*. According to the 'Nagar khand' of *Skanda Purana* the Kashi-kshetra was like the *trishul* (trident), in the Satya Yuga, a *chakra* (disc) in the Treta Yuga, *ratha* (chariot) in the Dwapara and the Kali Yuga it is like *shankha* (conch shell).

According to the *Skanda Purana* there are several hundreds of shrines in Kashi, of which today at least 450 shrines can be actually spotted. Of these 450 shrines, about 125 Pauranic shrines are located in the Chowk ward, about 51 in the Dasashwamedha ward, 43 in the Kotwali ward, and 33 in the Adampura ward. Some of the Pauranic sacred shrines have obviously become obsolete and can still be found in dilapidated condition or usurped by people for secular use.

The continuity[8] between the Pauranic and the contemporary sacred geography of Kashi is further strengthened by a description in the *Padma Purana* which makes the shrine of Madhyameshwar Mahadev as the centre of Kashi-kshetra. Even today this shrine continues to be at the centre of Kashi. It is also mentioned in this *Purana* that on the west of Manikarnikeshwar Mahadev is located Gokarneshwar Mahadev, on the west of Varanasi is Pasupani Vinayaka. Curiously the same arrangement continues today. The continuity in the Pauranic geography has been maintained largely by the system of the *parikrama* or the holy circumambulation. The *panchakosi parikrama*[9] and the *antargrahi parikrama* are made by thousands of pilgrims periodically exactly in the manner described in the *Puranas*. There are about 60 *yatras* periodically undertaken by the pilgrims making all the shrines of Kashi alive over again and again.

Some of the Pauranic shrines have been dislocated in time profile. Of this the most significant is the main temple of the Vishwanath which has been destroyed several times by the Muslim rulers and rebuilt by the Hindu devotees. In this process god Vishwanath has moved from one place to another. Yet, the overall continuity in the Pauranic geography at the contextual level cannot be ruled out without difficulty.

Extinction of Shrines

Of the shrines which have been extinct, mention may be made of Vasuki kund, Kashirod, Sanka, Vamana, Govinda,

Hayagriva, Girnar, Chitrangeshwar, Nilakantheshwar, Maruteshwar, Kaleshwar, Ganeshwar, Imleshwar, Someshwar, etc. Although some of these shrines are still fresh in the memories of the modern *pundits* of Kashi, large number of them have been destroyed in course of time. Some of the shrines are in the process of decay, such as Sringara Gauri (near Gyanvapi), Maheswar Mahakaleshwar, Gangeshwar, Abhimukteshwar, Moksheshwar, Pratignaneshwar, Nishkalankareshwar, Markandeshwar, etc., some others such as Hartirath, Panchpandeshwar, Akshay Vinayak, etc. are being used by local people for exclusively secular purposes. Such neglected shrines, lying on the roadside are sometimes quickly converted into shops or residential houses. This act though socially and religiously taboo is often done in the cover of darkness. In 1973, a sacred centre located near the Samudreshwar shrine in Bansphatak Mohalla was converted into a utencil shop overnight. The priest of the golden Vishwanath temple has recently constructed a house over a dilapidated sacred old shrine. Nobody seems to stop this kind of transformation of the sacred shrines into shops and houses. However, the organizations like the Tirthasudha Samiti and the Ganga Mahasabha have now come up to look after the shrines which are in the process of decay.

REFERENCES

[1] For details, see appendix III.

[2] On the basis of textual data it seems that in olden days the spatial distinction between Shiva Kashi and Vishnu Kashi was clearly marked; even today this distinction is orally maintained. The sacred centres located in the north of the Manikarnika ghat fall under Vishnu Kashi, while those lying south of the Manikarnika form Shiva Kashi.

[3] A *sannyasi* is a person who has renounced domestic life and has given up his distinction of caste. Here, the category of *sannyasi* has been enlisted with caste only, for a specific purpose, i.e. to make a distinct social category.

[4] For details, see appendix IV.

[5] It is the present site of the Gyanvapi koop which has witnessed the famous battle of 1664 fought between the army of Emperor Aurangzeb and the Dasnami Naga Sannyasis.

[6] For details, see appendix V.

[7] For details, see the *Kashi khanda* of the *Skanda Purana* where a detailed description of the various *Tirthas* of Kashi has been given.

[8] The continuity can be observed at various historic levels. Here we are discussing in brief, only the continuity between the *Pauranic* and the contemporary sacred geography.

[9] For details, see chapter on *parikrama* and Mas where different types of *parikrama* have been discussed.

Chapter II

THE SACRED PERFORMANCES

SACRED PERFORMANCES ORGANIZED BY THE MANAGEMENT

PERFORMANCES in a shrine are of two kinds : one, organized by the management and another by the devotees. The following description will illustrate the types of performances made by the management in various shrines of Kashi.

Arati

Arati is believed to be a symbol of respect. Its origin is traced to the return of Rama to Ayodhya after 14 years of exile. It is believed that that was the first occasion when the citizens of Ayodhya welcomed Rama by waving an earthen lamp. Since that day the custom of waving an earthen lamp in honour of gods and goddesses is in vogue.

Although *Arati* may be performed almost at any time one worships the deity, there are four principal occasions when it was waved in honour of the deities. These are *(1) mangala arati*, which means auspicious waving of earthen lamp; *(2) bhoga arati*, which is preformed at the time of lunch ; *(3) sringara arati*, which is preformed at the time of decorating the deities; and *(4) shayana arati*, which is waved at the time of the retirement of the deity to bed.

Mangala Arati

This is performed in the Brahma *muhurta* (usually between 3.00 and 3.30 a.m.) when the deities are supposed to get up from the bed. The priest must purify himself by reciting *Gayatri mantra* and *Sandhya vandan* before performing the *mangala arati*. First of all a conch shell is blown into the air with a belief that this will awaken the deity. This is followed by *mangala geet* or the auspicious song, generally sung in honour of god Ganesh.

for it is Ganesh who is appeased first in any auspicious act. Arati containing six wicks or *battis* soaked in *ghee* is waved round the deity with the right hand while with the left hand the priest continues to ring the bell. The number of priests participating in the *mangala arati* varies from shrine to shrine but nowhere they have been found less than four in numbers. In a Shiva temple, after performing the *mangala arati* the *damru*, (the favourite musical instrument of Shiva) is also played.

Bhoga Arati

Between 12.30 and 1.00 p.m., the *Bhoga Arati* is performed to the deity while serving him a course of lunch. First of all *Mukhashuddhi* (purification of mouth) is performed, and thereafter several dishes are offered. The dishes include boiled rice, pulses, vegetable soups, etc., and in each article a Tulsi leaf is placed with a belief that the eatables placed in the dishes will not be affected by evil eyes. Another interpretation of placing the Tulsi leaf is that owing to her presence there will never be any shortage of food. After placing the dishes the priests recite some *mantras* and wave *arati;* the door of the temple is closed for a while to let the deity have his lunch without disturbance. At the time of opening the door the priests make a few clappings and enters the shrine. The *bhoga arati* thus comes to an end.

Shringara Arati

When an *arati* is performed in course of decorating the deities it is called the *shringara arati*. The following description of the *shringara arati* performed in the main Vihwanath temple will provide the details. The *shringara arati* is performed with the help of 11 priests, who sit in the sanctum sanctorum surrounding the Shiva *linga*. Out of the 11 priests, only two are the servants of the *mahanti*, the owner of the temple; the rest perform *arati* on behalf of some of the Hindu priestly states and the representatives of the local rich devotees. First the *linga* is bathed with *Panchamrita* (five substances of immortality—milk, honey, *ghee*, curd and sugar) by the chief priest, and the deity is decorated with flowers, annointed with sandal paste, scented, clothed and ornamented. A silver replica of the Sheshanag is placed on the *linga*. Vedic verses are recited by all the priests in chorus. A *damru* and a small bell add rhythm to the Vedic enchantation. The *arati* is waved by all the priests simultaneously. The performance continues for about one and a half hour. The devotees having come for the *darshan* of the deity may offer flowers and incense with the help of the priests conducting the *arati*.

Shayana Arati

The *Shayana Arati* is performed at about 11 p.m. when the deity is to retire for the night. A cot is sometimes fitted with a mosquito net. A pair of wooden sandals and a pot of water for the use of the deity are placed near the cot. In brief, all the necessary articles which one requires during the night are kept there before the deity retires. An *arati* is waved and the deity is prayed to go to bed. Finally the doors of the temple are closed.

Modes of Worship

There are two modes of performing worship of the deities—*Shodashopchar* and *Panchopachar*.

In the *Shodashopchar pujan*, sixteen types of articles are offered to the deity, reciting Vedic *mantras* at offering each article. This method of worship is followed only in four centres—in the Vishwanath temple built by Karpatriji, in the Sankatamochan, in the Annapurna temple, and in the main golden Vishwanath temple. It takes nearly one and a half hours to complete the process of the *shodashopchar pujan*. First a lighted lamp is placed before the deity. This is known as Raksha or the protection lamp. Then the priest starts reciting *Shanti path*—verses from the Vedas. After Shantipath, *Sankalpa* (sacred vow) is taken by the priest by reciting *mantras*, and then a verse is sung in praise of Lord Ganesh and Gauri. After completing this course of prayer the deity is bathed in *Panchamrita*. This is followed by the purificatory bath, when the Ganges water is used. After this follows the *Abhisheka*, slow sprinkling of water through the narrow hole of a metal pot, when the verses from the *Shukla Yajurveda* are recited all through. The deity is again bathed with Ganges water. This completes bathing of the deity. A sacred thread is placed on the male deity. Among the things to be offered variation has been noted according to the sect and also the economic condition of the shrine. For instance, *Akshata* (sun-dried rice), *bibhooti* (sacred ashes), *Durba*, *Belapatra*-leaf, and

Dhatura flowers are offered to Lord Vishwanath, while Sankatamochan and other Vaishnava deities are worshipped only with *Tulsi* leaves and flowers. The performances of the *Shodashopchar Pujan* along with the waving of *Arati* comes to an end by undertaking three rounds of the deities known as *Pradakshina*.

Panchopachar Pujan is a short form of *Shodashopchar Pujan*. One important difference between the two is the recitation of the Vedic verses which is a must in the case of the latter form of worship, but not necessary in the former. In the Panchopachar *Paddhati* the five articles namely *Gandha*, *Pushpa*, *Dhoop*, *Deep*, and *Tambool* are offered whereas in the case of Shodashopchar *Paddhati* sixteen articles are offered to the deity.

Variations in Daily Performances

About 75 per cent of the sacred shrines do not perform all the four types of *Arati* and the details of worship described above. There is also variation in the modes of worship on the basis of the regional affiliation of a shrine. For instance, the Balaji temple, the Tara Mandir, the Tilabhandeshwar, the Gopala Mandir, the Kali Mandir, and the Nepali Mandir follow the Maharashtrian, the Tamilian, the Gujarati, the Bengali, the Maithili and the Nepali modes of worship respectively. The variation in the modes of worship takes place mostly on account of the variation in the Vedic *Sakhas* to which the priests of the management belong. For instance, in the Kedar temple and in the Tilabhandeshwar the Rig-Vedic hymns are recited, the deities are bathed with coconut water, and *Kumkum archana* is considered as one of the essential parts of the sacred performances. The Tara temple, which is owned by the Maithil Brahmins, follow the Tantric mode of worship. The verses are recited from Tantric literature. Linguistic influence on the modes of prayer can be seen at the time of performing Bhajan and Kirtan. For instance, in Kali temple *Bhajan* and *Kirtan* are performed in Bengali language; the Maithil temples follow the Maithili, and the Gujarati temples follow the Gujarati prayers.

Special performances are made on special occasions. For instance, the Maharashtrians perform the marriage ceremony of Balaji during the Aswin Navaratra. South Indians also perform the marriage ceremony of god Kedareswar with great pomp and show. The Tara temple of the Maithils observe special ceremonies called Kojagra on the full moon day of Ashwin. Thus varieties of regional traditions in the sacred performances can be observed in the shrines of Kashi.

SACRED PERFORMANCES BY THE DEVOTEES

All sacred performances organized in Kashi by the devotees fall into three broad categories: (*1*) *snan* (sacred bath), (*2*) *darshan* (sacred visitation), and (*3*) *puja* (worship).

Snan

A holy bath in the Ganges, known as the Ganga *snan* is the religious necessity for making all types of sacred performances. The sacred bath in the Ganges at any place is considered meritorious, for the Ganga is believed to be the remover of sins (*pap*), hence called *Pap Dhovani*. A bath in the Ganges at Kashi is considered to be endowed with special virtue; for here the sacred river flows from south to north (*Uttaravahini*) which is a unique phenomenon in the regular course of the Ganges. Besides being *Uttaravahini*, the river Ganges has acquired in Kashi a special significance: Lord Shiva resides in this sacred city permanently and the river is touching the feet of the Lord Shiva all the time. As mentioned earlier, there are several bathing *ghats* such as Dasashwamedha, Manikarnika, Panchaganga, and others with special religious significance where a bath is considered to be specially holy. All these factors contribute a special significance to the sacred bath in the Ganges at Kashi. Of the 500 pilgrims interviewed, 95 per cent reported to have taken holy bath in the Ganges, the remaining 5 per cent argued that it is unhygienic to take bath in the Ganges which is dirtied by the continuous inpour from the sewerage of the city. Bath in the Ganges is, of course, only a part of the pilgrimage, in the sense that 0.2 per cent of the pilgrims came to Kashi only for taking a holy bath.

It has been mentioned in the *Skanda Puran* that one should take bath only at the Panch Tirthaghats—Dasashwamedha, Manikarnika, Panchaganga, Assi and Varuna. In Kashi, 85 per cent of the pilgrims are reported to have taken bath at all these *ghats*. Besides these *ghats*, the pilgrims take bath at various other *ghats* mentioned as follows: Manikarnika ghat: 34.8 per cent; Harishchandra ghat: 7.2 per cent; Ahilyabai ghat: 13 per cent; Shitala ghat: 16.6 per cent; Assi ghat: 3 per cent; Durga ghat: 2.4 per cent; Kedar ghat: 7 per cent; Gauri ghat: 1.4 per cent; Brahma ghat: 2 per cent; Darbhanga ghat: 1.2 per cent; Adikeshva ghat: 3.2 per cent, and also Narainghat, Tulsighat, Munsighat, etc. (12 per cent).

While taking bath in the Ganges, no holy rite is performed. One simply offers '*pranam*' to the mother Ganges, and sometimes utters "*Maa Ganga ki jai*". Some may also offer flowers, *akshata* (unbroken rice), coconut, etc. at the time of taking bath, or immediately after taking bath.

Of the 500 citizens of Kashi interviewed, 90 per cent of them take holy dip in the Ganges regularly, and 61 per cent perform 'Ganga *pujan*'. Most of the regular bathers of the Ganges live along the banks of the river, some people living in other parts of the city also come to take bath regularly. Their number is of course negligible.

Among the bathers the number of women is generally large in the early hours of the morning. Most of these bathers are widows. The number of bathers vary according to season—during the winter, old men and women avoid taking bath in the Ganges.

The *ghatias*, who sit on the *ghats*, provide necessary facilities to the bathers. They look after the clothes and other personal belongings of their clients taking bath in the Ganges, offer them *chandan* and flowers, and help them in performing oblations. Some of the *ghatias* keep mirror and combs for the use of their clients. On some of these *ghats* there are specialists in applying oil and massages. Those who wish to have massage before taking bath, employ them. Scented oil, soaps, etc. are also sold at the *ghats*. The bathing scene at the *ghats* is enchanting, but the groups of beggars sitting in a row and expecting the bathers to give them alms, present a tragic scene.

After taking bath, one generally (particularly, if he is a Brahmin) makes a brief personal worship and recites *mantras* while making oblation to gods and ancestors; then one moves to a temple nearby and worship the deities, or goes away to a distant temple or back to home.

Although it is not possible to distinguish between an ordinary bath and a ritual bath in the Ganges, the distinction can be made on the basis of the time devoted to personal worship after the bath or the ritual followed immediately after the bath. An ordinary bath is generally not followed by the course of rituals. Thus the sanctity of taking bath in the Ganges is in practice directly linked with other rites and performances.

Pujan

After the bath in the holy river follows the worship of deities. Most of the pilgrims taking bath in the Ganges (or even those who do not do so) pay a visit to the shrine of Vishwanath for performing *Rudrabhisheka*. The word 'Rudhrabhisheka' is composed of *Rudra* (Shiva); *abhi* (maximum); *sheka* (respect) which means paying utmost respect to Lord Shiva. In some of the scriptures, particularly in the *Shukla Yajurveda* it has been mentioned that the 'Rudrabhisheka' is the best mode of appeasing the Lord Shiva; the *Vayu Puran* suggests that a barren woman desirous to be blessed with a son, should offer *Rudrabhisheka* to Shiva. There are various types of *Rudrabhisheka*, namely *laghu Rudrabhisheka*, *maha Rudrabhisheka*, and *ati Rudrabhisheka*. Some pundits add to this another type of *Rudrabhisheka* called *sarvanga ekadashi Rudrabhisheka*. The various types of *Rudrabhisheka* are distinguished from one another mostly on the basis of the number of priests employed for the purpose. For instance, in the *Rudrabhisheka* only one priest conducts the rites; in the *sarvanga ekadashi Rudrabhisheka*, 11 priests conduct the rites; in the *laghu Rudrabhisheka*, 12 priests; in the *maha Rudrabhisheka*, 1331 priests; and in the *ati Rudrabhisheka*, 1463 priests are required.

Because the *ati Rudrabhisheka* is very expensive, only a few rich people undertake to this mode of worship. It is said that in the olden days only Hindu princes could offer to organize the *ati Rudrabhisheka* in Kashi. Even *maha Rudrabhisheka* is uncommon, for it is an expensive performance. In August 1973, the Birla brothers performed the *maha Rudrabhisheka* in the temple of Vishwanath.

The *sarvanga ekadashi Rudrabhisheka* and *laghu Rudrabhisheka* are most frequent and could be generally seen to be taking place in the golden Vishwanath temple. The citizens of Kashi perform *laghu Rudrabhisheka* on such occasions as birth, marriage, or *Upanayan samskar*, with a view to appeasing Lord Shiva. Businessmen undertake this mode of worship while entering into a new business.

The *Rudrabhisheka* can be performed by all the *dwijas* themselves; the Sudras can perform it only with the help of a Brahmin priest. The one who performs *Rudrabhishekas* has to observe personal purity. Traditionally, the ladies, excepting the wives of the Agnihotris, are not allowed to perform any type of *Rudrabhisheka* mentioned above.

The actual mode of performing *Rudrabhisheka* is the same as described earlier in the *panchopachar* and the *shodashopchar* forms of worship. The third mode of worship was also reported as *rajopachar*. The *rajopachar* method of worship is significant because in so far as the amount of gift is concerned. Only a few years ago, the king of Nepal had performed this type of worship in the golden temple of Vishwanath, where he offered horses, elephants, silver and gold, clothes and eatables in large quantities to the priests who had officiated at the ceremony. The details of worship, such as in the use of *mantras*, in the articles to be offered, and in the ritual instruments to be used are practically the same for all forms of worship. The duration of worship and the articles offered at the time of worship may have personal variation, depending on the caste, economic condition and personal education of the worshipper.

SACRED PERFORMANCES ASSOCIATED WITH VOWS

Besides the performances made by the management of the shrine or by an individual on ordinary occasions, special performances are made on special occasions and in special contexts. Though the ultimate goal to which an orthodox Hindu wishes to arrive at is the *moksha* (salvation), there is no Hindu god which is exclusively worshipped for the attainment of salvation. Gods and goddesses are worshipped for the fulfilment of human desires which may be divided into three broad categories : *(1) artha*, *(2) kama*, and *(3) moksha*. The first two are associated with earthly considerations, the last is the desire to get rid of all worldly affairs of life and the cycle of birth and death. To fulfil the desires of *artha* and *kama* there are various gods and goddesses. In other words, there is a departmentalization of gods : certain gods are the givers of wealth, some cure particular ailments and sufferings, some promote excellence and scholarship. However, even in one god or goddess, all these functions may sometimes combine. The *Jyotirlinga* of Vishwanath is not only the giver of worldly pleasures (as is the *Jyotirlinga* of Deoghar), but he is also the bestower of *moksha*.

The specialization of the deities in Kashi are in some cases very minute. For instance, Khokhi Devi is specially worshipped and propitiated for recovery from cold and cough; Chatpati Mata is worshipped for quick recovery from high fever; Shitala is the well-known goddess of small pox; Sankatamochan bestows blessings for children and redresses worldly obstacles (*sankats*). Since these goddesses have the power to fulfil human desires, men and women in crisis approach them and pray for quick remedies.

Such worship as made in pursuance of a vow is quite frequent in Kashi. Some of the vows associated with worship, may briefly be described as follows : A couple generally keep a vow in connection with the desire to have a son; and when this is fulfilled the *mundan* ceremony (shaving off the head for the first time) of the boy takes place before Lord Shiva. Thirty cases of *mundan* ceremony performed in the Vishwanath temple have been recorded in detail. In all these cases, the performers from neighbouring districts of Varanasi, they were people from all the *varnas*.

The *mundan* ceremony may be also performed at the *ghats*. In it the role of the barber is important insofar as he shaves off the hair of the child, while the priest of the temple or the *ghatia* utters certain verses on this occasion. The *mundan* ceremony in a shrine is brief. The client may offer a piece of *dhoti* to the priest and also the barber, besides paying them in cash and making them available some eatables. The hair of the child is generally thrown in river Ganges. Pilgrims coming from distant places perform the *mundan* ceremony at the Dasashwamedh ghat or in the precinct of the golden Vishwanath temple. But the people of the Banaras Hindu University perform the *mundan* ceremony in the Vishwanath temple located in their campus.

Another sacred performance related to the fulfilment of a vow is called *dudhadharia* (pouring milk) over the Shiva *linga*. Milk is poured on the Shiva *linga* by those persons whose desires have been fulfilled. In Vishwanath temple if one wants to offer milk in large quantity, he has to pay two rupees to the management. The sacred specialist is employed for this purpose. Although this mode of worship is followed by all sections of

Hindus, it is largely the Maharashtrian Brahmins who perform the *dudhadharia* worship.

In 1973, a businessman who was suffering from paralysis had taken a vow that if he is cured of this disease he would perform the *tuladana* in Vishwanath temple. After recovery he came to perform *tuladana* in the Naya Vishwanath temple. A big *pandal* was erected and about 100 *Yajnikas* were engaged for reciting *mantras*, performing *homa*, on behalf of the person who had taken the vow. The ritual lasted for about 36 hours during which the chanting of the vedic *mantras*, the *abhisheka* of Lord Shiva, and *dana* to Brahmins were the main performances. In the *tuladan* ceremony, a performer has to donate silver or gold equal to his weight. Since these materials are very costly, one does not generally dare to keep a vow involving heavy expenditure. The number of *tuladana* performers in Kashi is, therefore, not much.

The *jaldalai* is another type of sacred performance generally made with a view to appeasing Shiva when there is no rain. This is performed mostly by agriculturists in the case of drought. Performers assemble at the Kedarghat and after taking a holy dip in the Ganges, fill up their vessels with the Ganges water to be offered to the Kedareshwar Mahadeva, to Tilabhadreshwar Mahadeva, and to Vishwanath. The performers stay in the temple for several hours engaging themselves in *bhajans* and *kirtan*. On this occasion, people are seen chanting *mantras* and raising slogans, such as '*Har har Shambhu*', '*Har har Mahadev*', and '*Baba Kashi Vishwanath ki jai*' etc. Sometime, the performers go to Saranath where water is offered to Saranganath Mahadeva.

Kabutar urana is a sacred performance peculiar to the pilgrims from Nepal. There is a belief among the Nepali pilgrims that if a *kabutar* (pigeon) is set free, the life of the bird is saved, and Lord Shiva is very pleased by this act and hence he fulfils the desire of the performer. The pigeon is brought before the deity and after taking off round the temple it is let free. No *mantra* is recited on this occasion.

Another performance which is quite common in Kashi is the engraving of silver coins in the temple precincts or on the gates of the temple. This is called *chandi thokana*. Large number of silver coins are engraved in the precincts of the Vishwanath temple by those whose desires have been fulfilled. At the time of engraving the silver coins the priest recites some *mantras*. The priest is paid special *dakshina* for this job, and the management of the temple is also paid a sum of one rupee as the fee for granting permission to perform this rite. Although this rite is nowhere mentioned in the ancient scriptures, it is in practice, and, indeed, very popular in Kashi, particularly among the north Indians.

God Satyanarayan is worshipped in every Hindu house periodically. The Satyanarayan *katha* is sometimes also organized at the Dasashwamedh ghat. Generally this is done in pursuance of a vow in connection with having a son or getting a job or promotion, or a daughter's marriage. The *ghatias* perform this *puja* on behalf of their Shudra clients. The other sections of the Hindu, i.e., the *dwijas* generally employ a special *karmakandi* for this purpose. The god Satyanarayan is worshipped, and the story of Lilawati is narrated on this occasion. *Prasada* is distributed to all those who are present on this occasion; the priest is paid *dakshina*.

The *Aar-Par* rite is generally performed by the newly married couple belonging to the so-called lower caste for leading a happy married life, and being blessed with a son. The newly married couple, accompanied by relatives, come to the *ghats* where the *ghatia* applies *chandan*, *rori*, *haldi* on their foreheads. The couple is asked to perform the *puja* of Gauri Ganesh made of sands. The *puja* is conducted by the boatman. The couple is asked whether the vow has been fulfilled; the answer has to be affirmative. A long rope, with mango leaves as flowers fastened in it, of the length of the western and the eastern banks of the Ganges, is taken from one end to another. A rich couple may offer clothes of the same length to mother Ganges. This rite is generally performed at the Dasashwamedha ghat. An offering of the cloth is called *chunari charhana*.

An offering of coconut in connection with the fulfilment of a vow is prevalent among the South Indian devotees. After recovery from an illness or having got the bridegroom for his daughter, one offers coconut to mother Ganges. The *ghatias* chant some *mantras* before asking the devotees to offer a coconut to the Ganges. The coconut one offers to the Ganges is received by the *ghatias* who may use it again for another devotee. It may be noted here that according to the Hindu tradition, the articles once offered to a god cannot be reoffered by the same person or any other person to the same deity or to any other deity.

nath temple. At the end of the *arati*, the devotees offer some flowers if they have brought these with them or may have a look at the deity which is enough for acquiring the *darshana*.

Many devotees pay periodical visits to the various shrines on fixed days. For instance, Monday is considered an auspicious day for visiting Shiva, while Tuesday is the day for Hanuman temple. One may himself also fix the days for visiting the various deities according to one's own convenience.

What makes the act of *darshana* different from *pujan* are the offerings and the necessary provisions for making a sacred performance. Although personal purity is necessarily required for any sacred performance, the *darshana* is the simplest of such acts, demanding no elaborate rite of purification, and yet rewarding with *punya* thereby.

ANTYESTHI KRIYA

Of all the places of Hindus pilgrimage, Kashi is the only one which is called as *Mahashmashan*, the great cremation ground. It is believed that those who leave their mortal body in Kashi would get *moksha*, for Lord Shiva would give the dying person the *tarak mantra* bestowing upon him salvation. Dying in Kashi is considered auspicious, and hence people from different parts of India come here to breathe their last, and be cremated at the Manikarnika ghat. Round the clock, dead bodies are cremated at this *ghat*. If there is a break in the process of cremation, the *kusha* grass is burnt in symbolic representation of the burning of the dead body and thus the cremation is completed. Thus the performances of the *antyesthi kriya* or the last rites is considered auspicious.

There are a number of *dharmasalas* meant for accommodating the persons who have come to die in this holy city. Among these mention may be made of *Dinahin Sadgati Niwas*, *Kashi Mukti Bhavan*, *Kashi Labha Bhavan*, etc., where various preparatory rites and necessary arrangements are performed immediately before death.

The performances before and after death may be described as follows:

Rites Before Death

At the approach of death two important rites known as *Godan* offering of cow) and *Vaitarani* are performed. In the *godan* ritual, the dying person, performs *chhourkarma* (shaving of hair) and a black cow is brought near him. The priest conducting this rite puts *kusha* grass in the ring finger of the performer and recites some *mantras* while the dyingperson throws *akshata* (rice), *tila* (sesame), barley, etc., at the cow. The ritual culminates with payment of *dakshina* to the priest. *Godan* signifies gifting away a milch cow to a 'worthy man' to expiate one's sins.

The rite of the *Vaitarani* is performed with a belief that the performer will be able to cross the mythical river Vaitarani while being carried to *yamaloka*. As a person nears his last, a cow is brought near him and the tail of the cow is placed in his right hand. The priest throws *akshata*, flowers, *tila*, barley, etc. at the dying person and the cow and recites *mantras*. The dying person is placed on a mat made of *kusha* grass and is given *charanamrita* (sacred water) of Lord Vishwanath and Kala Bhairava, with a belief that after drinking the sacred water, he would attain *moksha* after his death. Meanwhile the *Ramayana*, the *Gita*, and the *Garudapuran*, etc., are recited by the relatives or the priest. A dying person is sometimes given Ganges water (Gangajal), *tulsi*-leaf, and a piece of gold to touch, with a belief that by touching the Gangajal he is purified, the tulsi leaf makes him entitled for entering into Vishnuloka and the gold leads him to a way into the Devalok (land of the gods).

Rites After Death

As soon as a person dies, a bier is prepared for him. His body is placed upon it in such a way that the head faces north and the feet are towards south. Four persons, usually kinsmen, pick up the bier and bring it to the cremation *ghat* (Manikarnika ghat or the Harishchandra ghat).

At the cremation *ghat*, the chief mourner, who is to light the funeral pyre, goes to the Dom Raja[1] to obtain sacred fire from him. The Dom Raja who is considered to be the custodian of the sacred fire claims to be the descendants of the mythical Kalu Dom, under whom Raja Harishchandra of the Ikshavaku dynasty had served. A lot of higgling is done over the purchase of sacred fire and in the case of the death of a man of ripe age, say an octogenarian, the Dom Raja's demand is really exorbitant. Some South Indians and Gujaratis do not take sacred fire from the Dom Raja. Some local Brahmanas, Marwari Banias, Kayasthas and Khatris are also reported to have cremated their dead on the Manikarnika ghat without obtaining the sacred fire from the Dom Raja. However, most of the people still believe that the sacred fire has to be obtained from the Dom Raja for getting to *moksha*.

After obtaining the sacred fire from the Dom Raja, the chief mourner is asked to recite some *mantras* prompted by a *karma-kandi*. The chief mourner takes three rounds of the funeral pyre and then the priest recites some *mantras* and asks him to place *chandan*, *ghee*, barley, sesame, etc., on the funeral pyre.

The offerings which the relatives of the deceased offer on the funeral pyre may be classified into two types: (*1*) *dasang*, and (*2*) *ashtagandha*. In the *dasang* type of offerings, ten articles, namely barley, sesame, rice-powder, *ghee*, *bhojpatra* and *pancha-mewa* (consisting of five kinds of dry fruits) are offered on the funeral pyre. In the *ashtagandha* offerings eight kinds of articles, like *devadar*, *chandan*, *agar*, *dhup*, *ghee*, *kapoor*. *kurval* and wood of *tulsi* plant are offered. There is no hard and fast rule as to who should offer what type of offerings; the chief mourner generally takes a decision in this regard.

After the offerings have been made, the funeral pyre is lit by the chief mourner. The fire is lit on the mouth of the deceased and the flames creep over the whole funeral pyre, consuming the mortal remains of the deceased. Within a few hours the funeral pyre turns into a small mound of ashes.

After the cremation, a rite of 'pitcher breaking' is performed at the cremation *ghat*. The chief mourner is asked to collect some ashes and to fill them into a pitcher which is tied with a red thread. The pitcher is kept on the left shoulder of the chief mourner, he stands facing south and throws the pitcher on his back, so that it breaks into pieces. The breaking of pitcher is considered as the breaking of the existing relationship between the deceased and the chief mourner.

Purificatory Rites

The chief mourner and other kinsmen of the deceased have to undergo certain purificatory rites after cremating the dead body. First of all the chief mourner performs *chhourkriya*[2] (shaving off of hair and moustaches) and then all the members of the bereaved family go to take a holy dip in the Ganges. Usually they take five dips and offer *tilanjali* to the departed soul. *Til* (sesame) is offered along with water, following a belief that *til*, being black in colour, will protect the departed soul from evil eye. After taking a dip in the Ganges and after offering *tilanjali* all the mourners go to the residence of the chief mourner where they touch fire, water, iron, a piece of stone and chew black pepper before changing their wet clothes. On this occasion the Kanyakubja Brahmins and the Rajbhars chew *neem* leaves and the Saryuparin Brahmins chew molasses along with black pepper.

On the second day a *ghata* is hung under the *pipul* (*Ficus religiosa*) tree and an earthen lamp is lighted in honour of the departed soul. The barber assists in this rite. In the hanging of the *ghata* the following articles are required; two earthen pots, two *purai* (big lamp), *kusha* grass, few yards of rope, earthen lamp containing *ghee*, *tila* and a match box for lighting the lamp. The ritual of hanging *ghata* is performed by various castes on different days. For instance, the Rajbhars perform it on the third day, and the lamp is lighted by the chief mourner for seven days. The Doms hang it on the first day, just after the commencement of death, other castes perform it on the second day as mentioned above.

On the third day, the chief mourner offers *urad*, *tila* and water to the departed soul; this is called *shradhanjali*; he eats *doodh-bhata* (boiled rice and milk) with his relatives.

Two types of *shraddha*, viz., *panchadan* and *naryanibali* are performed in Kashi. The Naryanibali type of shraddha is performed in the case of immature death, like death by an accident (such as, due to a fall from the tree) but *panchadan* shraddha is commonly performed. In the *panchadan* shraddha articles like cooking utensils, bedding, clothes, shoes, cot, umbrella, etc., are offered to the *mahapatra*. There is yet another type of *shraddha*, called *Brkhotsarga* in which different types of animals like milch cow with calf, horse, elephant, etc. are offered. In it a calf is let loose after being brandished with hot iron (And that is why the city of Kashi is crowded with bulls). This type of shraddha involves considerable expenditure, and hence is uncommon. The performance of the *shraddha kriya*, ends with the feeding of Brahmins and worshipping the legs of the *mahapatra*, the specialists conducting death-rites. It is believed that the articles offered to the Brahmins on the occasion of *shraddha kriya*, would eventually reach to the departed soul in the next world.

Ancestor Worship

Like Gaya and Prayag, Kashi is no special offering place for offering *pindas* to the ancestors. The 'Kashi Khanda' of the *Skandapurana* however refers to some of the important sacred centres in Kashi, such as Pishachamochan kunda, Rameshwar, Panchatirth ghat, etc., where *pindas* should be offered by the people in the name of their ancestors, particularly during the *Pitri paksha*, which falls in the month of Ashwin.

During the *pitri paksha* of Ashwin many pilgrims from different parts of India come to Kashi to offer *pindas*. According to an estimate obtained from the pilgrim registers of the Pandas, during the *pitri paksha* in 1972, nearly forty thousand pilgrims from Rajasthan, Maharashtra, Gujarat, Madhya Pradesh, Punjab and Haryana, South India, West Bengal, Bihar and U.P. and about three hundred Nepali pilgrims came to Kashi to offer *pindas*.

The *pinda dan* rites vary according to caste, regions and the economic condition of the performer. The *pindas* are made of different articles, the pilgrims coming from Rajasthan and Punjab prepare *pindas* from the barley flour; the Bihari, the Bengali and the South Indian pilgrims prepare *pindas* from boiled *arba* (sundried) rice; the pilgrims from Madhya Pradesh prepare *pindas* from the powder of gram and of *khoa* (thick paste of milk).

Variation has been observed also in the number of *pindas* offered to the ancestors. The Brahmins offer 56 *pindas*, taking into consideration the long list of ancestors of both the paternal and maternal sides; other castes offer lesser number of *pindas*. The pilgrims from lower castes were seen offering only 21 *pindas*. The Brahmins and the other members of upper caste pilgrims were seen offering eight *pindas* to *rishis* and *devatas* also; the lower castes do not offer a *pinda* to the *rishi* and to the *devata*. The Brahmins and the members of the upper caste also offer *tarpan* (offering of water) to their ancestors, *rishis* and *devatas*. The members of the lower caste perform *tarpan* rites only perfunctorily.

The amount of *dakshina* to the *ghatias*, the *nais*, *tirtha-purohita*, *karmakandis*, etc., varies according to the economic condition of the performer.

REFERENCES

[1] The Dom Raja does not sit on the cremation *ghat* to give the sacred fire; the fire is purchased from one of his assistants, who sit there and give the fire in the name of the Dom Raja. The name of the Dom Raja in office is Shri Kailash Choudhary (age 38); Shri Lakshmi Narayan Choudhary, his father is also alive.

[2] Here there is a little difference. Some people do not perform *Chhour kriya* on the first day. For instance, the Maithil Brahmins perform *Chhour kriya* only on the 10th day, and not on the first day. For details see M. Jha (1966).

Chapter III

FAIRS AND FESTIVALS

A LARGE number of fairs and festivals are periodically organized in Kashi. Of these, some festivals are of all-India importance; others have local or regional significance. The festivals of Shivaratri and Kartik *purnima* (full-moon night) are attended by pilgrims from all over India; other festivals and fairs are celebrated locally. This may be described briefly as follows:

FESTIVALS OF ALL-INDIA IMPORTANCE

Shivaratri

According to Hindu calendar, Shivaratri falls on *Krishna paksha Chaturdashi* (fourteenth day of the dark lunar fortnight) in the month of Phalgun (falling in February-March). As the tradition has it, Shiva was married on this auspicious day. In this connection it may be pointed out that Shiva's first marriage with Sati (also known as Daksha Kumari), the daughter of Raja Daksha, is not celebrated by the devotees. It is only the anniversary of his second marriage with Parvati, the daughter of King Hemant of the Himalayas, which is celebrated as Shivaratri by the devotees all over India.

As Lord Shiva is believed to be permanently living in Kashi, his marriage anniversary in the form of Shivaratri is celebrated there with pomp and show, attracting a large number of pilgrims from all over India. The main concentration of pilgrims, however, is in the Adi Vishwanath temple, the Naya Vishwanath, and the B.H.U. Vishwanath. But those who are unable to cope with the rush at these places may visit other sacred centres of Shiva for having *darshan* and performing *puja*. Among such centres mention may be made of Kashi karvat

Dasashwamedheshwar, Bhimeshwar, Manikarneshwar, Agasteshwar, Brahmeshwar, etc

As regards its ritual observance, the festival of Shivaratri may be divided into two parts. First part is known as Shiva *upas* (fast in the name of Shiva), and the second part is called the Shiva *darshan*. The first part usually precedes the later, when the devotees keep fast for the whole day and night, Shiva's marriage is celebrated at midnight, and the devotees break their fast next morning, after having a *darshan* of Shiva-Parvati.

The second part of the ritual, i.e. Shiva *darshan*, starts after the culmination of the marriage of the divine couple. While the day marked for Shiva *upas* is spent on observing wedding rites, the Shiva *darshan* is meant for rejoicing giving *dana dakshina* to Brahmins and beggars.

In all the four important Vishwanath temples, the sacred specialists remain busy for 24 hours in the celebrations of Lord Shiva's marriage; the nature and extent of their involvement in the actual performance of Shivaratri may however differ from shrine to shrine depending on the organizational ability of the priests and the management. For instance, in the temple of Naya Vishwanath where the management follows orthodox mode of worship several learned *Veda-pathis* recite the Vedic verses for 24 hours, known as *akhanda path*. On this occasion, *havan* is also performed in the temple. In the golden Vishwanath temple this *akhanda path* or *havan* is not performed these days, although, as reported by the Mahanta of the temple, some fifty years ago this was being done regularly.

On the occasion of Shivaratri, the pilgrims as well as the local devotees organize *kirtan* and *bhajan*. In 1972-73, in addition to pilgrims, five groups of local devotees belonging to Brahmin, Kshatri, Nai and Ahir castes performed *kirtan* and *bhajan* in the precincts of the golden Vishwanath temple.

In the temple of B.H.U. Vishwanath and the Adi Vishwanath, Shivaratri is not celebrated as elaborately as is done in the other Vishwanath temples. While in the B. H. U. Vishwanath, a few additional *aratis* are done on this occasion, in the Adi Vishwanath, some offerings are also made besides the extra *aratis*. The influx of worshippers is also very low in these temples.

Besides the sacred centres of Lord Shiva, Shivaratri is performed with some variations in the sacred centres dedicated to other gods and goddesses, and also in the homes of the citizens of Kashi. In many families, the ladies remain engaged in *kirtan* and *bhajan* for the whole night of Shivaratri. Throwing of *abir* on one another, singing marriage songs, engaging themselves in jokes, and taking of *bhang* are the order of the day.

Kartik Purnima

The month of Kartik (coinciding with November) is believed to be the holiest month, and hence most orthodox Hindus perform various rites and observe the prescribed taboos in food articles (in vegetables and pulses) as well as suspend shaving of beard and pairing of nails during the month. According to the *Shivapuran*, in the month of Kartik all the Hindu gods and goddesses descend to *Mrityubhuvan* (earth) from the heaven. Among Hindus every full-moon day is considered sacred; the full-moon day of the holiest month Kartik is, therefore, most important. On this day large number of pilgrims take bath in the Ganges as also in other sacred rivers. Since in Kashi the Ganges is *Uttaravahini*, (flowing towards north) and Lord Vishwanath resides here permanently, a holy dip at this place is considered to be endowed with special merits. Hence pilgrims from all over India assemble here on this auspicious occasion.

On the occasion of the Kartik *purnima* (full-moon) people start taking bath in the Ganges from 2.30 a.m. onwards. On 20 November, 1972, the total number of people taking bath in the early hours of the dawn were estimated to be about two lakhs. The major concentration of pilgrims was at five main bathing *ghats* or the Panch Tirtha ghat, viz. the Panch-Ganga ghat, the Manikarnika ghat, the Dasashwamedha ghat, Assi ghat, and Varuna ghat. In addition to these *ghats*, where there was heavy rush of pilgrims, people took bath also at Meer ghat, Man Mandir ghat, Scindia ghat, and Darbhanga ghat. Most of the pilgrims who had come to take holy dip in the Ganges were from neighbouring districts of Varanasi, i.e. Mirzapur, Balia, Ghazipur, Gorakhpur, Azamgarh, Jaunpur, Chhapra, Arrah, etc.

On this occasion pilgrims generally do not perform any ritual in detail. After taking bath they offer water to the rising sun, recite some *mantras* or utter '*Ma Gange ki jai*', etc. The *ghatias* sitting on the different *ghats* hardly find time to assist the pilgrims in performing a ritual, for they are mostly busy in guarding the personal belongings of the pilgrims kept under their charge. After taking bath the pilgrims come to the place where the *ghatia* is sitting and change their wet clothes and then pay the latter a small amount ranging from ten paisa to one rupee as fee for guarding their belongings. The *ghatia* applies in return sandal wood paste on their forehead.

Regional variations in offerings at the *ghat* are noticed: the South Indians offer coconut, the Nepali pilgrims offer bananas, and those from the adjoining areas of Varanasi offer sugarcane. The pilgrims of Varanasi region believe that the offering of sugarcane to mother Ganga will yield them rich harvest.

After taking bath in the Ganges and observing certain rites at the *ghat* the pilgrims move towards the golden Vishwanath temple for having *darshan* of the deity, and offer *akshat*, flowers, etc. to Vinayak, Shiva *linga* and Ganesh, on the way.

The traffic of pilgrims is controlled by the police. The regular entrance door is used as exit and one way traffic is enforced. The pilgrims are allowed to enter from the Gyanvapi side, three sides of the sanctum sanctorum of the golden Vishwanath are fenced with iron bars, and the north side is occupied by the chief priest, known as the *gaddidar*. The pilgrims are allowed only to have *darshan* of the Shiva *linga* from a distance; they are not allowed to touch the idol. This arrangement is done only to keep the heavy rush of pilgrims under control.

FESTIVALS OF LOCAL AND REGIONAL IMPORTANCE

Annakut

The festival of Annakut is associated with the goddess of *anna* (crops), i.e. Lakshmi, and hence the Annapurna temple in Kashi is the main centre of the performance of the festival of annakut. It is celebrated also at other sacred centres, such as in all the Vishwanath temples in Kashikarvat, Bara Ganesh, Shitala Mandir, and Tulsi Manas Mandir.

The festival of Annakut falls on the Kartik *shudi pratipada* (the first day of the light fortnight of the month of Kartik) when different types of *bhogas* (eatables offered to the god) are offered to the deity. Regarding the origin of this festival the priests and the pundits of Kashi are of the opinion that originally it was associated with God Krishna, an incarnation of Vishnu, and along with Vishnu his consort Lakshmi, the goddess of wealth and prosperity, was also worshipped. Some 80 years ago, a Brahmin named Dhananjaya brought an idol of Annapurna and he kept fast on the first day of the light fortnight of Kartik and performed Annakut (festival), and since then the people of Kashi have started performing this festival.

This festival continues for three days. On this occasion tickets are printed and sold out in advance to the people desirous of having the *prasada* (left-overs from the *bhoga* distributed among the devotees). The minimum rate for a ticket in 1972 was one rupee (one could however pay any larger amount). On the third day *prasada* is given to the buyers of the tickets; the quantity of the *prasada* determined by the amount of tickets purchased. Fifty-six types of *bhoga* are offered to the deity.

As stated above, the Annapurna temple is the most important centre for the performance of Annakut. Here the gold idols of Annapurna, Vishwanath, Vishnu and Lakshmi are installed in a room on the first floor of the temple which remains closed throughout the year. It is believed that whosoever would attempt to open this room on any other day except of this festival would die. This special room is kept open for three days during the Annakut. In the collection of idols of Annapurna and Shiva, the latter is shown receiving alms from Annapurna.

On the first day of the Annakut festival, a *shodashopchar puja* is performed by the priests at about 6.30 a.m. It continues for about one and half hours and thereafter the devotees are allowed to enter the sanctum for having *darshan*. The devotees do not sleep during the night, some of them pass the night in *bhajan*, *kirtan*, *japa* and reciting the Annapurna *stotra* (verses in honour of the deity) etc. Next morning, the priest performs the *shringar arati* and offers 56 types of *bhoga* to the deities. The *bhoga* articles consist of various type of fruits, sweets, etc., in addition to 54 kgs. of boiled rice and 35 kgs. of pulses (particularly gram, *mung* and *arhar*) placed before the deities. The *bhoga* articles are placed before the deities in such a way that it appears like a small mountain; the priests and the devotees call it a mountain of *bhoga*. The devotees keep fast on the second day and they break their fast on the morning of the third day only after taking the *prasad* of Annakut.

From the counterfoils of receipts sold to the pilgrims in 1972, it could be assessed that at least one lakh and fifty thousand people participated in the Annakut festival in the Annapurna temple; out of this, 50 per cent tickets were purchased by the local devotees, 35 per cent were purchased by people from Varanasi region, and 15 per cent tickets were purchased by pilgrims from South India, Maharashtra, Bengal, Punjab, Gujarat, Rajasthan, etc.

Rangbhari Ekadashi

The Rangbhari Ekadashi is a colourful festival that falls on the eleventh day of the light fortnight in the month of Phalgun, when Lord Vishwanath is worshipped along with his consort Parvati and offered *abir* (coloured powder), sweets, *bhang*, etc. Originally the festival was associated with god Vishnu, particularly in Adikeshwar temple, but later, during 1880-1910, it was adopted by the followers of Shiva cult in the golden Vishwanath temple. In the beginning it was observed perfunctorily in the golden Vishwanath temple, but during the regime of the late Mahanta Mahabir Prasad Tripathi, it was elaborated, and today it is one of the most important festivals of the golden Vishwanath temple.

Besides the golden Vishwanath temple many other sacred centres such as Annapurna, Avimukteshwar, Shringar Gauri, Panchabadan Mahadeva, Hanuman, Ganesh, etc. also celebrate the Ranghbhari Ekadashi. But most of these sacred centres have been observing this festival only for the past 20 to 30 years.

In the golden Vishwanath temple two small idols of Shiva and Parvati, made of silver, are installed at about 4.00 p.m. On the head of Shiva is placed a beautiful umbrella-like silver structure with a narrow pipe placed on the back of Vishwanath; that shows the Ganges descending from the head of Shiva. These are covered with flowers, *belapatra* and garlands. The priests first offer *puja*, and then sprinkle *abir* on the deities while at the same time reciting sacred hymns from the scriptures. Thereafter the pilgrims come forward to offer *bhang*, flowers, sweets, *abir* to the deities. Lord Shiva and Parvati thus celebrate the holy festival. The festival comes to an end after 24 hours, at about 4.00 p.m. the following day.

Pilgrims mostly from the adjoining areas of Varanasi, viz.

Mirzapur, Azamgarh, Gorakhpur, Allahabad, Jaunpur, etc., gather on this occasion. In 1973 the number of people participating in this festival was estimated to have exceeded one lakh, but the pilgrims coming from distant places was only 5 per cent.

Vaikuntha Chaturdashi

The festival of Vaikuntha Chaturdashi falls on the fourteenth day of the month of Kartik when *deep* (lamp) and *batti* (wick) are offered to Lord Vishnu and Lord Shiva. Another significant aspect of this festival is that on the Vaikunth Chaturdashi day a special place is allotted to Lord Vishnu in the sanctum sanctorum of the golden Vishwanath temple, and people are told that it is the Vaikunth (heavenly abode). Both Vishnu and Shiva are worshipped together on this occasion; *belapatra* is offered to Vishnu and *tulsi* leaves to Shiva, which is otherwise taboo in the case of each other. It is believed that on this occasion gods Vishnu and Shiva worship one another; Vishnu offers *tulsi* leaf to Shiva and Shiva offers *belapatra* to Vishnu.

As the legend has it, a Brahmin named Dhaneshwar, who had committed various types of sins all his life, one day went to the bank of the Narmada river where people were performing *deep* and *batti* festival. Dhaneshwar mixed with the devout pilgrims and when he died, his soul was first taken away by Yamraj in order to punish him in hell, but Yamraj could not award him any punishment for he was told by god Shiva that Dhaneshwar got rid of all the sins committed during his life time simply by touching the pilgrims gathered on the occasion of Kartik Chaturdashi at the bank of the Narmada river. Dhaneshwar was eventually allotted a place in the *Vaikuntha* (heaven). The Vaikunth Chaturdashi is hence considered an important festival.

On this day the worshippers, after taking bath in the Ganges, visit the golden Vishwanath temple and offer *akshat*, *chandan*, *Gangajal*, etc. to both Vishnu and Shiva, and then place before the deities lighted *deeps* and *battis*. The offering of earthen *deeps* and the *battis* made of cotton are the specialities of the day.

The festival of Vaikunth Chaturdashi is observed mostly by the local devotees. Among the devotees old women outnumber men. In 1972, about ten thousand devotees participated in this festival, out of which about 50 per cent were local devotees, and the rest had come from the neighbourhood of Varanasi. Among the local devotees, about 75 per cent were old Brahmin ladies. They are experts in preparing *battis*, they worship the deities with one lakh and twentyfive thousand *battis*.

Ganga Dasehra

The festival of Ganga Dasehra falls on the tenth day of the light fortnight of the month of Jyeshtha (May-June). It is associated with King Bhagirath of the solar dynasty, who performed great tapa (penance) and is believed to have brought down the heavenly river Ganga from her heavenly abode on to the earth. On this day, finally the holy Ganga had descended on to the earth. To break her long downward fall, she was first received by Lord Shiva in his matted hair. Hence it is considered a very auspicious day by the Hindu devotees. This occasion is marked by taking a holy dip in the Ganges, and by worshipping mother Ganga. The Ganga Mahasabha makes special arrangements for the worship in the temple of the goddess Ganga; flowers, garlands, etc., are offered to the deities in huge quantity. A special *arati* consisting of 50 *battis* (wicks) is also offered to the deity; this type of *arati* is probably held only once a year.

On this occasion, the local people organize various cultural programmes like *bhajan* and *kirtan* accompanied by musical instruments (jhal, drum, harmonium, etc.). Brahmins, Khatris, Ahirs, Banias, Kurmis, Thakurs, belonging to Hindi, Maithili, Bhojpuri, Bengali and Marathi linguistic groups, are most active participants; the number of Punjabi, Gujarati and Tamilian devotees is much less; only a few pilgrims from North India come to attend this festival.

After taking bath in the Ganges people visit the golden Vishwanath temple for having *darshan* of the Shiva, because the goddess Ganga and Shiva are complimentary to one another, as if one is soul, the other is body, and the spiritual assimilation of the two makes Kashi *mokshadayini* (bestower of salvation).

Basant Panchami

The festival of Basant Panchami falls on the fifth day of the light fortnight in the month of Magh (January-February). It is associated with the worship of nature on the setting of *Basant*

Ritu which is considered the King of seasons (*ritu raj*). The festival is associated with the well known myth of *Kamadahan* by Shiva. People offer holy water of the Ganges to Shiva *linga*. But the most popular function on the day is the worship of Saraswati, the goddess of learning.

Since Kashi has been the most prominent seat of learning from time immemorial, the Saraswati *Puja* is performed here with great gusto and dedication. On this occasion, in all the educational centres of Kashi, the images of goddess Saraswati are installed and worshipped by students and teachers. Various cultural programmes, viz. drama, *bhajan*, *kirtan*, etc., are organized on this occasion. In the Banaras Hindu University and Kashi Vidyapith, Sanskrit dramas are staged as part of the celebrations.

The image of goddess Saraswati is installed in different parts of the city, cultural programmes are held in honour of the deity. Goddess Saraswati is worshipped in most of the families. This is also an occasion to initiate a young child to learning or what is known as *vidhyarambh*.

The Saraswati *puja* is organized in the golden Vishwanath, Annapurna, Sankatajee, Kala Bhairava, Sankatamochan, Kashi-karvat, Balaji and Gopal temples. Most of these sacred centres are visited by people for having *darshan* of the deities on this auspicious day. At some of the sacred centres the priests perform *shodashopchar puja* and offer the deities mango-flowers (*amra manjan*), *rori*, and mustary flowers. Saraswati *puja* is thus combined with the rejoicings of Basant *ritu*.

Mauni Amavasya

The festival of Mauni Amavasya falls on the full lunar eclipse day of Magh (January-February) which is believed to be a very auspicious day for worshipping the *Trimurti*, i.e. Brahma, Vishnu, and Mahesh. According to the 'Kashi Khand' of the *Skanda Puran* it is suggested that the golden idols of Brahma, Vishnu and Mahesh should be installed and worshipped by the people and, thereafter the worshipped golden idols of *Trimurti* should be offered to Brahmins as gifts. Because the worshippers are required to keep *maun* (complete silence) for the day falling on *amavasya*. That is why it is called Mauni Amavasya. On this day people take a holy dip at the Prayag *ghat* and then worship the *Trimurti.* While taking a holy dip at Prayag one must observe *maun* (silence). After bath pilgrims worship the idols of Brahma, Vishnu, and Mahesh kept in the temple at Prayag ghat, and then they visit Vishwanath temple and other shrines located in that cluster.

On this occasion again the influx of pilgrims is largely from the neighbouring districts of Varanasi.

On this occasion some devotees perform *homa* and *puja* at their residence. When the *homa* and *puja* are completed, the priests are given *dana dakshina*, and the devotees break their silence; the festival thus comes to end.

Krishnashtami

The birth day of Lord Krishna, the eighth incarnation of Vishnu falls on the eighth day of the dark fortnight of Bhadon (August-September). This is celebrated in Kashi by people belonging to different sects.

In the Gopal temple, the festival of Krishnashtami is performed with great enthusiasm. At midnight, the idol of Krishna is attired in princely garments. Since Krishna is believed to have been born in a prison, a model of the gaol is temporarily built near the shrine. A little later, the idol of Krishna is removed to another place, named Gokul, after the village so-called, where according to the mythology, Krishna was taken immediately after his birth and was brought up by his foster parents. The idol is installed there and then the rituals concerning the birth anniversary start. The devotees, particularly those who keep fast on this occasion spend the whole night in singing *bhajans* (hymns) and *kirtan*.

Although the main function is in the Gopal temple, the other shrines like that of the golden Vishwanath, Annapurna, etc. are also crowded by devotees and worshippers. In the morning of Krishnashtami the devotees take a holy dip in the Ganges and visit the temples of Vishwanath and other shrines for having *darshan* of the deities.

Durga Puja

The festival of Durga Puja is associated with the worship of the Shakti cult in which goddess Durga is worshipped in her different manifestations. In the *Puranas*, particularly in the 'Durga Saptashati Khanda' of the *Markandeya Puran* various names, forms and glorious deeds of the goddess have been described. Among the nine forms of Durga,[2] which is popularly called Nava Durga, are Shailaputri, Brahmacharini, Chitraghanta, Kusumanda, Skandamata, Katyayani, Kalaratri, Mahagauri and Siddhidatri.

The goddess Durga is worshipped during the *navaratra* of Ashwin (September-October), starting from the first day of the light fortnight of Ashwin to the tenth day, called Vijaya Dashami. On this occasion the devotees undertake a *parikrama* (circumambulation) of Kashi which is popularly known as 'Nava Durga Parikrama' which will be described at some length later on.

The temporary installation of Durga is made by various organizations, such as Youth Club, Students Club, Business Communities, etc., in different parts of Kashi. The number of temporary idols of Durga is increasing. Earlier only a few idols used to be installed in the Bengali *tola* and in the *Raja Darbaja* area, but at least 45 idols of Durga were installed in 1972 in various parts of this city; making the total number of idols to 50.

There is a great degree of variation at the level of sacred performances between the permanent shrines and the temporary installation of goddess Durga. At the permanent shrines of Durga the sacred performances are more elaborate and orthodox according to the textually prescribed procedures. In the temporary booths the ritualistic performances are simple and brief; the various modern means of entertainments, such as playing of film songs on loudspeakers, twist dances and pop songs (these are not at all found in the permanent shrines of goddess Durga) are employed. Smoking and putting on leather shoes at the time of having *darshan* of the deity are against the religious sanctity of the sacred performances, but at the time of immersion ceremony of Durga nobody seems to have such a consideration.

Chausathi Mela

The festival of Chausathi Mela falls on the first day of the month of Chaitra when *chausath* (sixty-four) *yoginis* are worshipped in Kashi. Regarding the origin of this festival it is said that sixty-four *yoginis* were sent to Kashi by Lord Shiva to captivate king Divodas who had ousted him from Kashi, but the *yoginis* instead of doing so were themselves so much attracted by the charming atmosphere and beauty of Kashi that they settled here and forgot to disturb the king. It was the first Chaitra when the *yoginis* had come to Kashi and hence this occasion is marked with festivity.

On the occasion of Chausathi festival the local people from different *mohallas* of Kashi assemble at the Chausathi ghat where the idols of yoginis are enshrined in a temple owned by a local Gujarati Brahmin. Throughout the year this shrine remains almost neglected, but on the occasion of the Chausathi Mela the temple is cleaned, painted and decorated with flowers, flags, etc. The *yoginis* are offered new clothes and other offerings. In the morning, *Shringar arati* is performed by the shrine priest, and thereafter the local devotees offer flowers, *abir* (red powder), sweets, etc., to the deity. After worshipping the deity the devotees also throw *abir* and sprinkle coloured water on one another.

In the Chausathi Mela of 1973, about ten thousand people participated, in which men outnumbered women (male participation was 80 to 85 per cent). Since men exchange colour and *abir* and visit the temple after drinking *bhang* the women folk usually do not come out fearing any ugly incidents.

Rath-Yatra

The festival of Rath-Yatra is not very old in Kashi. It is said that one Pundit Tripandi Brahmin started this festival in Vikram Samvatà 1964 (corresponding to A.D. 1907), and since then it is being performed by the local people. It is celebrated on *dwitiya* (second day) of the light fortnight in Asarh (June-July) every year.

Rath-Yatra or the chariot driving procession of Lord Jagannath is originally associated with Lord Jagannath of Puri in Orissa; but since he is believed to be the manifestation of god Vishnu, many vaishnavite shrines in Kashi observe this festival. Some of the sacred shrines of the Dasashwamedh ghat area, particularly the Vishnu mandir of Kotwali area, and the Rath Yatra chowk, are the main centres of attraction on the occasion of Rath-Yatra. The divine chariot of lord Jagannath is pulled by the devotees and brought at the Rath-Yatra Chowk where it is kept for three days, i.e. from *dwitiya* to *chaturthi*. The devotees feel proud of and take great pleasure in driving and pulling the Lord's chariot; they believe that by doing so they earn *punya*. Lord Jagannath is offered *khichri*[3], *halwa*, *puri*, curd, *karha*, *pera* and other sweets.

On this occasion the half-a-kilometre long route of the Rath-Yatra, i.e. from Gadoulia to the Rath-Yatra Chowk is heavily crowded, and many temporary shops are erected on either side of the route. These shops sell mainly toys, cosmetics, cheap quality of beads and other toilet articles as well as articles used in worship, such as flowers, *askhat*, etc. The rush of the devotees is seen around 8 a.m. in the morning and again in the evening between 6 to 8 p.m. when special *aratis* are performed. A rough estimate of the gathering of the local people goes up to ten thousand when the special *aratis* are performed in the morning and the evening.

PARIKRAMAS

The custom of circumambulation, which is popularly referred to as *parikrama*[4] in the various sacred scriptures, round certain sacred centres of Hindu pilgrimage, has been considered as the best method of blotting out all sins committed during one's life time. In India there are a number of sacred centres like Nimsar[5], Bithur, Mathura, Hari Parvat in Srinagar (Kashmir), Girnar hill in Junagarh, Barda in Jamnagar, Kashi, and Janakpur[6] in Nepal where the devout Hindus go for *parikrama* and attach great religious importance to these sacred centres. In Kashi large number of *parikramas* of various types are made.

The 'Kashi Khanda' of the *Skandapuran* gives an elaborate description and mentions 16 types of *parikramas* which are to be undertaken in the different shrines of Kashi. These are *nitya parikrama*, *anukrama parikrama*, *shadang parikrama*, *trikantak parikrama*, *ashtobasa parikrama*, Nava Gauri *parikrama*, *Nava-graha parikrama*, *Ekadas* Maharudra *parikrama*, *Dwadas* Aditya *parikrama*, 42 *linga parikrama*, 56 Vinayak *parikrama*, *antar-grihi parikrama*, and the Panchakosi *parikrama*.

According to the nature of *parikramas* and the pilgrims' participation therein, we may classify the *parikramas* into the *parikramas* of local, regional and all-India importance. Among the *parikramas* of local importance mention may be made of *nitya parikrama*, *anukrama*, *shadang*, *trikantak*, *ashtobasa*, *Navagrah*, *Ekadas*, Maharudra, 42 *linga*, and 56 Vinayak *parikramas*. Among the *parikramas* of regional importance mention may be made of Nava Durga, Nava Gauri and *antargrihi parikrama*. The Panchakosi *parikrama* is of all India importance.

Nitya Parikrama

The 'Kashi Khanda' of *Skandapuran* mentions that the *nitya parikramas* should be undertaken on each day by the citizens of Kashi. But nowadays only a few old ladies, and some priests and pundits do the *nitya parikrama*. Those going for *nitya parikrama* take a holy bath in the Ganges early in the morning and visit the shrines of Drupaditya, Vishnu Dandapani, Maheshwar, Dhundhiraj, Gyanvapi, Nandikeshwar, Tarakeshwar, Mahakaleshwar, etc., and offer them water, *akshat*, *dhup*, etc. In the *nitya parikrama*, elaborate ritual is neither required nor practised by the devotees.

Anukrama Parikrama

This *parikrama* is performed in the month of Chaitra. Also on some festive occasions, like Shivaratri, Annakut, Rangabhari Ekadashi, etc., old men and women of Kashi perform this *parikrama*. Before this *parikrama*, the devotees take a holy dip in the Ganges and then worship Lord Vishwanath, Bindu Mahadev, Dhundhiraj, Dandapani, Bhairava, Kashi Devi, Bhawani and Manikarnika Devi. It is believed that by performing this *parikrama*, one earns special *punya*.

Shadang Parikrama

Today this *parikrama* is only in the memory of the old priests and devotees of Kashi but not at all performed. In this *parikrama*, a *darshan* of Vishwanath, Vishalakshi, Mandakini, Kala-Bhairava, Dhundhiraj, Dandapani, etc., is traditionally prescribed.

Trikantak Parikrama

This *parikrama* is also mentioned in the *Lingapurana* and the *Skandapurana*. By undertaking the *trikantak parikrama* one gets rid of all difficulties faced in day-to-day life. In performing this *parikrama* one has to visit Abhimukteshwar, Lingeshwar,

Madhyameshwar, etc. But like the *shadang parikrama* it has also become extinct.

In addition to the *parikramas* mentioned above, there are a few more *parikramas* of local importance which have now become obsolete. Among these mention may be made of *ashtobasa parikrama*, *Navagraha parikrama*, *anga parikrama*, 42 *linga parikrama*, etc. Earlier, one who wished to undertake *ashtobasa parikrama* would visit Ganeshwar, Narmadeshwar, Gavastishwar, Satishwar, Tarakeshwar, etc. Similarly for undertaking *Navagraha parikrama* one is required to visit the shrines of Chandreshwar, Mangleshwar, Bundeshwar, Brihaspatishwar, Sukeshwar, Sanishwar, Rahu, Ketu etc.

Many sacred shrines which fell on the *parikrama* routes have now been completely defaced, most of them are being used for residential purposes and shops and have either disappeared or become inaccessible.

Nava Durga and Nava Gauri Parikrama

The Nava Durga and Nava Gauri *parikramas* attract people from the neighbouring districts of Varanasi. The Nava Durga *parikrama* begins on Ashwin *shudi parva* (i.e. first day of the light fortnight of the month of Ashwin corresponding to September-October) and continues up to *navami* (ninth day of the same fortnight). The Nava Gauri parikrama falls on the first day of the light fortnight of Chaitra (March-April). In both these *parikramas* various sacred centres belonging to different forms of goddess Durga, such as Shailaputri, Brahmacharini, Chitraghanta, Kusumanda, Skandamata, Katyayani, Kalaratri, Annapurna, Siddhidatri, etc., are visited by the pilgrims.

On the auspicious day of Ashwin *parva* pilgrims from the neighbouring areas of Kashi assemble here. After taking a holy dip in the Ganges they undertake the Nava Durga *parikrama* and visit the various shrines as mentioned above. The shrines are beautifully decorated on this occasion and special *aratis* are performed by the priests in honour of the deities.

On this occasion the *anushthanis* perform Chandipatha (recitation of verses from the *Markandey Purana*) for the welfare of their *jajmans*. One who is appointed to conduct *anushthan*, is supplied with a new *dhoti*, new towel, and some cash. The *anushthan* is performed for nine days. Those who do not employ *anushthanis*, take help of the *yatrawals* in conducting *pujas* and *parikramas* at various sacred centres. *Bhajans* and *kirtans* are arranged by rich devotees on the occasion of these *parikramas*. Old men and women take active part in these functions. One of the informants said, "I have earned a lot of money in my life time, and now I want to spend both time and money in doing *bhajan* and *kirtan* at the various sacred centres of gods and goddesses in Kashi." An old Marwari woman was found on this occasion distributing clothes, *dhoti*, towel, *buniyan*, etc. to the *anushthanis* and other sacred specialists associated with the shrines of Durga.

Antargrihi Parikrama

As discussed earlier, Kashi is divided into three *khandas* (segments), viz. Kedar khand, Onkar khand and Visheshwar khand. The circumambulation of the sacred centres located within the Visheshwar khand is called the *antargrihi parikrama*. It may be stated here that within the Visheshwar khand there are a number of sacred centres, but only a few important sacred centres are taken into consideration for undertaking the *antargrihi parikrama*. These centres are Sakshi Vinayak, Golden Vishwanath, Annapurna, Abhimukteshwar, Dhundhiraj Gangesh, Manikarnikeshwar, Mahadeva, Gokarneshwar, Bhuteshwar and Brahmeshwar.

Those who want to undertake the *antargrihi parikrama* first of all start it by visiting the shrine of Dhundhiraj Gangesh, and finally come to the golden Vishwanath temple where the *antargrihi parik-rama* comes to an end. In takes just one day. There is no fixed date for the *parikrama*; it can be performed on any day. Monday, the day of Shiva, is however, considered to be more meritorious for *parikrama*. The Visheshwar *khand*, of which *antargrihi parikrama* is performed, is also known as *abhimukta kshetra* (area of salvation) and, therefore, the devotees are told by the sacred specialists of Kashi that if the *antargrihi parikrama* of this *kshetra* is undertaken the performer will get *mukti* (salvation). Hence, its importance.

Panchakosi Parikrama

In the *panchakosi parikrama*, the performer has to undertake a *parikrama* in the radius of five *kosas* or 16 kms. where a large number of sacred centres belonging to the four *dhams* (Jagannathpuri, Rameshwaram, Dwarka, and Kedarnath), the seven sacred Puris (Mathura, Ayodhya, Dwarka, Awantika or Ujjain, Kanchi, Haridwar and Kashi), the 56 manifestations of Ganesh, nine Gauris, the 13 Narasingha, the 16 Keshava, the 12 Aditya, the eight Bhairavas and several Shiva *lingas* are located. The Panchakosi route, when drawn out on a map as per the description given in the *Skanda purana*, closely resembles the shape of a *shankha* (as also acclaimed by the *Skanda purana*). This forms the *pauranic* Kashi-kshetra.

Regarding the mythological origin of the *panchakosi parikrama* it is said that once Parvati requested Shiva to point out the process through which one can dissolve the sins committed by one during one's life time. Lord Shiva replied that there are three methods of dissolving the sins; firstly, a sinner should dig a well or pond for public use; secondly, he should construct a temple wherein deities particularly from Shiva's family (Ganesh, Parvati, Kartikeya, and Nandi) are enshrined and worshipped; and thirdly, he should undertake the *panchakosi parikrama*. Since then the *panchakosi parikrama* is in vogue.

The *panchakosi parikrama* was prevalent in the *satya yuga*. An interesting mythological story regarding its origin runs as follows:

> "A famous rishi named Kusmanda lived in Kashi. His son Mandap once committed a theft in the house of a rich man and decamped with gold and other valuables. In order to hide these valuables he went to the house of a prostitute. But there he got drunk and the prostitute ran away with all his loot. Mandap finally came to his own house and narrated the incident to his father. Rishi Kusmanda called a meeting of rishis and gods for conducting *prayashchita* for his son, but the rishi was told by the learned gathering that since his son had already undertaken a *panchakosi parikrama* his sins have been washed away and now no further punishment is required."

The legend has it that even in the *treta* and the *dwapar yugas* many divine personalities like god Rama and Krishna had undertaken *panchakosi parikrama* of Kashi. Thus the *panchakosi parikrama* of Kashi is believed to be of utmost religious importance, bestowing upon the performer all material enjoyments in this life and *moksha* in the life hereafter.

General Features of the Panchakosi Parikrama

People are encouraged to undertake *parikrama* usually on foot, but those who are physically unfit or very weak, may engage a motor car or a *rickshaw* for undertaking the *parikrama*. During 1972-73, it was found that many old ladies from Rajasthan had engaged *rickshaws* and motor cars for performing the *panchakosi parikrama*. Like other *parikramas*, performed at various sacred centres of India and Nepal, the rules of this *panchakosi parikrama* are also democratic. For instance, both men and women are allowed to undertake the *parikrama*. There is no caste and age restriction; persons of any caste or of any age can perform this *parikrama*. However, there are certain rules which are strictly followed even today. For instance, menstruating women do not undertake this *parikrama*. The pilgrims are neither allowed to put on shoes in course of the *parikrama* nor are they supposed to carry any cooked meal with them. Sexual intercourse during the period of *parikrama* is strictly prohibited. In addition to these general restrictions, people are always drawn to religious discourses and are encouraged to utter "*Har-Har-Mahadeva! Shambhu, Kashi Vishwanath ki jai*!"

Preparation for the Panchakosi Parikrama

A day before starting the *panchakosi parikrama*, the pilgrims take bath in the *Uttaravahini* Ganga and worship Dhundhiraj Ganesh and Lord Vishwanath. Early in the morning of the day of commencing the *parikrama*, they again take bath in the Ganges, specially at the Manikarnika ghat, and then go to Gyanvapi to perform *sankalpa* (sacred vow) reciting the names of 56 manifestations of Ganesh, 13 Narasingha, 16 Keshava, Vishwanath and Vishnu, etc. After doing the *sankalpa* and reciting the names of these gods, the pilgrims visit Vishwanath, Annapurna and then again come to the Manikarnika ghat keeping silence all along from the Vishwanath temple to the Manikarnikā ghat. The *parikrama* is thus started.

Five Halting Places of the Panchakosi Parikrama

There are five halting places on the *parikrama* route, these are called *chattis*. After leaving Kashi for *panchakosi parikrama*, the pilgrims arrive at the first *chatti*, called Kardameshwar. On the way they offer flowers, *akshat*, *chandan*, *Gangajal*, etc., to the idols of various gods and goddesses enshrined in and around the *parikrama* route.

After reaching the first *chatti* at Kardameshwar, the pilgrims look into the *Kardam kunda* (sacred well); this is done in the memory of the great rishi Kardam. Thereafter they take sacred bath and perform *puja* of the Kardameshwar *linga* to which *panch-anna* (five kinds of grains) are offered. After worshipping Kardameshwar *linga*, the pilgrims worship other deities, like Somnath, Birupaksha, Nilkanth, etc.

Next day, before leaving for the second *chatti*, the pilgrims offer *puja* to Nagnath, Chamunda Devi, Moksheshwar, Karneshwar, Birbhadreshwar, Unmatta Bhairava, Bimla Durga, Nandakeshwar, Gaupriya, Birupaksha, Kusheshwar, Bimleshwar, Gyaneshwar, Amriteshwar, Gandharva Sagar, etc. In this connection, it may be mentioned that the pilgrims do not make any elaborate ritual in these shrines; they simply throw *akshat* and *Gangajal* in these shrines and bow before them before leaving the place.

The next halting place is Bhimchandi. After arrival here, the pilgrims first of all take bath in the Gandharva Sagar and then worship the Bhimchandi Mata who is considered very *ugra* (of volatile temperament) and therefore, the pilgrims are told that even the slightest negligence in the performance of *puja* may put them into trouble and misfortune. The pilgrims are careful in performing *puja* at this shrine. Vermilion is offered to the goddess; other sacred ingredients, viz. red flower, sweets, *Gangajal*, etc. are also offered. In the night, special *shringar arati* of the Bhimchandi Devi is performed.

On the following day, before leaving for the third halting place, the pilgrims again offer *puja* to the Bhimchandi Devi with a request to accord permission to proceed ahead; this is called *anga puja*. While proceeding on to the third *chatti* the pilgrims offer worship to Mahabhim Bhairava, Bhutanath, Sindhurodees, Kalanatheshwar, Kameshwar, Birbhadra,

Chaumukh-Gyaneshwar, Delhi Vinayak, Khundas Vinayak, Udanad Vinayak, Tapobhumi, and many other gods and goddesses located on the *parikrama* route.

The third *chatti* is Rameshwar. After reaching there, the pilgrims first of all take bath in the Varuna river and then offer *pindas* to their ancestors. It is believed that in the *treta yug*, Lord Rama had undertaken the *panchakosi parikrama* and had offered here *pindas* in the name of his ancestors. Hence, the pilgrims also offer *pindas* in the name of their ancestors. After offering *pindas*, various deities such as Rameshwar Shiva *linga*, Bharateshwar, Lakshmaneshwar, Satrughneshwar, Bhumishwar, Hareshwar, etc., are worshipped. In the night special *shringar arati* is performed at the shrine of Rameshwar Shiva *linga*.

The fourth *chatti* on the route of the *panchakosi parikrama* is Shivapur. It is said that some hundred years ago it was not a halting place for the *panchakosi* pilgrims, and as such not mentioned in the Kashimahatmya of the *Skanda Puran*. Previously this area was a dense forest, and more than once the pilgrims were robbed by dacoits in this jungle. So the people of Shivapur and its neighbouring areas decided to make it a *chatti* for the *panchakosi* pilgrims. Two *dharmshalas* have been constructed for the pilgrims. The pilgrims offer *Gangajal*, *akshat*, etc., at the shrine of Panch Pandava. This shrine is not mentioned in the '*Kashi khand*'.

On the fifth day, the pilgrims arrive at the last *chatti* for the *panchakosi parikrama;* this is Kapildhara named after the famous *rishi*, Kapil Muni. At Kapildhara the pilgrims first of all take bath in the Kapildhara kunda and then perform *puja* at the shrine of Brishabhadwajeshwar Mahadeva. There is an interesting legend about the Kapildhara kunda and the Brishabhadwajeshwar Mahadeva; once the Lord Vishwanath came to Kapildhara where lived Kapil Muni in his *ashram*. The *rishi* had a beautiful cow. Lord Shiva was bathed by Kapil Muni in milk flowing from the cow's udders. This milk was accumulated in a *kunda*, 100 yards square. The *kunda* is today known as Kapildhara *kunda*. After being bathed in milk and worshipped by Kapil Muni, Lord Vishwanath rode on the *Brisha* (bull) and went towards Kashi, and hence, the Shivalingam at Kapildhara is called Brishabhadwajeshwar Shiva.

As the informants reported, about 20 years ago, many

karmakandis from Kashi used to come to Kapildhara on the last day of this *parikrama* to assist the pilgrims in performing the *puja*. But nowadays the *karmakandis* come to Kapildhara only on the occasion of Malmas *parikrama*. However, Kapildhara is the only *chatti*, where *bhandara* (community feast) is thrown by rich devotees.

Since Kapildhara is the last *chatti*, the pilgrims make all concluding sacred performances. While returning from Kapildhara they worship Jwala, Narsingh, Sarva Vinayak, Varuna Sangam, Panchganga, Bindu Mahadeva, Gavistineshwar, Mangala Gauri, Vaishitheshwar, Vateshwar Shiva, Sidhi Vinayak, Sapta Varuna Vinayak, Vishwanath, Annapurna, Dandapani, Dhundhiraj Ganesh, Kalabhairava, etc., on the way back home.

The *jau* (barley) throwing ceremony is an important performance in the *panchakosi parikrama*. Devout pilgrims are told that those who would throw *jau* on the *parikrama* route heavily from Sarva Vinayak to Sapta Varuna Vinayak, would attain *swarga* (heavenly abode), a ladder leading to the heaven is constructed for them. In the *panchakosi parikrama* of 1973, many old pilgrims were seen throwing *jau* on the route as well as in between the shrines of Sarva Vinayak to Sapta Varuna Vinayak. In the return journey of the *panchakosi parikrama*, the shrine of Sapta Varuna Vinayak is considered very important, particularly for those who have already performed the *panchakosi parikrama* five times, and now do not want to undertake it in future. Such pilgrims are told to offer wheat shaped gold article and a sickle to Sapta Varuna Vinayak. Those offering it are considered to be bidding a farewell to the *panchakosi parikrama*. On reaching Kashi, the final round of sacred performance of the *panchakosi parikrama* is made at the shrine of Gyanvapi where pilgrims had earlier made a *sankalpa*.

In the above pages we have described the general characteristics of the *panchakosi parikrama* which is performed in five days. The *panchakosi parikrama* may be performed also in one day, or in a few hours. The local devotees of Kashi perform one-day *panchakosi parikrama*, particularly on some festive days like Shivaratri, Dashehara, etc. Those who perform this one-day *parikrama* do not go for elaborate ritual; they simply run fast on the *parikrama* route and bow their heads at the important sacred centres.

The five-day *panchakosi parikarma* takes place once a year. The importance of a *panchakosi parikrama* is enhanced manifold during the Malemas (Leap year), on this special occasion the number of pilgrims also increases by several thousands. The Malemas *parikrama* is organized by some learned pundits of Kashi. They announce the date of the commencement of the *panchakosi parikrama* in newspapers; sometimes pamphlets are also distributed. Among the various institutions organizing the *panchakosi parikrama*, the *Panchakosi Jirnoddhar Samiti* is the best and the most trusted organizations. The *samiti* is managed by the orthodox and learned pundits of Kashi.

In 1973, the composition of 217 pilgrims surveyed by us was as follows :

TABLE 7

Showing the composition of pilgrims (Panchakosi parikrama)

Area	*No. Male*	%	*No. Female*	%	*Total*	%
Local	100	45 82	37	17.45	137	63.27
Regional	52	23.85	28	12.88	80	36.73
Total					217	100 00

The *panchakosi parikrama*, which is organized under the auspices of various organizations has many interesting features. Two days before the commencement of the *parikrama* a meeting is called by these organizations either in some *katha bhavan* or at some *ghat* where the *guru* of the respective team is appointed. The *guru* imparts training to the *parikrama yatris* regarding rules and various other procedures of the *panchakosi parikrama*.

In the institutions sponsored *panchakosi parikrama* the role of *guru* is very important. It is the *guru* of the team who guides and conducts the *sankalpa puja* at the Gyanvapi on the day of commencement; the *guru* leads the team on the *parikrama* route; or he is the first to offer worship at the shrines of each *chatti;* the pilgrims are supposed to worship the deities only after the *guru* has been offered *dhuli-pranam* (to bow upon the feet of the *guru*) by the *parikrama* pilgrims. At every *chatti* the *guru* is respectfully seated on a *gaddi;* the pilgrims perform *abhisheka* (a type of worship) of the *guru* and *tilak* is put on his forehead. The *guru* recites the *Puranas* to the pilgrims. In fact, the *guru* of the *panchakosi parikrama* is the chief in which the all religious powers are vested.

Mandali Panchakosi and Malemas Panchakosi

The *panchakosi parikrama* as stated earlier can be performed in one day, in a few hours, or in five days. The *panchakosi parikrama* may be extended to one month; this happens particularly in the month of *Malemas* or *adhikamas* (leap year) accordingly called *Malemas panchakosi.* The Mandali Panchakosi Parikrama is the organization of a grand feast called *bhandara* for which subscriptions, both in cash and kind, are collected from various groups of pilgrims locally called as *mandali.* Usually this grand feast, *bhandara* is organized at the last *chatti,* for which notice is circulated one day earlier to raise funds. The *bhandara* is thrown open to beggars, pundits and sannyasis. The *bhandara* is an important feature of the Mandali Panchakosi Parikrama which continues for five days.

The Mandali Panchakosi Parikrama, as reported by the pundits of Kashi, is not very old. It is said that about 80 to 85 years ago the father of Pundit Vishwanath Datar[7] started this Mandali Panchakosi Parikrama in which he used to arrange a big *bhandara* on the concluding day. In the beginning, the Maharaja of Kashi gave liberal donation for this purpose.

In the Mandali Panchakosi Parikrama there is no caste or sect restriction, either for giving donations or for participating in the grand feast, *bhandara.* During the Mandali Parikrama of 1973, a *bhandara* had been organized and it was observed that many castes and sects had dined together. About 500 persons were fed in the *bhandara* in which there were Brahmins, Shudras, sannyasis and beggars. It was also observed that all the invitees were fed respectfully, and as soon as the invitees finished their meals, many pilgrims, particularly women, rushed to pick up and throw away the *pattal* (leaf plates) on which they had taken meal.

The Malemas Parikrama continues for one month. For this the pilgrims come from different parts of India. On the occasion of the Malemas Parikrama of 1972, it was found that on one day out of 350 pilgrims, 93 pilgrims were local, 206 were from the neighbouring districts of Varanasi, and 52 pilgrims had come from different parts of India.

Unlike the Mandali Panchakosi Parikrama, the pilgrims of the Malemas Panchakosi are guided by professional Pandas and *bhadurs* of Kashi who instead of imparting *shastric* lessons to the pilgrims engage themselves in extracting money from them.

Another interesting feature of the Malemas Parikrama is the close interaction between the pilgrims belonging to various castes and sects; because they live together for about a month, they come very close to one another at various levels of interaction. Pilgrims coming from different parts of India spend their leisure hours in discussing among themselves things like prospect of crops in their respective areas, climatic conditions, particularly rain, drought, cold, etc., political situation, and even personal family affairs.

Malemas Pilgrimage

The system of living together for one month at a sacred centre and observing prescribed religious way of life is called Mas.[8] This typical sacred performance takes place in the months of the Kartik, Magh and Phalgun.

In Kashi, the Mas pilgrims were studied in October-November (Kartik) of 1972. A sample of 200 Mas pilgrims was also collected, of which 60.7 per cent were Brahmins, 39.3 per cent were from other castes. Like *parikrama*, Mas is also open to all castes and sects. In the Mas pilgrimage women out-number men, and among the women widows and old are in large number.

The Mas pilgrims stay in groups, either in some *dharamshalas* or temples located close to the bathing *ghats* of the Ganges. In early hours of the day they first take sacred bath in the Ganges, perform *Gangapuja* and then visit various temples for *puja* and *darshan*. All the Mas pilgrims of Kashi visit the golden Vishwanath temple, Annapurna temple, and Sakshi Vinayak temple regularly. After visiting the various sacred centres, the Mas pilgrims return to their respective places of stay, and after taking rest for an hour or so, they again assemble at the Dasashwamedh ghat or at the Manikarnika ghat to listen to the recitation of *katha* (fables from the Hindu scriptures) and

1. A Shivalinga of Kashi

2. Dashaswamedh Ghat

(Between Pages 88-89)

3. A Mandir at Kashi

4. A temple on the bank of Ganges

5. Country boats used for the transportation of pilgrims

6. The Scindia Ghat

7. A pilgrim performing Sandhya-Vandana

8. A view of Yajna performance

the *puranas* by the *kathakara* (one who tells the *katha*). After listening to the *katha* for about three or four hours, they offer *dakshina* to the *kathakars* and then go to offer the lighted *deep* to mother Ganga. The Mas pilgrims from Mithila generally offer lighted *deep* to mother Ganga, but those from Gujarat, Madhya Pradesh and Uttar Pradesh light *akashadeep*[8] At the Panchganga ghat the Mas pilgrims light *akashadeep* in large number. They believe that the souls of their ancestors hovering in the sky will get light and direction to come to Kashi to attain *moksha*. Another belief is that the devatas moving in the sky will be pleased to see light, and the pilgrims will be blessed by them. The Mas pilgrims lead very pious life, take cooked food only once in the night, and pass the day either by taking *phalahar* (diet of only fruits) or without taking any thing, even a drop of water.

REFERENCES

[1] The method of preparing *batti* may be described as follows: First of all the cotton bowl is kept in the right hand and by the left hand a thin thread is prepared. The thin thread is given three folds with the help of three fingers (pointer, middle finger and the ring finger); finally the three folds of the cotton thread are rubbed together in such a way that it comes out as a *batti*, which is to be offered to both Vishnu and Shiva.

[2] According to the *Markandey Puran*, the goddess Durga was born to kill the various asuras (demons) on earth who were harassing the gods and the sages in conducting *yajna* and *tapasya* (meditation). Among the notorious *asuras* whom she killed, mention may be made of Madhu Kaitab, Mahishasur, Chand Mund, Dhumra, Sumbh-Nisumbh, Raktabija etc. who had defeated various gods and had even conquered part of the Indraloka, the heavenly abode of the god Indra.

[3] In Puri, *Khichri* is first offered to the lord Jagannath, this is known as *Koth-bhoga*; the other types of *bhogas* are also offered to the god later (Jha 1975).

[4] As legends of the origin of *prikrama* has it, once the Gods were asked to undertake the *parikrama* of the world; they took part in it with their various speedy vehicles, but Ganesh, the son of Lord Shiva who was having a rat as his vehicle thought that it was very difficult to compete with these Gods who had very fast moving vehicles, and hence instead of undertaking a *parikrama* of the world, he moved three times around Shiva with a belief that since his father is called *Trilokinath* (Commander of the three worlds), his *parikrama* would be *equivalent to the parikrama* of the world. This attempt of Ganesh as well as His intelligence was very much appreciated by the fellow gods, and it is said that since then the

circumambulation of the gods manifested in the forms of sacred centre, is in vogue.

[5] For details see Saraswati (1962).

[6] For details see Jha (1971).

[7] Pundit Datar, a Maharashtrian Brahmin, has renovated many sacred centres of the Panchkosi *parikrama* and has also done many other valuable works for which he is very much praised by the people of Kashi.

[8] For details see Jha (1971).

Chapter IV

SACRED SPECIALISTS : TYPOLOGY

IN Kashi, there are groups of persons who cultivate, preserve and promote the classical cultural traditions. They are engaged in this pursuit of knowledge since time immemorial. The city of Kashi has been the seat of Brahmanic learning throughout the ages, attracting many saintly and scholarly personalities of India. Some of them have specialized themselves in the knowledges of the *Puranas*, the *Vedas*, the *Upanishads* and the *Darshans*. They are theorists. They are also practitioners of textual traditions, i.e. specialists of the second rank. In case of a dispute regarding the authenticity of a religious performance the matter is referred to the theorists—the pundits or the ascetics—for the final verdict. For instance, a temple priest is a specialist in temple rituals insofar as he actually practises it; but should some one challenge his method of performing a particular rite, his opinions cannot be taken for granted, and for that matter the only person who can give the final decision is the Dharmadhikari. Thus, among the sacred intelligentsia of Kashi there are two sets of persons: one group is called the theorists, those who are well versed in the sacred texts of the land; the other group is called the practitioners, those who have specialized in the applied aspects of the performances. The specialists in various sacred performances may be grouped as follows.

PROFESSIONAL SPECIALIZATION

The nature of specialization in various jobs at a place of pilgrimage is an important factor to be considered for the classification of the sacred specialists. This can be done at the observational level. For instance, on reaching Kashi one encounters various groups of persons operating from railway station or bus-stand to the bank of the Ganges, and from Gadaulia Chowk to the main entrance of the Vishwanath temple. He is guided, helped and taken to different sacred centres for performing various sacred performances, by various types of sacred specialists. Functionally these sacred specialists in Kashi are of the following kinds.

Pujari

The *pujaris* or the temple priests are of two kinds: *(1)* self-appointed, and *(2)* those appointed by the temple management. None of them form hereditary endogamous group, although there are a few cases of priests holding the occupation for four or five generations. The *pujaris* in all the four Vishwanath temples are the paid servants whose services can be terminated at any moment by the temple authorities. In some temples the proprietor is himself the priest.

Brahmins are the priests in most of the Brahmanic shrines; a few cases of non-Brahmins acting there as priests have also been recorded. For instance, in the Durga temp'e, located in village Adika Nagar on the Panchakosi route, a Kunbi (vegetable caste) is the priest. The number of such cases is however very negligible. In the non-Brahminic shrines there is no caste restriction, and both Brahmins and non-Brahmins can be appointed as priests.

All the priests of a shrine are not equal in their role and rank location. For instance, in the golden Vishwanath temple the priests are of two types: the *gaddidhari* and the *sthanadhari*. The former holds a superior rank and offers worship to lord Vishwanath; he is assisted by the latter in the performance of worship; they work in shifts.

Karmakandi

The term *karmakandi* (ritual performer) is literally used for such a group of persons who earn their livelihood by performing rituals for others. In common parlance, the term stands for all those who perform the Vedic rituals like *yajna*, *abhisheka*, *samskar*, etc. In Kashi, the learned *karmakandis* prefer to be called themselves as *yagnikas*—a term whereby they distinguish themselves from those who have no knowledge of the Vedic *karmakanda* (the method of performing the vedic rituals).

The main function of a *karmakandi* is to perform various Vedic rites for others, particularly for their *jajmans*. The *karmakandis* are neither endogamous nor do they adhere to their occupation hereditarily. However, there are also instances of persons practising it for three to five generations. Women are not allowed to adopt the profession of *karmakandis*, and hence it is absolutely a male profession.

The Maharashtrians and the South Indian Brahmins are considered to be good *karmakandis*, well known for performing the rituals strictly according to the Shastric injunctions. They are also the only group of *karmakandis* who correctly recite Sanskrit *mantras* at the time of performing a ritual; the local *karmakandis* generally recite the *mantras* either in Hindi or in faulty Sanskrit. For the distortion of *mantras* the pilgrims are also responsible, for some of them are unable to pronounce the Vedic *mantras* properly. An unscrupulous *karmakandi* does not take such trouble as to recite the Vedic *mantras* properly and cuts short the rituals.

The *karmakandis* of Kashi do not form an exclusive category. For instance, sometimes a *karmakandi* may be the *pujari* of a temple, or the *tirthapurohita* or an *anushthani* working temporarily for the welfare of his *jajman*. However, one thing is very clear that a *karmakandi* has to know necessarily the art of *karmakanda*. When the *karmakandis* take up a specific job such as of *pujari*, or of *anushthanis* for getting an extra earning, they are addressed accordingly.

Ghatias

There are several *ghats* (banks for bathing) on the Ganges. The *Ghatias* are those who perform rituals for others and accept *dan* (ritual gift) on these *ghats*. As their main source of livelihood is based on the rites and rituals performed on the *ghats* of the Ganges they prefer to be called as *Gangaputra* (sons of the Ganges). The profession of a *ghatia* is considered lowly, because the sacred texts have condemned the Brahmins taking *dan* in a *tirtha*. In order to overcome this disability and to sanctify their profession the *ghatias* call themselves *Gangaputra*, a prestigous term. A *ghatia* is different from a *karmakandi* who also performs rituals at the *ghats* of the Ganges but will not accept any *dan* from his *jajmans* on the bank of the Ganges (will take remuneration *dakshina* at his residence).

The average *ghatia* performs very little ritual, and his general function is to look after the clothes and other garments of the bathers and to put *tilak* mark on their forehead. The only sacred performance of which the *ghatia* is an authorized sacred specialist, is the *Ganga puja* (worship of the Ganges). Some *ghatias* keep with them the *saligram* (god Vishnu in the form of a rounded pebble) and small idols of Ganesh at their *takhata* (wooden platform). If the pilgrims express a desire to worship these gods, they may do so with the assistance of *ghatias*. A *ghatia* may also conduct such rituals as *godan* and *Vishnu puja* if these are to be performed at the *ghats* of the Ganges.

From the point of view of ownership of the *ghats*, the *ghatias* of Kashi can be divided into three groups: first, those who have proprietory rights on the *ghat* where they conduct rites and rituals; second, those who have taken the *ghat* on lease for conducting rituals; and third, those who are employed by the proprietors of the *ghats*. The *ghatias* of the first and the second categories are involved in this profession for several generations; those who belong to the third category are comparatively newcomers in this profession. In addition to these three principal categories, there are also a few *ghatias* who have taken the *ghats* on fifty per cent commission from their daily income, and on certain important occasions, the owner of the *ghats* himself sits for conducting rituals.

In all the 70 ghats[1] surveyed there were about 150 *ghatias* belonging to various linguistic regions, and sects. Out of 150 *ghatias*, there were 142 men and eight women. Like their male *ghatia* counterparts, the female *ghatias* also assist both male and female pilgrims.

The concentration of the *ghatias* is found mainly on the Panchtirtha *ghats*. However some of the *ghatias* are located also on the *ghats* constructed by the rulers of the former Princely States, like Scindia of Gwalior, etc. Of the 150 *ghatias* 45 were interviewed in depth, and it was found that according to their mother tongue 35 *ghatias* were Banarsi, five were Gujarati, three were Marathi, one Maithili and one Rajasthani. In this connection it is to be pointed out that almost all the *ghatias* whose mother tongue was not Banarsi speak many dialects and languages fluently. Out of the 45 *ghatias* interviewed in depth, six were illiterate, 28 had read upto seventh standard, four had studied upto Matriculation, two were matriculates and one was a Shastri, one was Acharya, and only three *ghatias* had knowledge of the *Vedas*. The *ghatias* are supposed to have the detailed knowledge of their profession. Out of the 45 *ghatias* only five got formal training in the Schools of Karmakanda located at Rajghat and Karnaghanta; others got trained in this profession by their elders.

As stated earlier, some of the *ghatias* have adopted this profession recently, in their life time, and as such they are treated as newcomers to the profession by those who follow it hereditarily. Out of the 45 *ghatias* six have taken up this profession in their life time; one of the newcomers was working previously as a temple priest in Mathura, another newcomer who was previously a private tutor came into contact with the Secretary of the Ganga Mahasabha and joined this profession subsequently, the third one had received training in the D.L.W. factory and the fourth was engaged in a business (selling vermilion).

The profession of *ghatia* is not very gainful; it keeps one on subsistence level of economy. And hence, some of the *ghatias* have gone into secondary profession for their livelihood such as part time work in some cloth shops, restaurants, and toy shops, also as part time tutors.

Pandas

The word *panda* is a generic term which is loosely applied to all categories of sacred specialists in Kashi. Sometimes even the *ghatias* are called *panda*. The *tirthapurohitas* and the *karmakandis* are also frequently addressed as *panda*. It may be clearly stated that the pilgrims coming from different parts of India apply the term *panda* for all such categories of specialists from whom they seek help in matters of accommodation, worship, visiting different shrines, etc. But from functional point of view, there is certainly a special group of people called *panda* which may be marked off from the rest of the sacred specialists, in so far as they exercise the right of entertaining the pilgrims with whom in most cases they have *jajmani* relationship. The pilgrims are received by the *pandas* at many places of their arrival in Kashi; the *panda* makes arrangement of the irstay either in a *dharamshala* or in a private house; or in his family suites as well. In fact it is only the *pandas* who look after the comforts of the pilgrim-*jajmans* in Kashi.

The *pandas* maintain contacts with their pilgrim-*jajmans* on the hereditary basis; they maintain registers where the address and the date of visit of their *jajmans* are very carefully recorded. They are keen in establishing a permanent relationship with the pilgrims; and in this respect they are quite different from the *pujaris*, the *karmakandis* and the *ghatias* whose relationship with the pilgrims, in most cases, is contractual, generally ending with the completion of the ritual.

In Kashi, *karmakandis* or *tirthapurohitas* have of late assumed the role of *panda*. It has happened mostly in the case of South Indian and Maharashtrian *karmakandis* who can conveniently interact with the pilgrims from their respective linguistic regions. They have also formed a Tirtha Purohita Sangha which has been functioning for the past several years as a South Indian pilgrim guide centre. In this connection it is worthwhile to mention that those who claim to be the descendants of the original seven families of the *pandas* in Kashi are all local Saryuparin Brahmins. At present, there are however several families of *pandas* who come from different linguistic groups. The institution of *pandas* in Kashi has created three allied groups—the *bhaddars*, the *yatrawals*, and the *gumashtas*—each claiming the right to receive pilgrims and interact in the manner of a *panda*. Unlike the Pandas of Gaya and Deoghar, the Kashi Pandas are thus heterogeneous and extremely divided.

Bhaddars

The *bhaddars* are the pilgrim hunters; they pick up pilgrims from the railway station or from the bus-stand and also make arrangement for their stay. They form an endogamous group of Joshi Brahmins, their professional organization is known as Joshi Brahmin Sangh, which looks after the interests of the *bhaddars* of Kashi. At present there are about 450 active members of the *Sangh*, and according to an estimate, the total population of the *bhaddars* is about 2,500. It is said that previously the *bhaddars* were employed as assistants of the *tirthapurohitas*, and their main duty was to bring the pilgrims from Railway stations to the place in charge of the *tirthapurohitas*.

Today they are functioning independently and several disputes on the rights of pilgrim-service have been registered. The major dispute arose when the Government of U.P. wanted to issue an identity card to the *bona fide pandas*, and subsequently inquiries were made thereof. At that time the *bhaddars* and the *tirthapurohitas* came out in open conflict, each claiming to be the *bona fide panda* of Kashi, and in order to prove their contention both the groups submitted their pilgrim-registers. Eventually both *bhaddars* and *tirthapurohitas* were successful in obtaining the identity card certifying that they are the genuine *pandas* of Kashi.

Sometime the *bhaddars* dispose of a pilgrim to some *ghatia* or a temple priest on a contract basis. Generally a pilgrim is not aware of how he was sold out to a *ghatia* by the person who has brought him from the railway station with the promise to guide him during his pilgrimage to Kashi. A *bhaddar* may also take the pilgrim to a hotel or to a Banarsi sari shop, and in all these places he will get some commission from the person to whom he has handed over the pilgrim customer. In this connection it should be recorded here that there are only a few *bhaddars* who really act as *panda* and keep the pilgrims in their private houses and maintain *jajmani* relationship with them. Majority of them indulge in pilgrims-hunting, and that is why they have earned very bad name in the city. The *bhaddars* are not well-educated either in scripture or in modern education. Of the 45 *bhaddars* interviewed, only one was matriculate, eight were none-Matric, 26 were educated upto seventh standard, and 10 *bhaddars* were semi-literate. The *bhaddars* believe that higher education is neither essential nor very useful for their profession which requires them to deal with the illiterate pilgrims coming from the countryside. The president of the Joshi Brahmin Sangh held that it is in their professional interest that the *bhaddar* boys do not attend schools. According to him as soon as a *bhaddar* boy attains the age of eight or 10 he starts assisting and guiding pilgrims and thus becomes an earning member of his family. Hence, the *bhaddar* boys are not encouraged to go to schools or colleges for education. A *bhaddar* boy receives primary training in priest-craft in his family, or in association with caste elders.

Though pilgrim-service is their primary source of income, some of the *bhaddars* have taken up secondary professions such as the wholesale business of betel leaves, tailoring, part-time booking clerks in cinema houses, and homoeopathic practice.

Yatrawals

Sometimes it becomes difficult to distinguish between a *yatrawal* and a *bhaddar*, because the former is not much different in his profession from the latter. The only important difference between the two is that while the *bhaddar* hunts pilgrims at the railway station or at the bus stand, the *yatrawals* pick up the pilgrims near the entrance of the Vishwanath gali (street) or near the temple gates. The main function of the *yatrawal* is to take the pilgrims to the neighbouring shrines and help them in having an easy access to the deity by keeping off the crowd.

The *yatrawals* come from different sections of Brahmins (unlike the *bhaddars* who are exclusively Joshi Brahmins) viz. Saryuparin, Joshi and Kashmiri. The majority of them are Saryuparin Brahmins. Though they come from different linguistic groups, they have acquired working knowledge of different Indian languages.

The *yatrawals* are totally dependent on the profession of *pandagiri* and unlike the *bhaddars* they have not gone for any other source of livelihood.

All the *yatrawals* are Shaivites; the *bhaddars* are from different sectarian orders.

Gumashtas

Persons employed to look after the pilgrims, to maintain the pilgrim-register, to go to the pilgrim's villages on routine tour or to bring them comfortably on festive occasions, are called *gumashtas*. The *gumashtas* follow the instructions of their *panda* masters, and have no independent role to play. They are recruited from Brahmin or any other upper caste; the pilgrims often address them as Pandajee.

Kathavachaks

The professional reciters of the *Pauranic* episodes are called *kathavachaks*. Sometimes they are also addressed as Vyasji. They organize their *katha* at the *ghats* of the Ganges or in some temples. The topic and nature of the *katha* called *prasang* is announced sufficiently in advance by the *kathavachaks* in order to attract large number of devotees. Sometimes a group of pilgrims employ them to recite the *Bhagawata* or any other scripture the devotees may like; for this the *kathavachaks* get *dakshina* both in cash and kind.

Tirthapurohita

The word *tirthapurohita* means the *purohit* of a *tirtha*, i.e., a sacred specialist who conducts rituals in a sacred centre. As discussed earlier, there are various *tirthas* in Kashi where there are sacred specialists working as *purohitas* and claiming to be the autochthonous *panda* of Kashi. There is no doubt that the *tirthapurohitas* are even today one of the important sacred specialists closely associated with the pilgrims. They are comparable to the *gayawals* of Gaya and the *pandas* of Deoghar.

The *tirthapurohitas* of Kashi claim their descent from the mythological *rishi* Vasistha who was for a long time the priest of the kings of the Ikshavaku dynasty of Ayodhya. It is said that Brahma, the creator of the Universe, had appointed Vasistha as the chief priest of the earth and because the *Trithapurohitas* are the progeny of this *rishi*, the entire world lies in their *jajamanika*. They also claim to be the first settlers of Kashi.

All the *Tirthapurohitas* of Kashi belong to the lineage of Naukulsardar (Nine chief lineages). The nine lineages are distinguished from one another by surnames—Upadhyaya, Chaturvedi, Dwivedi, Trivedi, Pathak, Mishra, Shukla and Pandey; all of them are the Kanyakubja Brahmins. Out of the nine lineages, it is said, only six lineages flourished and the remaining three became totally extinct. Even among the six lineages, the two lineages had no male issue—their last widows had only one daughter each and both the daughters had married Saryuparin Brahmins who not only inherited the property of these two widows of the *Naukulsardar* lineages but also adopted the profession of *tirthapurohitas*. This was vehemently opposed by the *tirthapurohitas* of the four original lineages of the Kanyakubja Brahmins without much success, and even today the two parties are frequently disputing.

The two Saryuparin Brahmins who married the daughters of the widows of the Kanyakubja *tirthapurohitas* are alive; they are Mahabir Tiwari and Gayananda Tiwari. Mahabir Tiwari is about 98 years old, possibly the oldest among the *tirthapurohitas* of Kashi. He married the daughter of the widow of the Kanyakubja *tirthapurohita* about 78 years ago and since then he is in this profession.

Several years ago a Saraswata Brahmin was appointed by a Kanyakubja *tirthapurohita* to look after the pilgrims from South India. The new recruit was a good scholar of Sanskrit, and he also knew many South Indian languages. In course of his long association with the South Indian pilgrims he eventually established with them a good *jajmanika* relationship and, thereafter, claimed himself to be the *tirthapurohita* of the South Indians. Although his claim was challenged by the Kanyakubja *tirthapurohitas* in the court of law, but nothing could stop him and his descendants from doing this job.

Thus, there are eight lineages of the *tirthapurohitas* in Kashi—five of Kanyakubja, two of Saryuparins and one of Saraswatas. In addition to the members of these eight families recently some Brahmins from South India, have taken up the profession of *tirthapurohita*, but they are not yet fully established in this profession.

All the *tirthapurohitas* belong to the Shaiva sect, and only male members are allowed to function as *tirthapurohitas*. Usually, the family is represented by the eldest male person as the *tirthapurohita*; the young male children assist their elders.

Out of the eight *tirthapurohitas* interviewed in depth, one was B.A., B.L.; two were holding 'Shastri' degree in Sanskrit; three were matriculates, and two had read up to seventh standard. After going through the sacred thread ceremony all the male children of the *tirthapurohitas* are given sufficient informal training in *karmakanda*; and thus in comparison to the other sacred specialists they are more versed in the performance of rituals.

Among the sacred specialists of Kashi, the *tirthapurohitas* are numerically small but economically well off. One of the Kanyakubja families of the *tirthapurohitas*, owns a coal mine which it received in *dan* by one of the *jajmans*. Two Saryuparin families of the *tirthapurohitas* have a large area of cultivable land in and around Kashi; this too was received in *dan*.

Kirtania

The *Kirtanias* are professional singers of devotional songs; they organize their performances either on the *ghats* of the Ganges or in the temples. When someone keeps a vow that on the fulfilment of certain desires, he would organize *kirtan* on a particular *ghat* of the Ganges or in a particular temple, the services of the *kirtania* are requisitioned, and in such cases the remuneration is also fixed in advance. A *kirtania* may himself organize a *kirtan* attracting pilgrims on the *ghats* or in temples, also to raise money. It has been found that the group singers are generally Brahmins, though other castes have also joined this profession. Individual devotional singers, both male and female are frequently met with on the banks of the Ganges, particularly on the Panchtirtha ghats. Thus, the devotional singers are also a group of specialists.

Anushthani

A Brahmin who has specialized in the performance of *anushthan* (a special type of rite which is performed on behalf of the *jajmans* for their welfare or for getting certain desire fulfilled) is called *anushthanis*. The sacred mantras uttered in course of an *anushthan* are kept secret; certain restrictions are imposed on an *anushthani* in matters of dress and food. For instance, the recitation of the *anushthan mantras* demands that the reciter, i.e. *anushthani*, should wear a *dhoti* of a particular colour or that he should take meal only once a day; the *anushthanis* would have to observe these rules. The *anushthanis* are found mostly in Devi temples, viz., the Durga temple, the Annapurna temple, and the Sankatamai temple. They are also located on the *ghats* of the Ganges.

Mahapatra

Some persons have specialized in conducting death-rites or *Shraddha-kriya;* they mainly operate at the two burning *ghats*—the Manikarnika and the Harishchandra. They are called the *mahapatra.* They are Brahmin but since they have specialized in conducting the Shraddha rites and they receive gifts offered to the deceased's soul, their social status is very low. Unlike the *pandas* and other ritual specialists, theirs is the only undisputed profession confined to the community of *mahapatras*.

In the foregoing pages we have described various categories of sacred specialists distinguishable on the basis of their specialized knowledge of various kinds of rituals. They are, indeed, functional groups, and since there is no complete monopoly on specialization an individual or a group may sometimes be found as having overlapping functions. For instance, a person may become temporarily a *pujari*, a *karmakandi*, an *anushthani*, or a *kathavachak*. This happens also because of the fact that all those who are engaged in these varied ritual occupations are Brahmins, and all Brahmins are entitled to perform all the rituals of the Brahmanic complex.

Ritual Associates

Besides these sacred specialists, who are fully and directly associated with the rituals of pilgrimage there are also persons who are indirectly associated with the ritual complex, though they are not entitled to perform *Shastric* rituals independently; these are generally non-Brahmins. For instance, the barbers, the boatmen, the musicians, as well as the Doms of Kashi come under this category; they may be properly called 'ritual associates.'

Among the ritual associates also there is a functional division often distinguishable by caste. Florists (Mali), barbers (Nai), boatmen (manjhi), and the custodian of sacred fire (Doms) are all the examples of such functional classification of ritual associates.

CLASSIFICATION ON THE BASIS OF CASTE

As has been indicated earlier the ritual specialists as also the ritual associates have been drawn from various castes. Socially, they may be placed under three broad categories; first, is the Brahmin group; second, consists of intermediate caste; and the third group is composed of those who are on the periphery of Hindu society and even outside Hindu society.

Brahmanic Group

The Brahmins of India are divided into two major groups, viz. Panch Gaur and the Panch Dravida, according to their geographical distribution—the demarcating line is the Narmada river. The Brahmins located in the south of Narmada are called the Panch Dravidas; the Brahmins inhabiting the northern part of this river are called Panch Gaur. These two blocks of Brahmins[2] are further sub-divided into a number of regional groups, each taking the name after the place of origin; such as Maithila (from Mithila), Gujarati (from Gujarat), Saraswata (from the bank of river Saraswati), Kanyakubja (from Kannauja), Utkal (from Utkal), Karnataka (from Karnataka), Maharashtrian (from Maharashtra) etc. Among the Brahmin ritual specialists in Kashi there are Kanyakubja, Saryuparin, Kashmiri, Gujarati, Maharashtrian, Tamilian, Telugu, Karnataka, Gaur, Saraswat, Maithil, Bengali, Oriya, etc. Of these groups, the Kanyakubja and the Saryuparin are in overwhelming majority.

The caste identity, however, becomes of little importance when professional identity is required. For instance, a Kanyakubja Brahmin may be a *ghatia*, a *karmakandi*, a *pujari*, or a *Tirthapurohita;* and so whenever he talks to a pilgrim he introduces himself according to his functional association, and not as a member of the Kanyakubja caste.

Except in case of Saryuparin and Kanyakubja Brahmins, all those who have taken up the profession of *ghatia*, *kathavachak*, *kirtania*, *pujari* are Brahmin immigrants to Kashi from different parts of India.

Intermediate Group

In the intermediate group we place all the castes below the Brahmins but above the so called untouchables. Among the intermediates group the following castes may specially be mentioned—Rajput, Bhumihar, Kurmi, Khatri, Bania, Koeri, Kahar, Halwai, Manjhi, Teli, Mali, Lohar, Nai, etc. In Kashi these castes are functioning, in many cases, as ritual associates and in some cases also as ritual specialists. For instance, Manjhi who is a ritual specialist in all those performances which are to be performed on the boat or on the other bank or as described above. Similarly, Nai (barber) is the lieutenant of the Brahmin ritual specialists.

In this group there are also persons who have taken up a ritual profession not in consonance with his traditional caste occupation. For instance, some of the Rajputs, who are traditionally warrior caste, act in Kashi as shrine priest.

The sellers of sacred ingredients such as vermilion, *chandan*, *rudraksha*, sacred threads, and ritual instruments belong to various castes, viz. Koeri, whose traditional occupation is to grow vegetables; Halwai, whose traditional occupation is confectionary; Teli, whose traditional occupation is to press oil seeds; Kahar, who are traditional palanquin carrier. Selling sacred ingredients is traditionally assigned to the members of the Bania caste. The caste profession of Nai is however untouched as nobody has so far entered into this profession.

To supply flowers to the pilgrims and local devotees at various sacred centres, for the worship of the deities, is the traditional occupation of the members of the Mali caste. But it has been found that in Kashi many persons from different castes have adopted this profession. These are from Mallah, Kumhar, Kahar, Kurmi, Koeri, Kayastha, as Rajput castes. The majority of the non-Mali (non-florists) caste, the profession of selling flowers is a primary occupation, to others it is secondary source of livelihood. Some members of the Kurmi and Koeri castes are working as *Jharudar* (sweeper) in various temples in Kashi, they also clean the personal utensils of the *mahants* as also of the temples. For instance, the *Jharudars* in the temples of the golden Vishwanath and Naya Vishwanath are Kurmi and Koeri caste. This is perhaps because those whose traditional occupation is sweeping (i.e. *mehtars*) are labelled as 'untouchables', not permitted to enter into the temple precinct.

Peripheral Group

Among the ritual specialists who are socially untouchables mention may be made of Doms and Mochis. The Doms, as stated earlier, function as specialists at the cremation *ghats*, insofar as it is they from whom the sacred fire is to be obtained for lighting the funeral pyre. The Doms of Kashi are divided into three groups, viz. (*i*) Gotakhors, (*ii*) Raddari or Magahiya, and (*iii*) Banarsi. The Gotakhors virtually control the *shmashan ghats.* As reported by the Gotakhor informants, there are 60 families of the Gotakhors in Kashi. They are also spread over to the neighbouring districts of Gazipur, Mirzapur, and Jaunpur where also they control the various burning ghats. The name

Gotakhor suggests that they are the people who dive into the river for collecting money and gold which the relatives of the dead throw in the Ganges on the occasion of cremation. The Gotakhors are further classified into two economic categories, viz. the masters and the servants. Out of 60 families of the Gotakhors, 12 families are masters and the rest are servants. However, all the Doms of Kashi claim to be the descendants of the Pauranic Kalu Dom—the master of Raja Harishchandra. In another stroy regarding the Doms of Kashi the Pauranic Dom Kalu is said to have attained *Vishnulok (moksha)*. Kalva had no sons to succeed him. His four friends belonging to four different castes, Lohar, Kahar, Yadav and Koeri, were attracted by the handsome income from the burning *ghat* and eventually adopted the profession of Dom. Thus, it is said that the present-day Doms of Kashi are neither the descendants of Kalu Dom nor do they really belong to Dom caste. (But this is a highly debatable claim, as these Doms marry in the Dom caste scattered all over Uttar Pradesh).

Similar is the case with the Chamars and Muslims, who are also considered 'untouchables', but have occupied a place in the sacred structure of Kashi. For instance, the Muslim musicians accompany the group or groups of pilgrims or local devotees from their lodging houses or from their residences, as the case may be, to the bank of Ganges where the musicians constantly play their musical instruments.

Similarly, Mochis or Chamars (and also Muslims) play musical instruments at the time of performing certain rituals on the *ghat* and also in temples. At the time of performing Ganga *puja*, musical instruments are played by Mochis.

In some of the important temples, Muslim musicians play *shehnai* during the early hours of the dawn in connection with a ritual called *mangala arati*. Among such temples mention may be made of Bara Ganesh, Annapurna, and Golden Vishwanath.

CLASSIFICATION ON THE BASIS OF ASSOCIATION WITH SHRINES

As discussed in Chapter I the sacred centres of Kashi have been classified on the basis of their local, regional, and all-India importance. The sacred specialists associated with these shrines may be also classified accordingly.

Specialists Associated with Local Shrines

All those sacred specialists who are associated with shrines of local importance, may be placed in one group. They are both Brahmins and non-Brahmins, self-appointed and appointed by the management. Their long association with the shrines of local importance makes them interact intensively with local population. Most of them are the original inhabitants of Kashi. Majority of these specialists do not have any permanent relationship, called *jajmanika* with the pilgrims coming from outside because they largely deal with the local devotees. It is also true that most of them do not have the requisite knowledge of the sacred texts, and they somehow carry on with their work, performing rituals generally in local dialect.

Specialists Associated with Regional Shrines

The sacred specialists functioning at the various regional shrines as discussed in chapter I, follow the regional customs of worship according to the need and tradition of the pilgrims coming from different parts of India. Unlike the sacred specialists working at the shrines of local importance, they come from different parts of India, speak different languages, and differ among themselves at different levels of living standards.

Specialists Associated with All-India Shrines

The sacred specialists, functioning at the shrines of all-India importance, assume special character which is widely reflected in their behaviour and performance. All of them are much multi-lingual and capable of performing rituals in greater detail. This happens because of their encounter with varieties of pilgrims. Since most of the shrines of all-India importance are affluent, a special group of sacred specialists, called *mahants*, has sprung up in these places. The *mahants* are distinguished from the *tirthapurohitas* insofar as they do not run after the pilgrims. They are the owner and proprietor of the shrines, and the pilgrims wanting to visit these shrines have to seek their help. Thus, in most of these shrines of all-India importance the *mahants* form a conspicuous group of sacred specialists. Under each *mahant* serve priests and other shrine servants. The mahant may perform temple rites only if the client is affluent or person in high office.

CLASSIFICATION ON THE BASIS OF SHASTRIC KNOWLEDGE

All the sacred specialists described in the foregoing sections may be classified into three broad categories according to the extent of their knowledge of Shastras:

(*1*) the sacred specialist conversant with *shastric* knowledge;
(*2*) the sacred specialist not at all conversant with *shastric* knowledge; and
(*3*) the sacred specialist having only working knowledge of the *shastras*, and thus acquiring the intermediate position.

In the first category of sacred specialists[3] mention may be made of the *dharmadhikaris*, the *tirthapurohitas*, the *karmakandis*, the *anushthanis*, the *Kathavachaks*, and also the *ghatias*. Of these, while the *dharmadhikaris* are the theorists, sufficiently advanced in the knowledge of scriptures others are the practitioners. There is however different levels of scholarship and knowledge where these categories of specialists can be individually placed differently. Considering them at professional level, it can be said that these *ghatias* are by and large the specialists of few rites demanding lesser degree of Shastric knowledge.

The ritual associates, of all types, have no Shastric knowledge, although they sometime chant *mantras* in vernacular (as the *manjhis* do in case of rituals of *malyarpan* or *chunari charhana* to the river Ganges). The Mochi and the Muslim musicians have also no knowledge of the *Shastric* form of music. The third category of the sacred specialists is of those who occupy the intermediate position in between the first and the second category, described above. In other words, they have working knowledge of the *Shastric* rites, but no formal learning of the *Shastras* as that of the Dharmadhikaris or even *karmakandis*, and *anushthanis*. Among this category of sacred specialists mention may be made of the *yatrawals*, the *bhaddars*, the *mahapatras*, the *kirtanias* and also some temple priests and *ghatias*. Most of them have acquired the requisite knowledge of their respective profession of audio-visual method, which is evident from their life-histories.[4]

The *Bhaddars* and the *Yatrawals* are pilgrim-hunters, and in fact they are not concerned with rites. Yet, most of them learn by heart a few Sanskrit verses in order to impress the pilgrims. If the *yatrawals* get an opportunity to conduct *puja*, for the pilgrims they perform it in Hindi or Banarsi medium. *Mohan Maharaj* (*L.H.No. 4*), a *yatrawal*, admitted that he did not join any Sanskrit Pathashala; he has learnt some Sanskrit *mantras* from his father, and that he performs rituals in local dialect.

CLASSIFICATION ON THE BASIS OF TRANSMISSION OF KNOWLEDGE

Considering the types of knowledge which they transmit, the sacred specialist may broadly be divided into three categories:—

(*1*) Sacred specialists transmitting the knowledge regarding *pap* and *punya* as described in scriputres—the philosophic and spiritual explanation of right conduct;

(*2*) Specialists transmitting the knowledge of ritual craft—modes of performance and the importance or *mahatmya* of sacred performances and pilgrimage; and

(*3*) Specialists transmitting the knowledge of various little traditions of worship.

In the first category of sacred specialists mention may be made of the *dharmadhikaris*, the ascetics, and the *Kathavachaks* who deliver to the people the core of the various philosophical, Vedantic and other transcendental elements of culture. As stated earlier, the *dharmadhikaris* are the authorities to pronounce the correctness and appropriateness of rituals as prescribed in scriptures. The ascetics preserve, protect and transmit the essence of transcendental culture and at societal level unite people across caste and linguistic differences. As Saraswati (1975:16) has rightly observed, "in Brahmanic tradition the ascetics are compared to the *dhruvatara* (pole star), for they symbolize the highest ideals which the *grihis* (houscholders) must try to attain". The Kathavachaks transmit the knowledge of the *Puranas*, and thus help maintain continuity with the past. They also transmit scriptural knowledge by word of mouth so that even those who are illiterate can have an access to the scriptures written in Sanskrit. In other words, they transmit great tradition to peoples belonging to both great and little traditions. They also unite people across regional traditions. The Tirthapurohitas, the Yatrawals, the Mahants, and the priests of sacred centres of all-India importance transmit the myths and *mahatamya* of Kashi and the importance of various sacred performances. They also transmit both great and little traditions to the pilgrims coming from different regions of India.[5]

The third category of specialists is comprised of those who transmit myths and *mahatamya* of the shrines of regional and local importance. These specialists promote the knowledge of little traditions particularly among those who are at the periphery of Sanskriti Hinduism. The priests of Satisthans and Birasthans are included in this category of specialists.

To sum up, there are almost innumerable centres in Kashi where different types of sacred specialists transmit the *shastric* and the *laukik* knowledge to the masses. The cultural phenomenon which thus appears may rightly be pin-pointed in the words of Vidyarthi (1961: 111): "The sacred complex of a Hindu place of pilgrimage. . . in itself is an intricate combination of the great and little traditions."

REFERENCES

[1] For details, see list of *ghats* as given in appendix-III.

[2] The Brahmins of India are also divided according to their traditional affiliation with the *Vedas* or *Vedic Sakhas*; and this also marks them off from one another in performance of rituals.

[3] In the first category of sacred specialists, who are the guardians of cultural traditions, Saraswati (1975) has also included the ascetics of Kashi who are the authors of the transcendental culture.

[4] For details, see appendix-I.

[5] For details see Milton Singer (1955) and McKim Marriott (1961).

Chapter V

SACRED SPECIALISTS : THEIR STYLE OF LIFE

ALTHOUGH the sacred specialists in Kashi come from different castes, belong to different linguistic and geographical regions, and are functionally heterogeneous, the pilgrims conceive them collectively and address them 'Pandajee', irrespective of their professional specialization like *tirthapurohitas*, *ghatias*, *yatrawals*, etc. The sacred specialists themselves share a common cultural consciousness of belonging to an institution called '*Pandagiri*', and thus, theirs is a part and whole relationship.

The life style of the 'pandas' of Kashi will be discussed here in terms of self identifiable 'panda culture'.

Brief Life Cycle

All the sacred specialists in Kashi, irrespective of their castes, sects and professional specialization, believe that a child is the gift of Lord Vishwanath. Hence if no child is born for sometimes after marriage, Lord Vishwanath and other deities are worshipped.

When a woman comes to know about the conception, she communicates it to her husband directly or through the elderly ladies of the family, and thereafter Lord Vishwanath is worshipped. During the period of pregnancy, delicious dishes are served to the pregnant lady and it has also been observed that quite often the pregnant lady is offered *charanamrita* of Lord Vishwanath. It is believed that the drinking of *charanamrita* removes all kinds of physical ailments of both the expectant mother and the foetus. During the period of pregnancy Gangamai, Sankatamai and other deities are also worshipped by womenfolk for safe delivery of the child. Previously a *chamaien* (traditional mid-wife of an untouchable caste) used to be called at the time of delivery, but these days, owing to the establishment of a hospital within the thickly populated locality of the sacred specialists, the pregnant ladies are either sent to hospitals or lady doctors and nurses are called to attend to them at the time of labour pain. After the period of birth pollution, known as *ashauch*, which continues upto six days, the women-folk go to worship lord Vishwanath and other deities for the welfare and longevity of the newly-born baby. It has been observed that a community dinner is also arranged on such occasion which takes place either on the sixth or the twenty-seventh day after the birth of the child. Usually members of the professional groups are invited to attend the dinner; however, family friends and relatives are also invited on such occasions. In some cases it has been found that the *jajmans* send gifts for the newly born child.

After birth, *upanayan* (sacred thread) ceremony is an important sacrament for the sacred specialists belonging to Brahmin caste in particular and *dwij* in general. Among the Brahmin sacred specialists, the *tirthapurohitas*, *karmakandis*, *anushthanis*, *kathavachak*, and *mahants* of a few important shrines, attach great importance to this secrament; but the *ghatias*, *bhaddars*, *yatrawals*, etc., however, do not perform it with equal seriousness. This fact may be further borne out by their professional requirement of sacred thread ceremony. For instance, not a single *tirthapurohita*, *karmakandi*, *anushthani* or *kathavachak*, etc. was found entering into the profession having performed sacred thread ceremony, but it is not the case with the other groups. Ghatias ask their minor sons who have not yet undergone the sacred thread ceremony to assist them in their profession; the uninitiated boy may sometimes conduct the ritual independently. But sacred thread ceremony is a primary requisite among the *tirthapurohitas*, *karmakandis*, *kathavachaks*, etc., without which they cannot assist and guide the *jajmans*.

The details of the sacred thread ceremony in the case of the sacred specialists are not different from what other Brahmins commonly practise. After performing this ceremony the sacred specialists are supposed to lead orthodox style of life—following all *shastric* injunctions scrupulously. Again it is only after this ceremony that they are supposed to learn the *Gayatri mantra*, which is considered one of the most powerful and popular *mantras* practised by the Brahmins and which is highly important for conducting any kind of ritual and at every stage of important ritual. Thus, from the point of view of priestcraft the sacred thread ceremony is absolutely essential.

After the sacred thread ceremony, marriage is another important event in the life of the sacred specialists. The Brahmin sacred specialists of Kashi, unlike their counterparts in Gaya, Deoghar and other places of pilgrimage, have established martimonial relations in different parts of the country, though more frequent in Varanasi region. Local marriages also take place in Kashi though there is no rule for town endogamy. Marriage is contracted according to the convenience and the availability of suitable match in or outside Kashi. Again most important of it is that professional considerations are never imposed on the contracting parties. For instance, if one is a Brahmin *ghatia* it is not essential that he should marry only a daughter of a *ghatia*. However, if *ghatia* is a Kanyakubja Brahmin he will search for a suitable match only in the families of Kanyakubja Brahmins irrespective of their location, residence and profession. The Doms of Kashi, particularly those who work at the Manikarnika and Harishchandra burning-ghats are the only exception to this rule. They marry only among those who are working at the burning ghats and do not establish matrimonial relations outside their professional group. While contracting matrimonial relation, they prohibit 'mother's milk'—i.e. boys and girls, who had been fed breast's milk by the same mother, cannot marry—the only restriction of marriage observed.

The *pandas* of Kashi believe that death is quite natural and they take it as the grace of Lord Vishwanath and it is their firm belief that since they pass their whole life under the feet of Lord Vishwanath and the mother Ganges, they attain *moksha* after death. Again it is their privilege to be cremated at the Manikarnika ghat, a place which is marked for bestowing *moksha*.

The death rites of the sacred specialists are performed in accordance with the textual procedures as followed by their caste members elsewhere.

Daily Life

The daily life of the sacred specialists of Kashi varies to a great extent according to their respective professions. For instance, the daily routine of a *karmakandi* who assists and guides in performing *abhisheka* and *pindadan* varies in some details from the *tirthapurohitas* who are fully associated with pilgrims or from the Doms who assist in the *antyesthi kriya*. However, except the Doms, the common routine followed by the sacred specialists of Kashi, irrespective of their sectarian and professional functions, is to take bath in the Ganges and then worship Lord Vishwanath and Shiva *lingas*. The Doms do not take bath regularly in the Ganges and most of the time they come to the cremation ghat after having a bath at their homes (or sometime even without having one), but all of them worship the Shiva *linga* enshrined at the cremation ghat.

A *tirthapurohita* leaves his bed early in the morning and after attending the call of nature, inquires from his assistants about the arrival of any new group of pilgrims. He also inquires, sometimes personally or through his assistants about the welfare and other programmes of those pilgrims who had come earlier. He then goes to take bath in the Ganges and offers *puja*, etc. which approximately continues upto 8 to 10 in the morning. After visiting some important shrines, viz. Golden Vishwanath, Annapurna, etc., he may go to conduct rituals, or if he has no such assignment on that day, he takes meals and retires for the day. In the afternoon he again inquires about the new arrivals and if anyone has come, he will call on the *jajman* to provide accommodation and to ask his welfare and then move on to the *ghats* or other sacred centres, if he is in the company of his *jajmans* he also narrates them the *mahatmya* of the shrines. In the evening he takes *bhang* (a type of intoxication) which is commonly known as '*thandai*' in Kashi, and thereafter, if he has no specific programme he may go for boating in the Ganges (almost all the *tirthapurohitas* own boats, they enjoy boating in the Ganges). After dusk he goes to the Vishwanath temple for *darshan*—most of the *tirthapurohitas* visit the Golden Vishwanath temple after the *sringar arati*, and then they go to their respective residences and retire for the night.

The *mahants* of temples have no specific assignment with the pilgrims, they devote their time in looking after the temple affairs. Like the *tirthapurohitas*, the *mahants* also take '*thandai*' in the evening, which is a part of their daily routine.

The *karmakandi's* daily routine include regular bath in the Ganges and visit to the golden Vishwanath temple. Some of them who worship the shrines located near their residences may not find time to visit the golden Vishwanath temple regularly; they visit at intervals. When there is no *jajman* to look after, a *karmakandi* is often seen passing time by playing chess, cards, etc., or gossiping with friends and relatives. The *karmakandis* also take *bhang* in the evening, most of them visit the golden Vishwanath temple after the *sringar arati* and then go to bed.

The *yatrawals* devote most of their time in search of pilgrims in and around the golden Vishwanath temple. After taking bath in the Ganges in the early morning they offer Ganges water, *belapatra*, etc., to Lord Vishwanath and thereafter till around 1 p.m. they remain busy in search of pilgrims. As stated earlier they are posted in and around the golden Vishwanath temple. After 1 p.m. most of them go to take meal at their residence (some of them take meals with their respective *jajmans*) and take rest for sometime and then again come to the golden Vishwanath temple in search of pilgrims. They remain there till around 9 p.m. During this period they also manage to take *bhang*; most of them consider it as the *prasad* of Lord Vishwanath. Thus the daily routine of a *yatrawal* moves round the search of pilgrims and sometimes they also adjust their programmes accordingly.

A *bhaddar*, like the *yatrawals*, also leaves his bed early in the morning, but unlike the latter he usually takes bath in his home instead of going to the Ganges. After wearing sandal wood paste mark quite prominently on their foreheads, they bow their heads in the direction of the golden Vishwanath temple and rush to the railway station or to the bus stand in search of pilgrims. As already stated they are pilgrim-hunters and for that they go out of Varanasi and board the incoming train one or two stations before Varanasi and subsequently hand over their clients to *ghatias*, *tirthapurohitas*, *karmakandis*, etc. for conducting rituals. In this way the *bhaddars* remain busy for the whole day in search of pilgrims. However, those *bhaddars* who attend the nearby stations and bus stands come home to take meal late in the afternoon. Sometimes a *bhaddar* may have to pass the whole day at the railway platforms. Even at some odd hours of the night one can locate a *bhaddar* at the Varanasi railway station. In other words their pilgrim-hunting goes on round the clock.

In the daily routine of a *ghatia*, the major activity is his work at the *ghat* on the bank of Ganges. After taking bath in the Ganges near his own *ghat* he offers *puja* to the mother Ganges and then sits on a *takhta* (wooden platform) fitted with a bamboo umbrella. Till late in the afternoon he guides the pilgrims in conducting sacred performances. After returning home the *ghatia* takes meal and rests a while. In the evening he meets his *jajmans* whom he had assisted during the day time, and takes *thandai*. He may spend some time on domestic works if any, or else he may go to visit shrines or attend cultural shows.

The *Mahapatra's* daily routine is, more or less, similar to that of the *karmakandi*. The difference may, however, occur in their professional activities; the former is a specialist only in the *antyesthi* and *shraddha kriya*, the latter has comparatively less work than who is specialised in conducting varieties of rites and rituals.

The florists and sacred article sellers remain busy from dawn to dusk in supplying the sacred ingredients to pilgrims and the local devotees and their daily routine moves round their profession. Their shops whether permanent or temporary, are not closed even at such hours of the day as when temples are closed and the influx of pilgrims ceases; they go for taking meals by rotation.

As stated earlier, the Doms of the Manikarnika ghat work in shift and each shift, is of about 8 to 10 hours. It has been observed that they usually do not take bath in the Ganges; they come to the ghat after taking bath in their houses. When off-duty at the cremation *ghat*, they either take rest at their residences or just move around the cremation *ghat*, and pass time in gossip either among themselves or with the relatives of the deceased.

The daily routine of the sacred specialists who are appointed by the shrine authorities is guided, to a great extent by their employer. Similarly those sacred specialists, who are working at local shrines, generally devote morning hours to manifold sacred activities as these shrines are opened only in the morning; the rest of the day these specialists either go for secondary sources of livelihood, or engage themselves in some domestic works.

Food Habits

As discussed earlier, the sacred specialists of Kashi come from different castes, and regions, and practise different professions; their food habits and tastes accordingly vary. For instance, the sacred specialists from South India, usually take rice, *sambhar* (a preparation of pulses) and curd in both the daily meals, while the Maharashtrians, the Gujaratis, the Rajasthanis, and even the Brahmin sacred specialists from M.P. and U.P. prefer to take *roti* (bread made of wheat flour), pulses, vegetables, etc., as principal meals. The Brahmin sacred specialist from Mithila and Bengal, however, prefer to eat rice and fish. Thus even among the Brahmin sacred specialists great diversity in food habits and tastes can be easily noticeable. There are also certain similarities of taste in their preference of such delicacies as *rabari* (a typical preparation of milk), *kachauri* and *raita* which they generally take as their morning breakfast, and also sometimes as the evening tiffin. It is in these special items of food where they cut across all the castes, sects, regional and linguistic barriers. These items are typically local and hence all of them have cultivated taste on account of their long association with this city.

These delicious sweets are usually not prepared at their homes; they purchase them mostly from the sweet shops of their locality. Most of the informants narrated that these confectionary items require expert knowledge and skill, which the ladies in the family lack. Hence they usually purchase such articles from the shops. In this connection it may be pointed out here that Kashi is a famous centre of the confectioners who are borrowed away to different parts of the state to prepare the articles of their speciality. Besides confectionary articles, betel leaves, spicy betel nuts, and scented chewing tobacco are exported to different places of India. The sacred specialists are also very fond of chewing betel leaves.

From the point of view of food-habits these sacred specialists may be divided into two broad categories, the vegetarian group and the non-vegetarian group. All Brahmin specialists, except a few, are vegetarians; the intermediate and lower caste sacred specialists are generally non-vegetarians. The Manjhi, the Doms, the Ahirs, the Nai, the Koeri, etc., are mostly non-vegetarians.

Meals are cooked in the families usually by the senior lady of the family. In a large family, the ladies cook meals by rotation, a menstruating woman is not allowed to cook. Generally, the children are fed first, and then the male members are served with meals. The ladies are invariably the last to take meals.

All the sacred specialists belonging to a caste group or a

functional group may have commensual relationship at least on ceremonial occasions. The exceptions are, however, not lacking. For instance, the *mahant* of the golden Vishwanath temple is a Saryuparin Brahmin, but friendship apart on principal he does not maintain food-relationship with the *tirthapurohitas* who are also Saryuparin Brahmins.

To sum up, it may be said that, although from the point of view of food habit, there are many similarities among the sacred specialists, there also are a few distinctive features on the basis of which they mark off from one another.

Dress and Dialects

In their dress and dialects the sacred specialists of Kashi are heterogeneous. Most of them have two sets of dresses—one set is worn at the time of meeting outsiders, or attending social functions or going on pilgrimage or visiting the relatives. For instance, when the *mahant* of the golden Vishwanath temple comes to worship Lord Vishwanath, he wears a *dhoti* and puts on a silken *chadar* on his shoulder, but for going out he wears *dhoti* and *kurta*, and puts on a silken *chadar* and a leather *chappal.* Some of the sacred specialists put on a silken *chadar* printed with such words as '*Om namah Shivayah*', or '*Ram Ram*', etc. Most of the time they use wooden sandals locally known as *paduka* or *kharaon.* Some smart *bhaddars* and *yatrawals* use leather shoes and chappals. Some young *mahants* and sacred specialists who are receiving education in the Banaras Hindu University, instead of the Varanasheya Sanskrit University, wear well-stitched suits when they are off from the duties of sacred specialists.

The traditional dress of most of the sacred specialists is not much different from one another. The dress consists of *dhoti*, *kurta* and silken *chadar*, *buniyan*, etc. which may vary in quality according to the economic condition of the person. Most sacred specialists, particularly the *tirthapurohitas*, *karmakandis*, *yatrawals*, *bhaddars*, *ghatias* and *mahapatras* put on a red *gamchha* or *angochha* (a thin long towel). The *gamchha* is hung on the shoulder or tied in the waist over the *dhoti*; the latter style is common with the *yatrawals*. Earlier the Brahmin sacred specialists used also to wear a headgear; even today a few old *tirthapurohitas* can be seen wearing a turban. However, the custom of wearing a turban is now out of fashion.

Wearing ashes, sandal-wood mark, or red vermilion dot on the foreheads in a design according to one's own sectarian affiliation, is common with the sacred specialists. Such distinctive features are however not found among the non-Brahmin sacred specialists.

The dress of the non-Brahmin sacred specialists particularly the Doms, and *manjhis* consists mainly of *dhoti*, covering the lower part of the body, and a *gamchha* on the shoulder. Most of the times the upper part of the body remains uncovered. Some of the *manjhis* have now started wearing readymade *bunyan* or a stitched *bunyan* called *gol-gala* even at the time of plying a boat or conducting a ritual. Among the Doms, the Dom Raja has a special dress; he wears a *dhoti*, *bunyan*, and shirt of fine quality and also a gold ring and a gold chain round his neck. When going out he puts on a well-stitched coat and shoes and takes a stick in his hand.

The womenfolk of the sacred specialists wear *sari* and *blouse*. Among them the South Indians and the Maharashtrians are distinguished from their North Indian counterparts in the style of wearing *saris*. Young girls and boys of the sacred specialists, who are attending schools and colleges, wear modern garments and fashionable dresses. On one occasion a *bhaddar* was found wearing *pyjama* and *kurta* when escorting pilgrims from the railway station. In brief, although most sacred specialists continue to live in their traditional dress, a change in respect of dress and personal decoration may sometime be noticed, particularly among the young generation.

It has already been mentioned that the sacred specialists of Kashi come from diffeient linguistic regions and since they have to assist various pilgrims of diffeient linguistic areas, they are multi-lingual. A *karmakandi* from South India is seen speaking fluent Hindi, Bengali, Marathi, and Bhojpuri; similarly the sacred specialists of North and Central India, Dravidian languages. This multi-linguism is born out of their professional necessity; but once they are with their kin and family members they switch on to their mother-tongue.

All the sacred specialists, irrespective of their linguistic affiliation, speak Banarsi dialect so fluently that sometimes it becomes difficult for an outsider to distinguish them from the autochthons of Varanasi. Most sacred specialists, particularly the *tirthapurohitas*, *karmakandis*, *ghatias*, *yatrawals*, *bhaddars* and *manjhis* use code words and a few catch sentences through which they pass on certain secret information to their co-professionals when dealing with the pilgrims. These code words carry secret information regarding pilgrims, and devotees, working condition, types of worship, location and economic condition and the amount to be extracted from them.

To sum up, in their dress and dialects, the sacred specialists of Kashi exhibit a distinct style of life; in the younger generation, however, a departure from traditional dress is easily noticeable.

Residence and Location

The sacred specialists live in different *mohallas* and this marks them off from their counterparts in Gaya[1] and Deoghar[2] who live in clusters formed round the place of their work. It is probably due to the linguistic heterogeneity of the sacred specialists of Kashi which has already been discussed. However, some sacred specialists are located around the areas of their language group. For instance, the *mahants* of the golden Vishwanath temple live in front of the temple, and most of the *tirthapurohitas* live in the Vishwanath gali. But the *karmakandis* of different linguistic regions live in their respective areas of linguistic dominance. For instance, the *karmakandis* from South India are concentrated in the Kedar and Hanuman ghat areas; the Bengali *karmakandis* live in and around the Bengali tola, close to the Chausathi ghat; the Maithil *karmakandis* live around Shyama temple; the Maharashtrian *karmakandis* reside around Brahma and Durga ghats and areas where the other Maharashtrians live. Thus we find that a parochial feature is prevalent in the residential pattern of the *karmakandis*.

Usually, the *ghatias* live very close to their *ghats* on the Ganges, but some of them also live in the heart of the city, particularly those who own the *ghats*. The *yatrawals* reside in various areas of Kashi, such as Chetganj, Sonarpura and Ramapura; it is interesting that in majority cases their residential areas are multilingual.

The *bhaddars* and the *mahapatras* are concentrated mainly at two places; the *bhaddars* live in the Benia park area, the *mahapatras* live in the Meer ghat mohalla. The *manjhis* live close to the ghats. The Doms live in a compact and congested areas of Manikarnika and Harischandra ghats. Other ritual associates like Mali, musicians, barbers, and the sacred article sellers are scattered all over, and some of them may be found in the remotest corner of the city.

Most of the Brahmin sacred specialists particularly the *tirthapurohitas*, the *karmakandis*, and the *ghatias*, have marked their preference for moving out of the congested and suffocative residential areas; some of them also own houses in open and newly planned areas. The younger generation of the sacred specialists, particularly those who are receiving modern education, decline to live in the old houses on hygienic grounds. However, change in residence is not frequent, because of economic factors and professional considerations.

Hobbies

The sacred specialists are so much involved in pilgrims industry that they have hardly any time to cultivate hobbies providing recreation and the pleasure of leisure. However, some of them have been able to learn classical music, both vocal and instrumental, and have earned name and fame in this field. Tobacco-chewing, snuff-taking, betel-leaf chewing, drinking of *bhang*, wrestling, *safa-pani* picnic, etc., may be enlisted as the favourite pastime of the sacred specialists.

Chewing *khaini*, made of tobacco mixed with dry lime is very common; one takes it even at the time of conducting rituals. A sacred specialist often shares tobacco with his *jajman*. Among the older generation of the sacred specialists snuff is also very popular.

The betel-leaf of Benaras is famous all over India, and betel-leaf chewing is indeed a must for all the sacred specialists. They consider it a prasad of Kashi, for it is offered to Lord Vishwanath during *bhog arati*, *sringar arati*, and specially on *shayan arati* when the Lord retires for the night. From the life history of the sacred specialists, it appears that from the very childhood they chew betel leaf.

Bhang locally called *thandai*, is a popular drink; it is usually taken in the afternoon. Like betel leaf, it is also considered as the *prasad* of Lord Shiva. There are some shops in Kashi famous for Benarasi *thandai;* but most of the sacred specialists prepare *bhang* at their homes or take it in the company of their friends. They have specialized in preparing delicious *bhang*.

Wrestling is one of the improtant hobbies of the sacred specialists, and that is why most of them possess robust health till the end of their life. Most of them have ancestral *akhara* (a place of wrestling) which they maintain and where in some cases outsiders are not allowed. The *akhara* is worshipped and the soil of the *akhara* is considered sacred. Generally before taking bath in the Ganges most of the sacred specialists go to an *akhara* for physical exercise.

Kashi is a famous seat of classical music. The sacred specialists of this city are lovers of classical music, and quite often they participate in the programme of classical music and dance. The father of Pandit Gajendra Nath Dube, a *tirthapurohita* of Kashi was a noted musician of his time. One of the *ghatia* informants narrated that he was loved by his teacher because he was a good singer. One of the *tirthapurohitas* narrated in his life history that his father used to play various musical instruments, such as *sitar*, *harmonium*, *tabla*, *veena*, *sarangi*, *pakhavaj*, etc., and he taught *sitar* to Raja Lakshman Singh, the then prince of the Gangabar estate in U.P. Among his royal disciples, two more important persons were Dilip Singh and Maharaja Bibhuti Singh of Kashi.

Going to *safa-pani* (in the mid-stream of the Ganges where there is clean water) for bath, and some times going outside Kashi or on the eastern bank of the Ganges on picnic may also be included in the list of hobbies of the sacred specialists.

Cooperation and Conflict

As indicated in the foregoing sections the profession of priestcraft has transcended the territorial, linguistic, caste and sectarian boundaries. Thus, at the intra-group level, they express solidarity in the institution of priestcraft. The occasions for the demonstration of their solidarity may however be few, but they do unite for their common interest. Practically all categories of sacred specialists united against the Harijans' entry into the golden Vishwanath temple in 1952. In their personal life all categories of the sacred specialists seem to compromise, for instance, in the linguistic matter. All of them speak Banarsi as noted earlier, have commonly developed a secret language, though they retain their mother tongue at home. Their professional specialization also demands co-operation among different groups. For instance, the *bhaddar* who are pilgrim hunters, escort the pilgrims from railway station and bus stand to the *ghats* of the Ganges. There, they hand over the clients to the *ghatias*, for which they receive some money from the latter. The *yatrawals* and the *karmakandis* have a similar understanding among themselves. Whenever a pilgrim is received by a *yatrawal* near the entrance of the Vishwanath gali or around the Vishwanath temple, he is asked whether he has to perform any ritual. If he replies in the affirmative he is taken to a *karmakandi*, for which the *yatrawal* receives commission. Practically no case of dispute between a *bhaddar* and a *ghatia* or a *yatrawal* and a *karmakandi* has been reported, so far as the transference of a client is concerned.

The *karmakandis* and the *ghatias* are always on good terms, for most often it is the latter who introduce the former to the pilgrims. On certain occasions when the *manjhi* has to act as a sacred specialist, he joins with the *ghatias* in guiding and assisting the pilgrims. The *manjhi* and the *ghatia* thus fall into a contractual relationship.

At the inter-group level also, there exist co-operation and compromise among the *bhaddars*, *ghatias*, *tirthapurohitas*, *manjhis* and Doms. Thus the *bhaddars* have formed their own association where they meet regularly for discussion on important social and professional matters. If a *bhaddar* is in litigation with a *tirthapurohita*, something not unusual, other *bhaddars* express full solidarity with this member of their community. Similarly, the *ghatias* also have professional unions. If the pilgrim (*jajman*) of a *ghatia* is assisted by another *ghatia* in absence, the latter is given in *dakshina* 75 per cent of the total money realized from the pilgrims. They have also formed an association which safeguards their interest. Although at the caste level these varied sacred specialists may not be interdining, but on account of their close professional integration they often disobey the caste rule in matters of food and 'touch' pollution.

Dom is a very closed functional group with whom others have little scope of interaction at functional level. The *yatrawal* is more a functional group than a caste, though most of them are Joshi Brahmins, they interact freely among themselves, but not so much with others. The *manjhis* have also caste association which safeguards the interest and welfare of their society.

In addition to these groups of sacred specialists, there are other groups which have no association, nor do they interact at functional level. Such are the *kirtanias*, *anushthanis* and *kathavachaks*.

The *bhaddars*, the *yatrawals*, and the *gumashtas* are most often involved in litigation with the *tirthapurohitas* who claim themselves to be the original priests of the *tirthas* of Kashi. These *tirthapurohitas* claim that the *bhaddars*, the *yatrawals*, and the *gumashtas* were once their employees, who are now functioning independently. Thus most often the right over the *jajman* is disputed between the two. Generally, the pilgrims are received at the railway station by the *bhaddars* who dispose of them to the *yatrawals*; the latter take the pilgrims to different sacred centres and finally hand them over to the *karmakandis* who assist the pilgrims in conducting rituals. In this way of handling pilgrims, the *tirthapurohitas* who have the traditional *jajmanika* relationship with the pilgrims are not even informed. Later, when the *tirthapurohitas* come to know that their *jajmans* have been taken away by the *Bhaddars* and the *karmakandis* they pick up quarrel with them. It is true that sometimes the *bhaddars* do bring pilgrims for the *tirthapurohitas* in lieu of commission, but on many occasions when a wealthy pilgrim does not know the name and address of his *tirthapurohita* or *Panda*, he is prevailed upon by the *bhaddars* and the *yatrawals*.

As no one has the monopoly on the profession of *Pandagiri* anyone can take up this profession, and hence, the *jajmanika* relationship is often disputed. One of the learned *tirthapurohita* informants, Pt. Gajendra Nath Dube,[3] said, "since the *pandagiri* profession is open to all, the family members of the *gumashtas* are claiming to be the old *tirthapurohitas*. We are helpless to impose any restrictions on them, because the Government has allowed them to adopt this profession. Though we have lodged several suits in the courts of law against them but the decision of the court always goes in their favour."

Some sort of professional competition exists between the Barbers, the Malis, the *kirtanias*, and the *kathavachaks*. Each of them try to attract more pilgrims and devotees for having good income. Some of the *tirthapurohitas*, *jyotishis* (astrologers), owners of the shrines, *anushthanis*, *ghatias*, *Manjhis* and *karmakandis* may also enter into such professional competition at individual level: many of them employ touts to convass and attract more clients. There are many *jyotishis* in Kashi who employ modern media of advertisement. They also post touts in some of the posh restaurants of the city seeking affluent and wealthy clients. Such competition sometimes leads to personality assassination resulting in conflict and tension among the members of a professional group.

Competition among the sacred specialists is prominently reflected in the field of establishing permanent and stable *jajmanika* relationship with the pilgrims. We have already stated that the *tirthapurohitas* were once the sole member of the *jajmanika* geography of India and Nepal, and, as claimed by the *tirthapurohitas*, the *bhaddars*, the *gumashtas*, and the *yatrawals* used to be employed by them as servants to escort and bring pilgrims from different places, and also visit the *jajmans* from time to time to encourage them to undertake pilgrimage to Kashi. But now since most of the old servants of the *tirthapurohitas* have become independent functional groups, they are caught up in professional rivalries. Although some of the *bhaddars* have established permanent *jajmanika* relationship with the pilgrims, yet they have to keep a constant watch on their clients so that others may not attract them away. Thus, interaction of the sacred specialists with the pilgrims is often subjected to competition and conflict.

The influx of tourists and the Hippies have also accelerated competition and conflict among the sacred specialists. A healthy competition in the decoration of the deity and the shrine has also been noticed. Since tourists and the Hippies are good pay-clients all the sacred specialists try to win them over.

To sum up, it can be said that although the nature and the extent of these processes of interaction may vary at a place of pilgrimage among the various categories of the sacred specialists according to their distinctive local, social and cultural conditions, their presence in one form or the other is marked everywhere.

REFERENCES

[1] In Gaya, as *Vidyarthi* (1961) observes there is a prominent residential proximit y among the sacred specialits, this strengthens the formation of sacred segments.

[2] Like Gaya, the sacred specialists of Deoghar (Narayan 1975) live in one compact area and thus their residential proximity seems to be very prominent.

[3] For details, see life-history No. 2 of Pandit Gajendra Nath Dube (40).

Chapter VI

PILGRIMS AND PILGRIMAGE

INSTITUTION OF PILGRIMAGE[1]

THE institution of pilgrimage can be traced back to the early phase of Hindu cultural traditions. Its antiquity is evidenced by both the Brahminist and the Buddhist literature. The holy rivers of the Punjab and Madhyadesha are described in the *Vedas*. The sanctity of the rivers was stressed in the *Smritis* which use the term *tirtha* in describing them. The water of the rivers, particularly of the Ganges, the Saraswati and the Jamuna, was believed to have been endowed with special merits. The *Vishnusmriti* gives an exhaustive list of the *tirthas* spread over the whole of India; it recommends *tirtha yatra* (pilgrimage) which is equated with *ashvamedha* (horse sacrifice) as the effective means of expiation for all sins. The *Manusmriti* also attaches great importance to pilgrimage to the Ganges and to Kurukshetra. In Kautilya's time there used to be large congregation of pilgrims at various holy places. The epics mention *tirthayatra*; the epic of pilgrimage par excellence is the *Mahabharata*. A section of the *Vanaparva* (chapter 78-158) entitled 'Tirthayatra Parva', is exclusively devoted to pilgrimage. The *Puranas* and the *Upapuranas* are the main sources of information on pilgrimage. *Tirthasthala* and *Kshetra Mahatmya* are the important parts of the *Puranas* dealing in great detail with the efficacy of pilgrimage and the righteous way of life a pilgrim is required to lead during *tirtha yatra*.

Tirthas : Their Number and Classification

Tirthas are countless. The list of *tirthas* as given in all the major *Puranas* and the *Mahabharata* is really a large one. The *Shabdakalpadruma* which has utilized information from the *Puranas* and the epics gives a list of 264 *tirthas* arranged in the order of their due circumambulation from the left to the right. Thirty-five millions of Tirthas are believed to be in existence in three worlds (*Bhuri*, *Divi* and *Antariksha*). Many *tirthas* are named at one place. According to some *puranas*, there are more than three hundred *tirthas* at Kashi alone. Of the various *tirthas*, the rivers like the Ganges (the best of rivers), the Jamuna, the Narmada, the Tapti, the Gautami (Godavari), the Panjara (Banganga), the Bhimarathi (Bhima), the Krishnaveni (Krishna), the Brahannadi (Mahanadi), the Malapaharini (Malaparbha) at its junction with the Krishna and the Tungabhadra have been mentioned as very sacred. Prayag, Kashi and Gaya are some of the leading places of pilgrimage which have received universal homage.

The *Brahmapuran* gives an ancient classification of *tirtha* and mentions them as *Daiva*, *Asura*, *Arsha* and *Manushya*, according to their origin. The *daiva* type of *tirthas* are those which were revealed by the Trinity (Brahma, Vishnu and Mahesh) and as such they are endowed with the utmost sanctity. Kashi, Pushkar and Prabhash are examples of this type. The Ganges, the Jumna, the Saraswati, the Jhelum, the Beas, the Godavari, the Bhima, the Tungabhadra, the Krishnaveni, the Tapti, and the Banganga are also listed among the Daiva type of Tirthas. Gaya is an *Asura tirtha*. The *Arsha tirthas* derived their origin from sages. The Manusha Tirthas are those which were made holy by rulers of the solar and lunar dynasties.

Tirtha Phala

The merit of pilgrimage is often equated with that of a *yajna*. The *tirthas* vary in their potency and some are more powerful in their effect than others. According to the orthodox view a pilgrimage is not a pleasure tour, and if undertaken with such motive it fails to become a *tirtha yatra*. The scriptures have laid utmost emphasis on the purity of motive and intensely devout feeling for pilgrimage.

> "The *Yatra* must be one-pointed. It must be undertaken in a spirit of faith in its efficacy. The mystic potency of a sacred stream may confer a minor benefit on the person who immerses himself in its holy waters, without even believing in its value. But to attain the full spiritual advantages of a

yatra, it must be commenced with a definite purpose and in the full faith that the journey, when completed in the proper frame of mind and without any lapse of the austerities prescribed, will yield the highest unworldly advantage. The assurance in the *sthal-mahatmyas* that in certain tirthas sin does not penetrate, is a tribute to their austere atmosphere and associations. Life affords numerous opportunities for the ascent to spiritual perfection, which will end re-birth. One of such opportunities is furnished by the discipline of pilgrimage which is not an end in itself but only one of the means to the highest end.

The merits of pilgrimage range from immediate relief from mundane troubles to the expiation of sins and gaining the Ultimate Reality. But the efficacy of *tirtha yatra* is proportioned to the degree of the purity of mind and body. The ancient authorities have repeatedly pointed out that the holy rivers would not wash away spiritual dirt by mere immersion; for acquiring a spiritual merit the pilgrimage must add a spirituality to his conduct. There is no automatic spiritual reaction to the mechanical act or rite; the mental *tirthas* are more effective than the physical ones. The *Mahabharata* elaborates this idea and holds that the best of the *tirthas* is a pure heart. The *Puranas* are also replete with this idea. *Tirtha yatra* is in fact aimed at securing a coordination between pious life and highest knowledge.

Commended Tirtha Practices

Fasting, sexual abstinence, abstinence from unguents, soft bed and luxuries, rejection of the aid of vehicles or animals for making journey, and walking without shoes in *tirtha* have been enjoined on the pilgrims with a view to producing righteous mind by disciplining the body.

Some of the recommended performances at almost every important *tirtha* are holy bath, vow, prayer, worship, gift, cremation, *pinda dan*, *tarpana* and *shraddha*. The gods and goddesses of a *tirtha* are to be propitiated by chanting their names, by remembering their sanctity, by cultivating devotion, and by performing *puja* and *arati* to them.

The throwing of flowers, coconuts, fruits, betel leaves and money into holy rivers is considered meritorious. The throwing of bones, which remain after cremation of the dead body, into the holy rivers is also recommended. To live in a *tirtha* till death is regarded as an important means of obtaining salvation. The circumambulation of a *tirtha* is considered an important part of pilgrimage.

A peculiar custom which finds mention in some of the *tirtha* literature is the suicide at a place of pilgrimage. Although the authorities are sharply divided on the question of suicide as a commendable practice, there seems to be a considerable weight on the merit of religious suicide. The ancient custom of self-slaughter in the Ganges, at Prayag and at Kashi has been reported. Suicide at Pehova near Thaneshwar is mentioned in the *Mahabharata*. The *Lingapuran* recommends the merits of suicide at Kurukshetra. Suicide by fire or water and above all by falling head-long from a cliff at Amarkantak is mentioned by Lakshmidhar, the author of the *Kalpataru* in the twelfth century A.D.

The pilgrims are enjoined to observe *upavas* or fast, and to worship and propitiate Ganesh and gods, ancestors and Brahmins before undertaking a tirtha yatra as well as after it is completed. The practice of the *shraddha* is considered an act of supreme merit. The liberal feeding, accompanied by *dakshina* to Brahmins and hungry is also a commendable practice during pilgrimage. At some of the *tirthas* the solemnity of pilgrimage is enforced by *mundana* (tonsure), while at others it is not obligatory. But to do the *pitripuja* at all the *tirthas* is an obligation of all the pilgrims. Every gift at a *tirtha* has far more efficacy than when made elsewhere. But gift should not be accepted lightly because they bless more the giver than the recipient.

A special merit is assigned to pilgrimage on special occasions, such as on the occurrence of astronomical conjunctions, for instance, eclipses of the sun and moon. The *Puranas* have described at great length the merit of taking holy bath in certain rivers on these occasions. The Ganges is however always pure and endowed with special sanctity.

IMPORTANCE OF KASHI

As has been described in Chapter I, Kashi finds prominent mention in various scriptures. In most of the treatises on *tirtha*, Kashi has been referred to as a very important place of pilgrimage. The most important shrine and *linga* which has been repeatedly mentioned by the *Puranas* and the later texts is that of Vishweshwara (today popularly known as Vishwanatha) as the lord of Kashi. But the Swayambhu or the Jyotirlinga of this Vishweshwara was destroyed when the Muslims ransacked Kashi, and according to the canons of scriptures there is no substitute for this *linga*. The *Tristhalisetu* makes the following remarks on this issue: "Though here the *linga* of Vishweshwara is removed and another is brought in its place by human beings, owing to the times, the pilgrims must worship whatever *linga* is in this place. Sometimes, owing to the action of tyrannical Mlechcha rulers, there may be no *linga* in that place. In that case, circumambulation, *namaskara* and other forms of salutation must be made to the spot only. By that action the fruit of the pilgrimage is attained. The *abhisheka*, etc. which can only be done (to the *linga*) can of course not be done."[3] However, as the new *linga* has been accepted by most *sisthas*, modern authorities on scriptures, it is being worshipped and venerated as the old Vishweshwara—the authentic one.

The sanctity of the Manikarnika is mentioned in various scriptures. The Dasashwamedha also finds mention both as Tirtha at which bath is meritorious and as the shrine of a *linga* of the name.

Now famous *panchakosi* circumambulation of Kashi does not find mention in the Krityakalpataru, and hence possibly, this tradition was introduced only after the twelfth century.

The rules of pilgrimage prescribed for other *tirthas* are equally applicable to Kashi. Also there are certain customs peculiar to this holy city. For instance, according to the *Krityakalpataru*, sweeping the streets of Kashi is a specially meritorious act. Suicide at Kashi by the usual means of starvation, drowning, or self-immolation is a recognized practice according to the *Puranas*. "But suicide is unnecessary at Kashi owing to a special power conferred on the *kshetra*. Shiva himself ensures *mukti* to everyone who dies within the sacred limits by whispering into the right ear of the dying person a *mantra* which is appropriately called the *taraka*."[4]

Another peculiar recommendation of the ancient scripture for the pilgrims of Kashi is to break their legs on a stone so that they may not run away from this holy city !

The scriptures have tried to banish the fear of death in the devout pilgrims. It may be pointed-out that generally a cremation ground carried impurity and conveys mortality to all who tread it. But Kashi, the greatest cremation ground of all, is the exception.

It is only at Kashi that mere death grants release from rebirth. Obviously, this guarantee makes such practices of the pilgrims as baths, fasts, vows, sacrifices and prayers unnecessary. Yet, these are recommended to the laities for providing moral and spiritual force.

In brief, according to the scriptures, Kashi is the city of living and also the city of the dying and the dead. (See Table 8 on next page).

PILGRIMAGE TO KASHI IN MODERN TIMES

Composition of Pilgrims

To analyse the pilgrimage to Kashi in modern times a sample of 500 pilgrims representing the various cross-sections of Hindu society was drawn up from Dharamshala,[5] hotels and the houses of the *pandas*.

As it may be seen from Table 8, pilgrims from all over India visit this sacred city. Of these, most numerous are the pilgrims from Bihar (19.8), U.P. (18.2), and West Bengal (13.6). The flow of pilgrims visiting the city is almost uniformly large round the year. On certain special occasions such as Shivaratri, Shravana, and *Pitripaksha* their number increases considerably.

The composition of pilgrims is heterogeneous insofar as their caste, class, and education are concerned. As shown in Table 8, among the pilgrims, the Brahmins, as expected, are in majority (32.8). Next to the Brahmins are the Kshatrias (16.4) and then come the Vaishyas (13.8). The rest of the pilgrims come from different castes, often disputing their rank in the *varna* order. It is interesting that only 6 per cent of the pilgrims fall under the category of illiterates. From what appears in Table 9, educated persons in both modern and traditional learning are enlisted among the devout pilgrims. Men and women in different professions are also making pilgrimage to Kashi. Although we have not been able to record the origin of pilgrims in rural and urban contexts, it came out (Table 10) that 16.4

TABLE 8

Showing the composition

Name of the State (Linguistic region)	*Number (percentages of*					
	Brahmin	*Kshatriya*	*Vaishya*	*Bhumihar*	*Kayastha*	*Maratha*
1	2	3	4	5	6	7
Andhra Pradesh	9 (1.80)	3 (0.60)	3 (0.60)		2 (0.40)	
Assam	3 (0.60)				1 (0.20)	
Bengal	35 (7.00)		7 (1.40)		25 (5.00)	
Bihar	19 (3.80)	27 (5.40)	7 (1.40)	11 (2.20)	13 (2 60)	
Delhi	8 (1.80)	1 (0.20)	3 (0.60)		1 (0.20)	
Gujarat	2 (0.40)	1 (0.20)	4 (0.80)			
Himachal Pradesh	1 (0.20)					
Jammu & Kashmir		1 (0.20)				
Karnataka	10 (2.00)					
Kerala	1 (0.20)					
Madhya Pradesh	13 (2.60)	10 (2.00)	9 (1.80)		4 (0.80)	
Maharashtra	19 (3.80)	8 (1.60)	7 (1.40)			5 (1.00)
Orissa	2 (0.40)		2 (0.40)			
Punjab					1 (0.20)	
Rajasthan	2 (0.40)		14 (2.80)			
Tamil Nadu	9 (1.80)	3 (0.60)				
Uttar Pradesh	29 (5.80)	24 (4.80)	13 (2.60)	5 (1.00)	9 (1 80)	
Nepal	1 (0.20)	7 (1.40)				
Ceylon	1 (0 20)					
Total	164 (32.80)	82 (16.40)	69 (13.80)	16 (3.20)	56 (11.20)	5 (1.00)

of pilgrims (General)

pilgrims according to caste)

Khatri	*Kurmi*	*Ahir*	*Kahar*	*Koeri*	*Other castes*	*Total*	*Percentage*
8	9	10	11	12	13	14	15
1 (0.20)						18	(3.00)
						4	(0.80)
1 (0.20)		2 (0.40)				68	(13.60)
	4 (0.80)	2 (0.40)	3 (0.60)	8 (1.60)		94	(18.80)
						13	(2.60)
	1 (0.20)					8	(1.60)
						1	(0.20)
						1	(0.20)
						10	(2.00)
		1 (0.20)				2	(0.40
1 (0.20)		1 (0.20)		1 (0.20)		39	(7.80)
2 (0.40)						41	(8.20)
						4	(0.80)
2 (0.40)						3	(0.60)
	1 (0.20)					17	(3.40)
						12	(2.40)
3 (0.60)	3 (0.60)	3 (0.60)	1 (0.20)	3 (0.60)		91	(18.20)
2 (0.40)						10	(2.00)
						1	(0.20)
12 (2.40)	9 (1.80)	7 (1.40)	4 (0.80)	10 (2.00)	66 (13.20)	500	(100.00)

per cent of the pilgrims were peasants. The number of pilgrims coming from business (20.2) and higher professions[6] (19.8) is considerable, but men and women engaged in menial services (20.0) are also represented well; and therefore we can safely conclude that Hindus from all walks and ages visit Kashi.

Preparation

As has been indicated in the preceding sections, the Brahmanic scriptures have prescribed in great detail the rules regarding pilgrimage. From what has come out in the interviews of pilgrims it seems that the canons of the scriptures regarding the motive of pilgrimage and the commended *tirtha* practices have been considerably vulgarized in actual practice. Yet, one

TABLE 9

Showing percentage of literacy among the pilgrims

Sl. No.	*Educational qualification*	*No. of pilgrims*	*Percentage*
1	Illiterate	30	6.00
2	Literate	146	29.20
3	Matriculate	107	21.40
4	Graduate	118	23.60
5	Post-Graduate	51	10.20
6	Sanskritist	19	3.80
7	Professional qualification (Technicians, Drivers)	29	5.80
	Total	500	100.00

TABLE 10

Showing professions of the pilgrims

Sl. No.	*Profession*	*No. of pilgrims*	*Percentage*
1	Peasant	82	16.4
2	Business	101	20.2
3	Higher professions (Doctors, Lawyers etc.)	99	19.8
4	Menial Services	100	20.00
5	Other professions	118	23.6
	Total	500	100.00

cannot quite say that today the attraction towards pilgrimage, particularly towards Kashi, has diminished. The respectability attached to pilgrimage is not lost anywhere in India, for the pilgrims from different regions of the country have reported that the belief in the efficacy of *tirtha yatra* is well founded in their respective villages and towns, and among people of all categories. Attraction to pilgrimage to Kashi is evidenced from the fact that among the pilgrims interviewed 146 (29.2) were those who visited Kashi for the first time and the rest (70.8) had visited this sacred city more than once (Table 11) that 29.6 of pilgrims visited Kashi for more than six times in their life time is indeed remarkable. (One should find out whether such a large proportion of Indian population visits a secular town more than six times.)

In South Indian villages sometimes subscriptions are collected and those who wish to make a pilgrimage to Kashi enlist their names sufficiently in advance to the organizers. A collective pilgrimage is thus arranged. Special trains, railway coaches, and chartered buses are arranged by the organizers of the pilgrim party. This type of commissioned and collective pilgrimage has been reported from all parts of India.

In some of the villages in Uttar Pradesh the custom has been that a person going on pilgrimage will announce his intention to the villagers, who will assemble in his house where the family deity will be worshipped and later on all the villagers will see off that person at the boundary of the village. Once having made a *sankalpa* of this type, one cannot return to his village unless he or she has performed the intended pilgrimage. On return from pilgrimage he or she is to organize Satyanarayan Katha, generally followed by the feasting of villagers. The *prasad* which one has brought from *tirtha* is also distributed among the villagers and kinsmen. A visit to a place of pilgrimage adds to one's social esteem. The pilgrims by and large visit in groups; among the 500 pilgrims interviewed 268 (53.6) had come with family members, 60 (12.0) came with friends, and only 172 (34.4) came all alone.

Participation in Sacred Complex

The varieties of rituals and the modes of sacred performances have already been described in Chapter II. So far as the prescribed rules regarding the sacred performances are concerned, it appears that today most of the pilgrims visiting Kashi do not adhere to the scriptural recommendations For instance, according to the *Pauranic* recommendations, one is required to stay at least for three nights at a place of pilgrimage. But this rule is defied by 64.2 per cent of the pilgrims interviewed in course of our survey. The detailed figures for the duration of the stay are as follows : 38 per cent pilgrims stayed in Kashi for one day; 26.2 per cent stayed for two days, 13.6 per cent stayed for three days, 5.8 per cent for six days, and 4.8 per cent pilgrims stayed for more than six days (answers from 5.7 per cent persons could not be obtained).

Similarly, of the various rituals prescribed in the scriptures only a few are performed today and that too in most cases, perfunctorily. When asked about the main purpose of their visit the pilgrims replied as shown in Table 11.

TABLE 11

Showing the main purpose of pilgrim's visit

Sl. No.	*Main purpose of visit*		*Response in percentage*
1.	Tirthayatra (as a part of normal religious duty)		12.8
2.	Special Tirthayatra (on the occurrence of astronomical conjunctions and festive occasions) more effective than ordinary pilgrimage		4.2
3.	For making special performances		59.0
	Viswanath pujan	57.2	
	Ganga puian	0.2	
	Sankatamochan pujan	0.2	
	Listening Katha	1.2	
	Performing *anushthan*	0.2	
4.	To die in Kashi		0.2
5.	Funeral ceremonies		13.0
	Cremation	2.4	
	Asthi-pravaha	2.8	
	Pind.idana	7.8	
6.	Mundan		2.0
7.	Answers not obtained		8.8

Considering the movement of pilgrims in the sacred geography of Kashi, it transpires that all the pilgrims do not visit all the sacred centres, and that, except the main golden Vishwanath temple and its clusters, no sacred centre is visited by all the pilgrims. The response (in percentage) of the pilgrims regarding their visit to the following important sacred centres has been as follows :

(*1*)	Golden Vishwanath temple and all other shrines in its cluster	100.00
(*2*)	Naya Vishwanath Temple	19.3
(*3*)	Vishwanath temple located at the B.H.U. and all the shrines such as Durga kunda, Tulsi Manas Mandir, and Sankatamochan, that are located on the way	45.6
(*4*)	Kedar Temple	5.8
(*5*)	Sankta Temple	12.8
(*6*)	Kalabhairava Temple	15.0

Similarly, the sacred bathing *ghats* on the Ganges are not equally used by all the pilgrims. The figures (in percentage) obtained in this regard are as follows: (The percentage of pilgrims taking bath on different *ghats* has been indicated in brackets):

Dasashwamedha ghat (85.6), Manikarnika ghat (34.8), Sheetala ghat (16.7), Ahilyabai ghat (13.0), Ram ghat (9.4), Harishchandra ghat (7.2), Kedar ghat (7.0), Adikeshwar ghat (3.2), Assi ghat (3.0), Meer ghat (2.6), Raj ghat (2.6), Durga ghat (2.4), Tripurabhairavi ghat (1.7), Man Mandir ghat (1.6), Chausathi ghat (1.4), Gauri ghat (1.4), Darbhanga ghat (1.2), Munshi ghat (1.2); less than one per cent pilgrims bathed on Brahma ghat, Hanuman ghat, Lalit ghat, Manasarovar ghat, Mysore ghat, Niranjani ghat, Ranamahal ghat, Sankat ghat, Scindia ghat and Tulsi ghat.

The sacred wells (*kundas*) are generally visited for performing special rites associated with them; and hence all the pilgrims may not visit all the *kundas*. In the sample survey only 25 per cent pilgrims visited *kundas*; and of these 23.4 per cent visited Manikarnika Kunda, 21.0 per cent visited Durga Kunda, 3.6 per cent visited Lolarka Kunda, 1.8 per cent visited Gauri Kunda and Bakaria Kunda.

There are various shrines dedicated to *Birs* and *Sati*, but only 0.8 per cent pilgrims visited these shrines. All the pilgrims who visited these places were non-Brahmins or, what has been called, the pilgrims of *laukik* culture.[7]

In Kashi, there are more than two hundred religious institutions called *mathas*, *ashrams*, *akharas* etc. Pilgrims visit these institutions which, in some cases, may happen to be their *gurupitha;* or that may be visiting some *siddha mahatma* of that place. However, only 7.4 per cent pilgrims reported to have visited these *mathas* and *ashrams.*

After making sacred performances some pilgrims visit places of tourists interest in the neighbourhood of Kashi. For instance, 15.6 per cent pilgrims visited Ramnagar to see the palace of Maharaja of Banaras (a part of which has been converted into a museum), and 27.8 per cent pilgrims visited Sarnath, where the Lord Buddha had delivered his first sermon, and which is now an archaeological site (the museum and the archaeological remains of Sarnath are great attraction for pilgrims). Although at both these places, the Brahmanic gods and goddesses are also located, but the primary motive of the pilgrim visitors has been secular, i.e. site-seeing.

The daily routine of the pilgrims, irrespective of age, sex, caste, education and profession, may be briefly recorded as follows: A pilgrim remembers Lord Vishwanath at the time of taking holy bath in the Ganges in the early hours of the day. After taking bath he performs some rituals at the *ghats* and then proceeds to worship Vishwanath and other shrines located in that cluster. He usually takes *satwika* (vegetarian) food in the day, and rests in the afternoon. In the evening he goes to Vishwanath temple for having *darshana* (sacred visitation) of the Lord at the time of *Shringar arati.* On the second day, he goes for *puja* and *darshana* of the various shrines such as Vishwanath temple located at the Banaras Hindu University, Sankaṭamochan, Tulsi Manas Mandir, Durga Kunda, Kalabhairava, and Sankataji. On the third day, he goes for site-seeing to Ramnagar and Sarnath. In the daily routine of a pilgrim a holy bath in the Ganges and the Vishwanath *puja* are essential (the minimum sacred performance to be followed everyday), and common to all; the performance of ritual depends upon one's own requirement. Hence there are personal variations. Before going to the bed one remembers Lord Vishwanath, in the belief that it is his sacred duty to pay homage to the Lord in whose city he has come to spend a few days in peace. Generally in the first two days of stay, particularly in the morning, he is very busy in making sacred performances; in the first few days of stay the rituals are also elaborate. In the afternoon, he participates in *katha* and *kirtan* at the *ghats*. Since the merit of pilgrimage is proportioned to the time one devotes to sacred performance, the daily routine of the devout pilgrims is crowded with religious activities.

Although the type of accommodation one chooses at a place of pilgrimage is no index of his religiosity, but that can, at least, suggest his attitude towards some of the institutions in sacred complex. For instance, of the pilgrims interviewed, 44.0 per cent stayed in *dharamshalas*, 16.4 per cent stayed with the Pandas, 13.2 per cent stayed with their relatives, 14.0 per cent stayed in hotels, and 12.4 per cent left Kashi without staying anywhere. To most pilgrims, who stayed in Dharamshalas, cheaper accommodation (*dharamshalas* do not charge any rent for stay; hence, they are cheaper than hotels) was no consideration. For many wealthy informants who could afford to live in luxurious hotels preferred to stay in Dharamshalas because they believed that the hotels which are generally open to people of all castes and religions are no good for stay during pilgrimage, and since *dharamshalas* are not open to non-Hindus (most of the Dharamshalas are sectarian and parochial) they can maintain their standard of purity by having private arrangement of cooking (which is generally not permissible in hotels). Thus, the pilgrims staying in *dharamshalas* are, by and large, orthodox in their attitude towards purity and pollution. The pilgrims staying with the *pandas* were also guided by a similar consideration.

The extent and nature of relationship between pilgrims and sacred specialists may reflect the attitude of the former towards the latter. It has come out significantly that maximum number (65.2) of pilgrims have contractual and temporary relationship with the sacred specialists: and that only 33.8 per cent pilgrims have hereditary relationship with the *Pandas*, and one per cent with the *Bhaddars*. Although 2.5 per cent pilgrims did not utilize the services of the sacred specialists at all—they themselves performed the rituals of worship, *tarpan* and *darshan*—but the fact that 50.5 per cent pilgrims took help of the *tirthapurohitas*, *Karmakandis* and *Pandas*, and 12.5 per cent utilized the services of the *bhaddars* and the *yatrawals*, (data for 34.5 per cent pilgrims were not obtained) shows that these institutions have not lost their relevance.

In an attempt to assess the attitude of pilgrims towards the sacred complex in general we enquired about their pilgrims' cycle, their motivators, and their knowledge of the sacred complex in Kashi. Although much that we expected from this enquiry would have come if the data were collected in depth, yet the responses obtained in this regard indicate a general trend.

Most of the pilgrims interviewed were those who had visited more than one pilgrim centre; all the informants had visited most of the holy places located in their respective regions. That 85.5 per cent pilgrims had visited holy places outside their home regions is a clear proof of their attraction towards pilgrimage. It has also been found that 14 per cent pilgrims follow pilgrim's cycle, when pilgrimage is made periodically at the interval of one, two or three years. The frequency of pilgrimage to Kashi, as stated earlier, shows that nearly 70 per cent pilgrims have visited this holy city more than once; such is the attraction of Kashi.

An enquiry into the motivating factor that brought the pilgrims to Kashi reveals that 27 per cent pilgrims were motivated by their family members, kinsmen and friends, 30 per cent came to perform necessary and obligatory rituals, 21 per cent themselves desired to undertake pilgrimage, 2.5 per cent followed the advice of the astrologers and family priests (to overcome their misfortune and problems), and 19.5 per cent pilgrims did not clarify the motivating factor of their pilgrimage to Kashi.

From what has come out in the interviews, there seems to be no doubt that most pilgrims do not have adequate knowledge of the sacred geography of Kashi; only 42 per cent pilgrims could rightly identify the boundary of Kashi-kshetra, as described in scriptures. But the fact that 99 per cent pilgrims had heard the *mahatmya* of Kashi (either through villagers and kinsmen, or through sacred specialists and sacred literature) before coming to this place, testifies the strength of the traditional media of communication through which the knowledge of pilgrimage is continually transmitted. Once the pilgrims arrive in this holy city the varieties of sacred specialists interact with them; and it is this interaction and personal experiencing of the sacred phenomena which add to the knowledge of the pilgrims and sustain their interest and faith in the institution of pilgrimage.

REFERENCES

[1] The principal source material for this section has been drawn from K.V. Rangaswami Aiyangar's (1942) Introduction to the *Tirthavivechankhanda of Krityakalpataru* by Lakshmidhara Bhatta.

[2] Aiyangar (*op. cit.* XXIX).

[3] Tristhalisetu, p. 208 quoted by Aiyangar (*op. cit.* LXXV).

[4] Aiyangar (*op. cit.* LXXVI).

[5] The Dharamshalas in Kashi are easily distinguishable from one another by the caste and linguistic composition of their visitors.

[6] In the category of persons in higher profession are included gazetted officers, doctors, lawyers engineers, college teachers, business executives, and those earning more than Rs. 500.

[7] See Saraswati (1972 : 96).

[8] See Saraswati (1970 : 28).

Chapter VII

CONCLUSIONS

STRUCTURE OF SACRED COMPLEX

FROM what has been described in the foregoing chapter, it becomes fairly established that the Gaya-model of sacred complex (Vidyarthi 1961) is widely applicable to Kashi, and also, perhaps, to all the Puranic Tirthas of India. This is largely so because the three elements which build up the structure of sacred complex, viz., the sacred geography, the sacred performances, and the sacred specialists, are formed on scriptural canons, upheld by Hindus of all categories, of all places, and of all times. In conclusion, we might say that the structure of the sacred complex is so built that it sustains heterogeneous population and varieties of traditions. To illustrate this point, the main findings of the present study may briefly be stated as under :

Sacred Geography

As has been described in Chapter I, the *Puranas* have given a detailed plan of the Kashi-kshetra; its outer boundaries have been clearly marked, and its inner division into three *khandas* or segments has also been mentioned. The boundaries and the description of the Kashi-kshetra, however, vary from one scripture to another, and it is also said that the physical appearance of Kashi has been changing in different *yugas*. Yet, if the contemporary map of Kashi is juxtaposed on the Puranic geography of Kashi, a conspicuous continuity of the present with the past can be easily traced. This continuity has been maintained largely by the system of *parikrama*—both Panchakosi and Antargrahi—and the periodical *yatras* performed collectively by the pilgrims.

The change in the sacred geography has also been noticed; the reasons assigned for this are largely historical and secular. The destruction of temples by the Muslim rulers has caused a great stir in the sacred geography of Kashi. The location of the Golden Vishwanath temple, for instance, has been altered several times. There has also been a natural rise and fall of the shrines; some of the Puranic shrines have now fallen into disuse because of mismanagement, or have been usurped by people and are now being used for secular purposes. Many new temples have also come up into existence, since the time *Puranas* were written. Some of these are of very great attraction to pilgrims.

Looking at its physical extension and location of old and new temples, the contemporary sacred geography of Kashi roughly falls into two parts which may be called the sacred and secular zones. The sacred zone, as has been shown in Table 1 (Chapter I), is further divided into 11 segments and within each of these segments there are clusters of shrines. The number of clusters in each segment varies from one to three; and in each cluster the number of shrines is invariably large.

As discussed earlier, there is a popular tradition which divides Kashi into two sectarian zones, called 'Shiva Kashi' which is spread from Assi Sangam to Manikarnika ghat; and 'Vishnu Kashi' which lies between Manikarnika and Varuna Sangam. But this sectarian division of Kashi cannot be empirically established on the basis of the distribution of the Shaiva and the Vaishnava shrines.

This pattern of the sacred geography of Kashi has a close resemblance to that of Gaya.

Sacred Performances

In the Brahmanic scriptures the methods of sacred performances are elaborately laid down. They form into two broad categories—Vedic and Tantric. The Brahmanic shrines of Kashi follow both these types which may be grouped into a single class of sacred performance, called *shastric*. In the non-Brahmanic shrines, the sacred performances are made according to oral traditions or what is called *laukik parampara*, distinguishable both in content and manner from the shastric performances.

Each of the sacred performances, is composed of a number of rites. For instance, for performing *Abhisheka*, one has to go through various rites, such as personal purity, cleaning of god, decoration of god, offering of water, offering of coconut, waving of lamp, and circumambulation of the deity. All these acts are described in the *Shastras* as the essential elements of the *Abhisheka* ceremony. Thus, *Abhisheka* is not a single act of performance but a series of acts. This, of course, is true only in the case of such performances as are directed towards worship and *samskar* ceremonies.

On the basis of *(a)* the motive or purpose of performance, *(b)* the use of ritual instruments and mode of performance, and *(c)* the merit of performance, the sacred performances may be further classified into *(1) Pujan* (worship of the deity), *(2) Pindadan* (ancestor worship), and *(3) Prayashchita* (personal purification). The *Pujan* may be in the form of either actual worship or symbolic worship. In actual worship the performer is directly or indirectly involved in a variety of actions, such as bathing and decorating the image, waving *arati*, ringing the bell, and, above all, uttering *mantras* specific to a ritual. In the symbolic worship, the performer is involved in a single act, such as *darshana, kirtan* and *katha shravana*.

The sacred performances made for the fulfilment of 'this-worldly' desires vary greatly in their contents. Their differences can be identified easily at both Brahmanic and non-Brahmanic shrines. For instance, in the sacred performances made in the Vishwanath temples, the offering of wine is taboo, whereas this is a preferential offering at the non-Brahmanic shrines, namely at Daitrabir. The offerings may vary even in a single shrine, depending upon the type of vows of the performer. For instance, wishing to be cured of an eye disease, one offers a silver eye to Shitala, but a silver leg is offered to this deity when one wants to be cured of paralysis. If the same deity is to be propitiated for the general welfare, the offerings of sweets, flowers, incense, etc., are welcome.

The object and the method of offering may vary according to the sex and the sect of the deity. The Shakta shrines, for instance, employ the *Tantric paddhati* in which vermilion is the most common offering, but in the temples dedicated to the male deity the *puja paddhati* is largely Vaidika. No vermilion is offered to Shiva or to Vishnu, but there are, of course, certain notable exceptions to this rule. For instance, the *Jyotirlinga* of

Vishwanath is believed to be combining Shiva and Parvati in its monolithic *linga*, and hence vermilion is offered to the Lord Shiva in the form of *Jyotirlinga*. The ritual instruments used for Vaishnava and Shaiva deities are also different. For instance, *Damru* is essential for the worship of Shiva, but it is taboo for the Vaishnava deities who are propitiated best by bells.

This structure of the sacred performances is operative at all Hindu shrines, and hence all the places of Hindu pilgrimage have the unity of beliefs and practices. But the places of pilgrimage may be differentiated from one another also on the basis of the sacred performances peculiar to them. For instance, in Gaya the main sacred performance is the ancestor worship or what is known as *Pindadan*, but in Kashi it is difficult to say what the main sacred performance is, for all kinds of sacred performances are made here. Kashi thus, appears as a centre of varieties of rituals.

Sacred Specialists

As there are varieties of rituals, there are also varieties of ritual specialists. There are specialists in *Shastric* rituals, specialists in *Laukik* rituals. In the category of specialists in *Shastric* rituals are included the Dharmadhikaris, the Karmakandis, the Tirthapurohitas, the Pandas, the Ghatias and the Brahmanic shrine priests who have the requisite knowledge of the *Shastric* rituals, however little that knowledge may be. In this category of specialists, we may place the *katha vachaks*, the *kirtanias* and the *anushthanis*, but they are a class by themselves—different from the former category of specialists insofar as the extent and nature of their participation in the sacred performances are concerned. The *katha vachaks*, for instance, actually perform a sacred act in which the pilgrims join to share the merit; the karmakandis, on the contrary, act merely as helpers to the pilgrims who are the actual performers.

Among the specialists in *Laukik* rituals mention may be made of the boatmen and the barbers who perform *Laukik* rituals free from *Shastric* injunctions, though they may sometimes be appended to *Shastric* rituals.

Besides the specialists who direct the rituals there are also some persons who assist at the time of performance. These persons have only a peripheral role in the rituals, and as such they cannot be appropriately placed in the category of sacred specialists. The florists and the musicians are the examples of ritual associates. Among these ritual associates we may also place the pilgrim guides who assist the pilgrims to find out accommodation and the way to shrines, for instance, the Yatrawals and the Bhaddars of Kashi. In the category of ritual associates the Doms of Kashi, who are the custodian of sacred fire, also find a place. They not only give sacred fire for cremation (on receipt of some payment which they call tax), but also assist the pilgrims in cremating the dead. One of their functions is to bring wood for the preparation of pyre and finally to clean the ashes at the cremation *ghats*.

All the priests in a shrine do not hold equal rank, nor do they have equal role in the performance of rituals. The social status of a ritual specialist is determined by the nature of gifts he receives from the pilgrims. It may be stated here that receiving gift in a place of pilgrimage is not at all a meritorious act. Hence all those who receive gifts are ranked low in social status. Among these, the Karmakandis who receive only *dakshina* (fee for performing rituals and *not* gifts) are placed higher than the Ghatias who receive gifts at the *ghats*. The Mahapatras are however ranked lowest because they accept gifts on behalf of the dead at the time of Shraddha rituals.

The role of the priests may also sometimes divide them into distinct classes. In the Vishwanath temple, for instance, there are *gaddi-dharis* and *sthan-dharis*. The *gaddi-dharis* are the chief priests whose function is to worship the deity with all the paraphernalia involved in it. The *sthan-dharis* only assist the *gaddi-dharis* in the performance of worship; they operate in shifts.

There are both male and female priests; they come from different castes and linguistic groups. In most cases, they are identified with the linguistic composition of the managers of the shrines.

Thus, it comes out that the ritual specialists and associates in Kashi are not homogeneous groups. Among them there are both Brahmins and non-Brahmins. Most of the functional categories of ritual specialists are not endogamous; the Bhaddars and the Mahapatras are the only exceptions. In fact, among the aforementioned categories of specialists there is a good deal of confusion as one tries to place them accurately in a specific category. For instance, the shrine priests may act as domestic priests, they may also act as Ghatias or Pandas or Tirthapurohitas, or Yatrawals, and so on. Therefore, unlike their counterparts in Gaya and Deoghar, the sacred specialists in Kashi are heterogeneous both in their social composition and in their specialization of functions in sacred performances.

SACRED SECULAR CONTINUUM

Looking at the structure of sacred complex in the totality of Kashi's cultural traditions, it seems extremely difficult to dissociate it completely with what might be called the structure of 'secular' complex. This brings us to a fundamental question as to whether in Indian tradition there exists a clear dichotomy between the sacred and the secular, as it is in Semitic traditions. The question has been tried out briefly by Saraswati (1975:41-47); his main arguments are:

> "The intrinsic relationship between sacred and secular is truly reflected in Kashi's cultural complex—in its settlement pattern, sacred performances, and the professions involved in the sacred complex."

Settlement Pattern

> "As has been discussed in the foregoing section, Kashi is roughly divided into sacred and secular zones on the basis of the bulk distribution of shrines and places where the activities of sacred performances are incessant. But the area which has been marked out as a sacred zone is also the area which shelters a large proportion of the population of the city, both Hindus and Muslims. It is decidedly the main business area in Kashi. It covers the total area of *pucca mahal* and reflects the cultural life of Kashi—arts, crafts, commerce, sacred-secular, *gundas*, *thugs*, and everything. In this area, are concentrated people from all parts of India in linguistic and regional pockets. The importance of this area lies not merely in the performance of the hub of the ritual but in all aspects of Kashi's cultural life. If this area is taken out from the map of Kashi, there remains nothing of Kashi. In the circumstances, it is impossible to mark a clear boundary

between sacred and secular on the physical map of Kashi. The two are linked up with one another so inseparably that even the most veteran geographer may fail to decide where to begin and where to end drawing the boundaries of sacred and secular."

Sacred Performances

"The human desires are of three classes: 1) *Artha*, (2) *Kama*, and (3) *Moksha*. The Hindus gods have been assigned accordingly various functions to fulfil human desires. In other words, there is a specialization among gods. Certain gods are the givers of wealth; others cure particular ailments and sufferings; and still some others promote skills and scholarships. But in some of the Brahmanic gods and goddesses all these functions may also combine, and therefore, people worship the same god for the fulfilment of various desires. The *Jyotirlinga* at Deoghar is called *manokamana linga* (the phallus of Shiva which fulfils. . . earthly human desires). But the *Jyotirlinga* at Kashi has not been put to such limitation, he is the bestower of *moksha*; and the one who takes shelter in his favourite city gets all worldly pleasure and no pain. Therefore, the god Vishwanath combines in himself both what might be called sacred and secular.

"Besides Vishwanath, there are innumerable gods, both Brahmanic and non-Brahmanic, to fulfil various desires of man. The 'specialization' of these gods, in some cases has been very precise.

"Certain types of sacred performances are consciously conducted with earthly considerations. Man's final desire of enjoying beauty and his sense of aesthetics are amply fulfilled in his sacred performances. This is truly reflected in the selection of sacred objects or motifs, in the style of performances, in the choice of place, the choice of time and season, and such other considerations which make a ritual pleasing and absorbing. . . In Kashi, a ritual bath in the Ganges is not only a matter of gaining religious merit but also an occasion of going through an exciting experience in life. . . Similarly, when one visits the Viswanath temple at the time of *arati* he is completely lost in the beauteous surroundings.

. . .All ritual performances are made with a perfect sense of aesthetics held with deep devotion.

"Indeed, no ritual of whatsoever merit can persist for a long time without lending a sensual pleasure to the performer, and no religion can draw people simply on abstract philosophy untenanted with human emotions involved in the exquisite beauty of Nature."

Sacred—An Industry

"About three-fourths of Kashi's population is dependent upon the pilgrim 'industry'. Several thousands of people are employed in sacerdotal occupations of various kinds.

"But what is more revealing about the sacred complex is that those who are professionally involved in it, consider sacred as a mere means of livelihood and not something to be treated in a special manner. This attitude towards sacred is discerned by any conscious observer visiting a temple or observing a priest conducting rituals.

"The shrines are personal properties of individuals; these can be transacted in the manner of immovable property. A shrine may be owned individually or collectively. In most of the shrines there is *pari* (turn) system whereby the revenue of the temple is shared by turn. The *pari* can be bought and sold, and can also be mortgaged to anyone—to a Brahmin or Ahir, to a Hindu or Muslim. The collection of the cash gifts and offerings from a temple is called *galla*, a term which the merchants use for their day's earnings. All these are undeniable facts and both the devotees and the professionals in sacred crafts are aware of them. Indeed, it is hard to make a distinction between sacred and secular so far as the style of earning, the attitude towards earning, and the professional ethics are concerned."

Sacred in Tune with Secular

"From the preceding discussion it becomes obvious that sacred is more or less used as a tool in the various spheres of man's creativity, and in achieving this earthly goal a Hindu seems to have no reservations whatsoever. . .

"In the circumstances, in Indian cultural traditions one fails to put 'sacred' and 'secular' into two water-tight compartments. In the drudgery of social life one may find certain diacritical marks artificially dividing people into high and low, but as one comes to a place like Kashi, this difference begins to evaporate. A Brahmin—the tallest in the society—comes to Manikarnika cremation *ghat* and asks for sacred fire from its custodian, the untouchable Dom; for without this sacred fire his deceased kinsman cannot attain *moksha*—the supreme sacred. From such examples how can one really dichotomize 'sacred' and 'secular', or 'sacred' and 'profane'? Indeed, they are the two sides of the same coin, the difference lies in the perception of the man, depending from what angle he looks at it."

FUNCTIONS OF SACRED COMPLEX

Summing up his observation on the sacred complex in Gaya, Vidyarthi (1974) made the following remarks:

> "The Gaya sacred complex can thus be described as a local grouping of sacred centres, performances and specialists, which is in intricate interdependence, both culturally and structurally with the whole-breadth of Hindu civilization. The Gaya complex is predominantly great traditional in its content, but incorporates, and in the past has both incorporated and transformed centres, elements of performances, and specialists of little-traditional origin. At the same time, it has played an integrating role in Hindu civilization by providing a traditional meeting place of different kinds of peoples and traditions, of castes and sects, of classes and statuses; and by communicating with every corner of India through texts and through priestly relationships."

These remarks, it may be pointed out, are literally true for Kashi, and also, perhaps, for all such great centres of civilization. We shall discuss them briefly in the following pages.

Patterning of Cultures

One of the important functions of the sacred complex is the patterning of cultures. As has been discussed in the foregoing chapters, on the basis of their physical features, organization of functionaries, and clientele, the sacred centres of Kashi are characterized as local, regional and all-India. In the sacred geography of Kashi, people from all over India are settled in linguistic clusters or pockets, each preserving its identity in respect of food, dress, language, rituals, ceremonies, and shrines; and at the same time they also commonly interact at the all-India sacred centres. In the sacred performances also, there are varieties of traditions (Saraswati 1975:35-6), distinguishable in the modes of performances (such as, *Vedic*, *Tantric*, and *Laukik*), in the local and regional customs of worship, as also in objects of offerings. There are varieties of sacred specialists each having a distinctive function in the organization of pilgrimage and sacred performances. These specialists belong to different linguistic groups (though majority of them are from local-language group) castes and classes; they maintain their caste and linguistic character almost in their prestine purity, but closely interact with all-India pilgrims.

It has been pointed out (Saraswati 1975:37) that pilgrims belonging to different cultural traditions (oral or *Laukik*, textual or *Shastric*, and transcendental or *Parasanskritik*), and accordingly their participation in the sacred complex of Kashi is unequal. In other words, by taking into account, the totality of traditions synchronically, one finds different levels of cultures in the sacred complex of Kashi.

Even by examining a single element in the sacred complex, the levelling of cultures becomes emanent. In Gaya, for instance, the different levels of culture are identifiable in the organization of sacred specialists which Prof. Vidyarthi (1974:3) has analysed both synchronically and diachronically as follows:

> "Three sub-cultural divisions may be distinguished today among the Gayawal (the sacred specialists of Gaya)—Sanskritic, feudalistic and proletarian: Sanskritic priests are marked by orthodoxy, ceremonialism and strict adherence to the Brahmanic rules of priesthood; the feudalistic priests are distinguished by their wealth and aristocratic way of life as well as by their employment of servants to perform their priestly and demestic work; and the proletarian priests are noted for their commercial and mercenary orientation, professional rivalry and group disorganization, while pretending to maintain priestly life.
>
> "The distinctive features of these three sub-cultures seem

to characterize three probable phases in the development of the Gayawal through time. Earliest is the Sanskritic phase; it is followed by an intermediate feudalistic phase, and finally by the present proletarian phase brought on by the recent transformation of Indian civilization under the influence of western industrialization, education and mass communication.

"Another and still earlier formative phase can be conjectured, a phase in which the Gayawal would have been 'folk priests'. The Gayawal of today still reflect some of the characteristic of folk priests.

"All four aspects of the Gayawal priesthood—folk, Sanskritic, Feudalistic and proletarians—postulated above as successive phases, continue, of course, to exist among the Gayawal of today, three of them being very distinct. Since all are found together in the present, one may assume that each earlier variety of priesthood persisted along side of each later type without replacing it entirely. These sub-cultures and phases of Gayawal cultural development may be understood, in part, as effect of the impacts of the larger Hindu universe upon the sacred complex of Gaya."

The aforementioned four-fold classification of the Gayawal priesthood holds equally good for the sacred specialists in Kashi. The boatmen, the barbers, and the priests officiating at the shrines of Birs and Satis fall under the category of folk priests; the *karmakandis*, the *anushthanis* and the *kathavachaks* form the core of Sanskritic priests; the Mahantas of the various shrines and the affluent Tirthapurohitas or Pandas are included in feudalistic category; and the Gumashtas, the Bhaddars, the Yatrawals and the Ghatias are the proletariats. Although it cannot be accurately reconstructed whether 'folk' tradition in Kashi gave a way to Sanskritic tradition, but it seems that the Birs, whom the autochthon of Kashi (viz. Ahirs, Doms and Gonds) claim as their caste deity, must have been in existence much before the Brahmins made inroad into this ancient city. That the proletarian priests appeared in Kashi at the recent phase is evidenced by the fact (as they themselves admit) that they were separated from the Tirthapurohitas or Pandas—their one time masters—only recently.

Thus, Kashi appears as mini-India, accommodating varieties of peoples and cultures, allowing each of them to maintain its distinctiveness, and to grow according to their respective traditions. This sort of cultural patterning is possible primarily because the binding force in the organization of sacred complex is the belief that there are various ways to unite with the Ultimate, and all the gods and goddesses enshrined in Kashi are only the manifestations of that Ultimate. Hence one can choose the way one likes.

Integration of Cultures

The belief which lies at the root of cultural differences is also the potent factor integrating the heterogeneous cultures. The sacred myth that Kashi is *mokshadayani* and that all the Tirthas of India are enshrined in Kashi bring Hindus from all over the world to share in common the totality of its sacred complex—the space, the performance, and the services of specialists.

The institution of pilgrimage, as has been discussed in the previous chapter, has undoubtedly been a levelling influence on diverse social life. Sex, colour, civil condition, economic inequality, traditions of servitude which have made some people untouchables, become unreal distinctions in course of pilgrimage. It is only during the pilgrimage that unity of faith in Hindu society and religion can be seen at its best.

The institution of pilgrimage is largely maintained by the sacred specialists. The role of these specialists has been thoroughly discussed by Vidyarthi (1961) in his work on the *Sacred Complex in Gaya*, and also in the preceding chapters of this monograph. It is, indeed, through the network of pilgrimage that Kashi operates as a civilizational centre. And it is also by this mechanism that Indian civilization has been integrating through the ages the geographical and cultural diversities of India.

The pattern and processes of the territorial extensions of civilizations have been adequately described by M. Jha (1971). According to him, the sacred town of Janakpur, which lies in the political boundary of Nepal, is undoubtedly an integral part of Indian civilization. And thus, the civilizational boundaries cut across the national boundaries.

In brief, the solidarious elements in sacred complex function as the linchpins in the Indian modes of cultural integration.

Cultivation of Excellence

The third important function of the sacred complex is to cultivate excellence in varieties of creative arts and literature. Much of Kashi's secular arts and crafts have flourished on account of pilgrim industry. Pilgrims' continual inflow in Kashi provide a good market for the varieties of utility and luxury goods. As has been stated in the preceding chapter, 51 per cent sample pilgrims visiting Kashi had spent the major portion of their budget on buying Banarasi *sarees*, toys and cosmetics for which the city has been famous through the ages.

The sacred complex in Kashi has decidedly been responsible for the cultivation of excellence in music. Most of the world-famous musicians of Kashi, both Hindus and Muslims, have performed their *sadhana* at different shrines and *ghats*, and *mathas* and *akharas*.

It is the sacred myth of Kashi that has attracted Pundits from all over India to settle here; this eventually leads to the cultivation of excellence in various fields of traditional learning. It was this attraction of Kashi that brought Sant Tulsidas to compose here his celebrated work, the *Ramacharita Manas*, as well as many other saints and scholars with whom this sacred city of the Hindus still abounds come here to spend the last days of their life.

Preservation of Ideal Types

The fourth most important function of the sacred complex is the preservation of the 'ideal types' that serve as an index to grandeur of Hindu civilization. In Kashi, nearly two thousand ascetics reside permanently; besides there is a floating stream of ascetic pilgrims. This means, the proportion of ascetics to the total Hindu population is nearly 1:150, or one out of every 240 persons in Kashi is an ascetic (Saraswati 1975:15). In Hindu society, the ascetics have been compared to the Dhruvatara (pole star), for they symbolize the highest ideals which the *grihis* (householders) must try to attain.

Besides the ascetics, there are large number of Pundits who are not only great scholars, but also the champions of orthodox traditions. They lead austere life and exemplify the type of Brahmins described in the scriptures.

In an attempt to assess the overall impact of sacred complex on the life and ways of the 500 samples of common citizens, the samples showed a high degree of religiosity, regardless of their heterogeneous social categories (Brahmins 182, Kshatriya 80, Vaishya 62, Shudra 166, others 10), diverse educational background (illiterate 80, literate 189, matriculates 84, graduates 70, post-graduates 9, Sanskritists 46, technicians 22), and varied professional specialization (business 144, higher professions 48, political and social work 4, priestcraft 44, ascetics 5, menial services 124, hawkers 11, rickshaw-pullers 28, beggars 10, others 82). As shown in Table 12, the varieties of sacred performances indicate the range and the foci of the religious behaviour of the citizens of Kashi.

TABLE 12

Showing the major types of sacred performances made by the citizens

Sl. No.	*Name of the sacred performance*	*Percentage of citizens*
1.	*Gangasnan*	90.00
2.	*Gangapujan*	61.6
3.	*Abhisheka* to Vishwanath (once or twice a month)	15.00
4.	Vishwanath *darshan*	100.00
5.	*Sringar arati darshan*	53.4
6.	Weekly *darshan* of some important deities	27.00
7.	*Antargrahi parikrama*	4.00
8.	*Panchakosi parikrama*	32.4
9.	*Chardham parikrama*	1.0
10.	Brahmin *bhojan*	27.0
11.	*Madhukari* to Sannyasi	7.4
12.	*Kangali bhojan*	12.4
13.	*Pindadan*	21.4
14.	*Katha-kirtan* at sacred centres	34.4
15.	Satyanarain *katha-pujan* at home	51.4
16.	*Havana*	13.2

The intensity of their faith in the sacred complex can be judged by the fact that cent per cent of the Hindu citizens reported to have visited temples and bathed at the Panchatirtha *ghats*. Although comparable data from the citizens of a secular town are not available, yet in all likelihood they do not seem to make such detailed and varied sacred performances (perhaps, owing to the lack of opportunities) as the citizens of Kashi do. Hence, from the point of view of leading a religion-oriented life, the citizens of Kashi verily represent the ideal type.

Summing Up

Finally, we might say that the sacred complex is not an abstruse philosophy but a reality that binds us together against the geographical diversities, and social and linguistic heterogeneities. Whether the modern secular mechanism and institutions are equally viable and lasting means of cultural integration is a question that awaits time. But there is no doubt that the mechanism of sacred complex and the institution of pilgrimage are dependable and effective means of integration; for they have already stood the test of time, and hence their relevance.

REFERENCES

Aiyangar, V.K. Rangaswami, "Introduction", *Krityakalpataru of Bhatta Lakshmidhara* (Tirthakanda), Oriental Institute, Baroda, 1942.

Bose, N.K., "Organisation of Services in Bhubaneshwar Temple", *Culture and Society in India*, Asia Publishing House, Calcutta, 1967.

Chakrabarti, P., "Some Observations on the Pilgrims and their Pilgrimage: A Case Study at Tarkeshwar", *Journal of Social Research*, Ranchi, 1974, **XVII-1**, pp. 104-15.

Goswami, B.B. and Morab, S.G., "Castes and Temples", *Research Programmes in Cultural Anthropology and Other Related Disciplines*, (ed.) Surajit Sinha, Anthropological Survey of India, Calcutta, 1970.

———"Temple as a Civilizational Centre : A Case Study of Chamundesvari Temple in Mysore", *Journal of Social Research*, Ranchi, 1974, **XVII-1**, pp. 116-123.

————*Chamundesvari Temple in Mysore*, Anthropological Survey of India, Calcutta, 1975.

Jha, Magna Nand, "Sacred Performances at Kashi", *Journal of Social Research*, Ranchi, 1974, **XVII-1**, pp. 23-28.

Jha, Makhan, "Death-rites among Maithil Brahmans", *Man in India*, 1966, **46**, No. III.

————*The Sacred Complex in Janakpur*, The United Publishers, Allahabad, 1971.

————"Aspects of Hindu Traditions in Nepal", *Research Journal of Ranchi University*, Ranchi, 1972, **8**, pp. 137-42.

————"Ratanpur: Some Aspects of a Sacred City in Chhatisgarh", *Journal of Social Research*, Ranchi, 1973, **16-1**, pp. 49-58.

————"Pilgrims and Centres of Pilgrimage in Chhatisgarh", *Journal of Social Research*, Ranchi, 1974, **XVII-1**, 96-103.

Mahapatra, M., *Lingaraj Temple : Its Structure and Change, ca 1900-62* (Mss), Unpublished Ph.D. Dissertation, Utkal University, Bhubaneshwar.

————"The Sacred Geography of Gupta Kashi", *Journal of Social Research*, Ranchi, 1974, **XVII-1**, pp. 75-87.

Marriott, McKim, and Guha, B.S., "Networks and Centres in Integration of Indian Civilization", *Journal of Social Research*, Ranchi, 1958, **1-1**, pp. 1-9.

Narayan, Sachindra, *The Sacred Complex of Deoghar*, unpublished Ph.D. dissertation, Ranchi University, Ranchi, 1972.

————"Pilgrimage to Kashi", *Journal of Social Research*, Ranchi, 1974, **XVII-1**, pp. 20-22.

Prasad, Onkar, "Cult of the Smashan at Kashi", *Journal of Social Research*, Ranchi, 1974, **XVII-1**, pp. 35-41.

Redfield, Robert, *Peasant, Society and Culture : An Anthropological Approach to Civilization*, The University of Chicago Press, Chicago, 1974.

Sahay, B.N., "The Sacred Geography in Kashi", *Journal of Social Research*, Ranchi, 1974, **XVII-1**, pp. 14-19.

Sahay, K.N., "The Sacred Geography of Rameshwaram and Tirupati", *Journal of Social Research*, Ranchi, 1974, **XVII-1**, pp. 49-51.

Saraswati, B.N., "The Holy Circuit of Nimsar", *Bull. of the Anthropological Survey of India*, Calcutta, 1962, **VI**, 3-4, pp. 211-216.

———"Temple Organisation in Goa", *Man in India*, Ranchi, 1963, 43, 2.

———*Contributions to the Understanding of Indian Civilization*, Karnatak University, Dharwar, 1970.

———"Sacred Complexes in Indian Cultural Traditions", *Anthropological Approaches to the Study of a Complex Society*, (*ed.*) Binod Chand Agrawal, Indian Academy of Social Sciences, New Delhi, 1972.

———"Studying Sacred Gomplex in Kashi", *Journal of Social Research*, Ranchi, 1974, **XVII-1**, 6-13.

———*Kashi: Myth and Reality of a Classical Cultural Tradition*, Indian Institute of Advanced Study, Simla, 1975.

Singer, Milton, "The Great Tradition in a Metropolitan Centre: Madras", in Milton Singer (*ed.*) *Traditional India : Structure and Change*, 1955, pp. 207-15.

S inha, Arvinda Kumar, "Specialists in Sacred Performances at Kashi", *Journal of Social Research*, Ranchi, 1974, **XVII-1**, pp 29-34.

Sinha, S.C., *Research Programmes in Cultural Anthropology and Other Related Disciplines*, Anthropological Survey of India, Calcutta, 1970.

Upadhyay, Basudeva, "Some Bibliographical Notes on Sacred Kashi", *Journal of Social Research*, Ranchi, 1974, **XVII-1**, pp. 42-48.

Upadhyay, V.S., 'The Sacred Geography of Dwarka", *Journal of Social Research*, Ranchi, 1974, **XVII-1**, pp. 52-74.

Vidyarthi, L.P., "Origin and Development of the Gayawal: A priestly community", *Journal of Bihar Research Society*, 1954, **XI**, Part 2.

———The Extensions of an Indian Priestly caste, *Man in India*, 1959, 39, No. 1.

———"Thinking about a sacred city", *Eastern Anthropologists*, 1960, XIII, No. 4.

———"City and Civilization : A Case of Sacred Complex", Proceedings of the 47th Session of All India Science Congress, Bombay, 1960, Part III (Abstract).

———*Sacred Complex in Hindu Gaya*, Asia Publishing House, Bombay, 1961.

———"Aspects of Religion in Indian Society", (*ed.*), Meerut City, Kedar Nath Ram Nath, Hill Tribal Village, *Journal of Social Research*, 1961, **IV**, Nos. 1 and 2.

———*The Maler: Nature-Man-Spirit Complex in a Hill Tribe*, Bookland Pvt. Ltd., Calcutta, 1963.

———— "The Changing life of an Indian priestly caste : A Case of Desanskritisation, *Indian Sociological Bulletin*, 1965, **II**, No. IV.

—————Foreword to Dr. M. Jha's book *Sacred Complex in Janakpur*, United Publishers, Allahabad, 1971.

—————"Cultural Personality of a Priestly Community of India", *Journal of Social Research*, 1970, **XIII**, No. 2.

—————"Sacred Complex as a dimension of Indian Civilization", *Journal of Social Research*, Ranchi, 1974, **XVII**, No. 1.

Vidyarthi, L.P., and Jha, M. (ed.) Symposium on the Sacred Complex in India; published by the Council of Social and Cultural Research, Bihar and Department of Anthropology, Ranchi University, 1974.

APPENDIX 1

SCHEDULE

PILGRIMS

Serial No. Code No. Date:

1. Name:

   Permanent Address:

   Local Address:

   Age:

   Sex:

   Caste:

   Sect:

   Education:

   Profession:

2. I Planning pilgrimage to Kashi:

   (*a*) Main purpose of visit

   (*b*) No. of visits: Duration of each visit:

   (*c*) Stayed with *Panda*/*Karmakandi*/relatives/friends. Accommodation in Dharmashala/Hotel arranged by *Panda*/*Karmakandi*/self.

   (*d*) Visiting alone/with family members/friends.

   II Sacred Centres visited

   (*a*) Ghats:

   (*b*) Temples:

   (*c*) Kundas:

   (*d*) Bir/Satisthan:

   (*e*) Matha/Ashram:

   (*f*) Other places:

III Sacred performances

(a)

Name of the ritual	*Place where ritual was performed*	*Frequency of performance*	*Assistance of the priest/ specialist sought*
1.			
2.			
3.			
4.			
5.			
6.			
7.			
8.			
9.			
10.			

(b) Sacred circumambulation : Antargrih/Panchakosi/ Chaurasikosi/Charodham.

IV Relationship with specialists

Pattern of relationship	*Ascetics*	*Pundits*	*Pandas*	*KarmaKandis/ Ghatia Pilgrim guide*
(*a*) Hereditary				
(*b*) Casual/contractual				
(*c*) Linguistic affiliation				
(*d*) Regional affiliation				

3. Daily routine during pilgrimage
(Specify activities related to sacred performances: distribution of time devoted to sacred/secular activities).

4. Notes:
(What are the places of pilgrimage the informant has visited ? Does he/she follow any pilgrimage cycle ? How was he/she motivated to make a pilgrimage of Kashi ? Whether he/she had read/heard Kashi mahatam before undertaking the pilgrimage ? In the present visit, what new things about the mahatam of Kashi have been added to his/her knowledge ? What are the sources of such knowledge and how it was acquired ? Please note the informant's existing knowledge of the sacred geography of

Kashi, i.e. the beliefs related to the Tirthas of Kashi, and the rituals one is required to perform in Kashi. Also note how much money the informant has actually spent on the performance of rituals, feeding Brahmins and beggars, and on buying ritual articles, sacred literature, and articles of secular use. Please obtain a list of articles.)

CITIZENS

Serial No. Code No. Date:

1. Name House No. Own House/Rented house

Age: Sex: Caste: Sect:
Education Profession
Period of stay in Kashi
Total No. of family members M: F:

2. I Sacred centres visited

Name of the sacred centre *Frequency and purpose of visit* *Remarks*

(*a*) Ghat:
(*b*) Temple:
(*c*) Kunda:
(*d*) Bir/Sati/Sthan:
(*e*) Matha/Ashram:
(*f*) Other places:

II Sacred performances

Name of the performance *Frequency and purpose* *Assistance of the priest/specialist sought*

(*a*) Ganga snan
(*b*) Ganga Poojan
(*c*) Pindadan
(*d*) Abhisheka to Vishwanath
(*e*) Sringar Arati Darshan
(*f*) Weekly Darshan
(*g*) Katha/Kirtan
(*h*) Kangali Bhojan
(*i*) Brahman Bhojan

(*j*) Madhukari to Sannyasis
(*k*) Yajna/Havan
(*l*) Satyanarain katha pooja
(*m*) Antargrihi parikrama
(*n*) Panchakosi parikrama
(*o*) Chaurasikosi parikrama
(*p*) Charodham parikrama

3. Daily routine

(Specify activities related to sacred performances, distribution of time devoted to sacred/secular activities.)

4. Notes:

(What are the places of pilgrimage the informant has visited ? Does he/she follow any pilgrimage cycle ? Please note his/her existing knowledge of the sacred geography of Kashi or the beliefs related to the Tirthas of Kashi. Also note the sources of such cultural knowledge. Whether he/she is a member of a religiousinstitution/academic institution/political party ? Whether he/she has the requisite knowledge of the sacred performances? Whether or not the informant's sacred performances are confined to the sacred centres of his/her locality ? Whether his/her association with sacred centres is governed largely by linguistic consideration, locational consideration, or purely religious consideration ? Explain, give examples.)

TIRTHAS

Serial No. Code No. Date:

1. I (*a*) Name of the shrine (*b*) Location
(*c*) Whether it is Kashikhandokta Tirtha ? Yes/No
If yes,
(i) Name of the Tirtha as mentioned in Kashikhanda:
(ii) Pauranic location of the Tirtha

II (*a*) Structure of the shrine:
(*b*) No. of temples/Kunda within the precinct of the Tirtha:
(*c*) Name of the deity/deities enshrined:
(*d*) (Principal deity)

III Shrine functionaries Caste Nature of appointment

IV (*a*) Whether the shrine is visited only by local devotees or by pilgrims from outside?

(*b*) If it is latter, average number of pilgrims visiting the shrine daily :/on festive occasions:

V Name of the sacred performances for which the shrine is popular:

2. Notes:

(Please note the caste/linguistic/religious group inhabiting region where the shrine is located. Whether the shrine is managed by individual, a particular caste, or a linguistic or religious group ? Whether the shrine is visited by members belonging to a particular linguistic group, caste, or sect ? Also note if the shrine is visited by both Hindus and Muslims, Special offerings, such as, animal sacrifice; special functions, such as, dancing of prostitutes, should also be recorded.)

APPENDIX II

LIST OF SACRED CENTRES STUDIED AT KASHI

Sl. No.	*Name of the Tirtha*	*Location Present*
1	Yaksh Vinayak Ganesh	CK37/18
2	Sakshi Ganesh	D10/7
3	Vishwasen Janard	Karmjitpur (near B.H.U.)
4	Durgamai Mandir	Adik Nagar
5	Kardaneshwar Mahadeo	Kardaneshwar chatti
6	Kauleshwar Mahadeo	Kandwa village
7	Birro Paksha	Kandwa village
8	Shomanath	Kandwa village
9	Kardam Koop	Kandwa village
10	Nilakantha Mahadeo	Kandwa village
11	Chaurasi Mahadeo	Amara
12	Naganath	Amara
13	Chamunda	Anurhi
14	Vir Bhadreshwar Gelhan	Gelhana
15	Vikataksha Durga	Deghana
16	Unmatta Bhairava	Kashipur Dewra
17	Nilagana	Dewra
18	Kalakut Gana	Dewra
19	Vimala Durga	Kashi Rampur
20	Mahadeo	Kashipur
21	Nandi Keshava Ganesh	Kashipur
22	Bhringiriti Gana	Kashipur
23	Gana Priya	Gaura Gaon
24	Virupaksha	Gaura Gaon
25	Yaksheshwar	Chakmatal Devi
26	Mokshadeshwar	Prayagpur gaon
27	Vimaleshwar	Prayagpur
28	Gyanadeshwar	Ashwari
29	Amniteshwar	Ashwari

Sl. No	*Name of the Tirtha*	*Location Present*
30	Bhimachandi	Bhimchandi
31	Chandavinayak	Chand Vinayak
32	Ravi Raktaksha Gandharva	Bhimchandi
33	Navakarnar Taraka Gana	Bhimchandi
34	Ekpada Gana	Kachnar village
35	Bhootabhairava	Haraiya
36	Mahabhim Bhairava	Haraiya
37	Kalanatheshwar	Gansha
38	Kapardishwar	Gansha
39	Kameshwar	Gansha
40	Ganeshwar	Chaukhandi
41	Virabhadra Gana	Chaukhandi
42	Charumukhi	Bhookpur
43	Ganothishwar	Bhookpur
44	Sodashak Vinayaka	Bhatauli
45	Dehlivinayaka	Bhatauli
46	Udadand Vinayaka	Bhuyali
47	Utkaleshwar	Bhuyali
48	Rudram Tapobhumi	Hirampur village
49	Rameshwar	Rameshwar
50	Someshwar	Rameshwar
51	Bharateshwar	Rameshwar
52	Lakshamneshwar	Rameshwar
53	Shatrughaneshwar	Rameshwar
54	Dyabhumishwar	Rameshwar
55	Nrihsheshwar	Rameshwar
56	Agreshwar	Rameshwar
57	Asankhyateshwar	Rameshwar
58	Shri Vishwanath	Vishwanath Gali
59	Panchapandeshwar	Shivapur
60	Panchakosimandir	CK 5/32
61	Gananath	Beside Gyanvapi Kund
62	Prithvishvar	Kharjur village
63	Sona Talab	Dinadayalpur village
64	Kapiladhara Temple and Shrine of Patu Guru	Kapiladhara village
65	Jwala Narsingh	Kotana village
66	Adikeshwar	Near Varuna sangama

Sl. No.	*Name of the Tirtha*	*Location Present*
67	Sangameshwar	Near Varuna sangam
68	Varuna Sangama	Varuna sangama
69	Kharva Vinayak	Raj Ghat
70	Prahladeshwar	Prahalad Ghat
71	Trilochana Temple	Trilochan Ghat
72	Vindu Madhava	Panchganga Ghat
73	Kal Bhairava	Bhairawnath Mohalla
74	Panchaganga shrine	Panchaganga Ghat
75	Danda Pani Bhairava	Kalabhairava Mohalla
76	Mangladevi Mandir	Mangladevi Mandir Mohalla
77	Vashishtheshwar	Near Sankta Ghat
78	Annapurna Temple	Vishwanath Gali
79	Dhundhiraj Ganesh	Vishvanath Ghat
80	Agasteshwar	Agastya Kunda
81	Nandikeshwar	Gyanvapi
82	Gaurishanker	Gyanvapi
83	Tarakeshwar	Gyanvapi
84	Mahakaleshwar	Gyanvapi
85	Maheshwar	Gyanvapi
86	Gyanvapi Koop	Gyanvapi
87	Gauri Bhavani	Sri Ram Mandir Vishvanath Gali
88	Gangeshwar	Gyanvapi
89	Avimukteshwar	Gyanvapi
90	Moksheshwar	Gyanvapi
91	Dandapanishwar	Gyanvapi
92	Virabhadreshwar	Gyanvapi
93	Present Avimukteshwar	Golden Vishwanath
94	Manikarnika Kund	Manikarnika Ghat
95	Parvateshwar	Sindhia Ghat
96	Manikarnika Ghat	Manikarnika Ghat
97	Siddhi Vinayak	Manikarnika Ghat
98	Manikarnikeshwar	Manikarnika Ghat
99	Dasashwamedha	Shitala Temple
100	Paraneshwar	Gyanvapi
101	Patigraheshwar	Gyanvapi
102	Paradraveshwar	Gyanvapi
103	Nishakalankeshwar	Gyanvapi
104	Markandeyeshwar	Gyanvapi

Sl. No.	Name of the Tirtha	Location Present
105	Harishachandreshwar	CK7/124
106	Siddheshwaridevi	CK7/124
107	Chintamanivinayaka	At Vamdeshwar West to South
108	Nakuleshwar	Golden Vishwanath
109	Suraja Kund	Suraj Kund
110	Suraja Narayan Mandir	Suraj Kund
111	Lakshami Kunda Tirtha	Lakshami Kund D52/40
112	Lakshami Tirtha	Lakshami Kund
113	Bhoga Annapurna	Golden Vishwanath Temple
114	Kuvereshwar	Annapurna Temple
115	Ashtang Bhairava	Suraj Kund
116	Vishnu Mandir	Golden Vishwanath
117	Gangeshwar	CK13/79
118	Pashupateshwar	CK13/66
119	Chitraghanta Devi	CK23/24
120	Chitraghanta Vinayaka	CK23/24
121	Saptavarun Vinayaka	CK Nepali Khapra
122	Amriteshwar	CK33/28
123	Durga Mandir	Durga Kund
124	Durga Kunda	Durga Kund
125	Pitamaheshwar & Khokhi Devi	CK7/92
126	Amba Devi	CK7/106
127	Brihaspateshwar	CK7/133
128	Mitra Vinayaka	In Atmavireshwar Temple
129	Mangaleshwar	In Atmavireshwar Temple
130	Buddheshwar	In Atmavireshwar Temple
131	Atmavireshwar	Near Sankata Mandir
132	Katyayani Devi	In Atmavireshwar Temple
133	Seema Vinayaka	Near Sankata Temple
134	Agneshwar	CK1/4
135	Seva Vinayaka	Near Sankata Temple
136	Yamadharmeshwar	North of Sankata Ghat
137	Harishchandreshwar	Near Sankata Temple
138	Ypsanteshwar	Near Panchaganga Ghat
139	Bridhkal Kund	Daranagar in the campus of Mahavir Temple.
140	Amrita Kund	—do—
141	Mahamrityunjaya	K52/39

Sl. No.	*Name of the Tirtha*	*Location Present*
142	Brihadkaleshwar	D52/39
143	Mahakaleshwar	K52/39
144	Kashi Karvata	CK31/12
145	Modavinayaka	CK31/12
146	Vimaladitya	D35/273
147	Baba Harikeshanath	D35/273
148	Khandeshwar Mahadeo	Near Baba Harikeshnath
149	Maltishwar	K52/39
150	Chandihandishwar	In Kalikagali
151	Srishti Vinayaka	—do—
152	Shukreshwar	—do—
153	Devasharneshwar	—do—
154	Manakeshwar	K53/40
155	Churahreshwar	K53/40
156	Ratneshwar	K53/40
157	Pataleshwar	Near Ratneshwar
158	Hartirtha Pokhara	Hartirtha Mohalla
159	Kritivasheshwar	Hartirtha Mohalla
160	Nadyameshwar	Maidagin
161	Sultankeshwar	Dasashwamedh Ghat
162	Markandeshwar	Daranagar
163	Kali Mandir	Daranager
164	Brahmeshwar	Prayag Ghat
165	Gankeshwar and Tarkeshwar	Manikarnika Ghat
166	Kartikeshwar	Prayag Ghat
167	Kamleshwar	Manikarnika Ghat
168	Dharmeshwar	—do—
169	Dharma Koopa	D2/21
170	Vishwa Bhuja Devi	Dharmeshwar Tirtha near D2/21
171	Ratneshwar	D2/21
172	Batsavitree	D2/21
173	Adi Mahalaxmi	Near Laxmi Kund
174	Kuritaksha Vinayak	Near Laxmi Kund
175	Onkareshwar	Koyala Bazar (Machahda)
176	Makareshwar	—do—
177	Akareshwar	—do—
178	Rasotak Koop	—do—

Sl. No.	Name of the Tirtha	Location Present
179	Tara Tirath (Kunda)	Koyala Bazar (Machahda)
180	Paryageshwar	Dasashwamedh Ghat
181	Shivarateshwar	North of Narsingh Temple
182	Mankeshwar	Mansarovar Kund
183	Akash Chandi	Near Mansarovar Kund
184	Mansarovar Tirtha	Popular Tirtha Kund
185	Mandagini Ganga	Mandgin Park Kund K Ward
186	Mandagini Mai	K59/16
187	Nagkunwa Kunda	Near Jaitpura Kotwali K wood
188	Nageshwar Mahadeo	—do—
189	Kashi Devi	Sapta Saper K wood
190	Sapta Sagar Koop	Sapta Saper K wood
191	Bhoot Bhairaw	Sapta Saper K wood
192	Pancheshwar or Maruteshwar	Boot Bhairaw Mohalla
193	Kauleshwar Nath	—do—
194	Byaghreshwar	—do—
195	Niwasheshwar	—do—
196	Ganeshwar	—do—
197	Imleshwar	—do—
198	Someshwar	—do—
199	Jaistha Gauri	—do—
200	Jaistheshwar Mahadeo	Sapat Sagar Mohalla
201	Ash Bhairaw	Ash Bhairav Mohalla
202	Karnaghanta	K60/35
203	Modvinayak	In the dilapidated wall of Gyanvapi Mosque
204	Durmukh Vinayak	In west-south corner of Gyanvapi under a Pipal tree
205	Saubhagya Gauri	Missing
206	Sumukha Vinayak	In east of Ganga Devi and Hanuman Mandir under the buildings wall of Vyasji of Gyan Vayapi
207	Gyan Vinayak	South of Gyanvapi Koop
208	Pramod Vinayak	North of Gyanvapi mosque graves

Sl. No.	Name of the Tirtha	Location Present
209	Draupadaditya	In centre of Marble floor of Gyanvapi Mandap
210	Sringar Gauri I	In back dilapidated wall of Gyanvapi
211	Apsareshwar	Currently Graveyard
212	Pritikeshwar	D10/16
213	Manh Prakameshwar	D10/50
214	Kali Priyavinayak Kalratri Durga	D10/50
215	Kalratri Durga	D8/17
216	Madalsheshwar	D5/33
217	Sanishwar	Vishwanath Gali
218	Rajrajeshwar	CK35/33
219	Gautameshwar	Gadaulia near Kashi Naresh Shivala
220	Gajkarnvinayak	CK35/33
221	Ishaneshwar	Near Press
222	Langlishwar	Khowa Bazar CK28/4
223	Kamaleshwar	CK8/14
224	Rahu	On north of Manikarnikeshwar, now missing
225	Jyotirupeshwar	CK8/10
226	Rudreshwar Tirtha	On south of Manikarnikeshwar, now missing
227	Dwintunda Vinayak	In the building of Shambdity temple near Kund
228	Pulasteshwar	CK33/43
229	Salthula dant Vinayak	Shomeshwar Shrine
230	Adalbhayeshwar	Near Someshwar Shrine
231	Someshwar	Manmandir Ghat
232	Asha Vinayak	D3/79
233	Jarasandheshwar	D3/79
234	Bridhaditya	D3/79
235	Rurubhairav	D3/79
236	Samudreshwar	CK37/32 Borsphalk
237	Samudreshwar Koop	CK37/32
238	Purusottam Bhagwan	D38/21
239	Trayankeshwar	D38/21
240	Brahmuseshwar	Sakarkand Gali D7/37

Sl. No.	*Name of the Tirtha*	*Location Present*
241	Swargaduawari	CK10/16
242	Dandkhat Tirtha	Piyala Sahib Kund missing
243	Dwarka Trisandheshwar	Missing
244	Trisandheshwar	D/40
245	Dwarvinayak	CK28/10
246	Dwarvinayak II	In Kashi Karwat Temple
247	Chaturwakreshwar	D7/19
248	Vashukishwar	CK7/155
249	Kalas Koop	CK7/102
250	Kauleshwar	CK7/102
251	Trimbakeshwar	CK7/165
252	Brahmeshwar	D33/67
253	Mukundeshwar	CK7/160
254	Ekdanta Vinayak	D33/67
255	Janbukeshwar	Near Bose
256	Danta Hosthavinayak	Near Bare Ganesh Temple
257	Bare Ganesh	Bare Ganesh Mohalla
258	Sankat Mochan	Sankat Mochan
259	Vidhishwar	Near Agasta Kund Temple
260	Loharavir	Loharavir Chowk
261	Skandmata	J6/33
262	Doksheshwar	K52/39
263	Assisting Bhairav	K52/39
264	Awantika or Ujjaini	K52/39
265	Sidheshwar Mahadeo	K6/8
266	Ratan Koop	Near K46/32
267	Jawahareshwar	J6/8
268	Sarang Nath	Near Sarnath Rly. Station
269	Sarang Nath Kund	Near Sarnath Temple
270	Kapardishwar Mahadeo	Near Pisachmochan Kund
271	Panchvinayak	East to Pisachmochan temple
272	Pisachmochan	Near Pisachmochan Kund
273	Pisachmochan Kund	Popular Pisachmochan Kund
274	Paphareshwar	Near Kedarghat in Ganga missing
275	Tarkeshwar	—do—
276	Gauri Kund	Kedarghat
277	Nilkantheshwar	Near Kedar Temple
278	Kedar Temple	Kedarghat

Sl No.	Name of the Tirtha	Location Present
279	Baikuntheshwar	Kedarghat
280	Tirtha Vasistha	South to Dasashwamedh Ghat Chausathighat in Ganga
281	Vasuki Kunda	Piyari Mohalla near Aughar-nath Takiya
282	Takshak Kunda	—do—
283	Nageshwar Tirtha	Near Gayghat in Ganga river
284	Manipradip Temple	On east of Bridhakal, Daranagar
285	Sanghar Bhairaw	D15/45
286	Tilperneshwar	In the precinct of Durga Temple
287	Tilsarthoshwar	—do—
288	Chand Bhairaw	—do—
289	Durga Vinayak	On east of Durga Temple
290	Varahi Devi	DS/84
291	Bhisan Bhairav	Near Bhoot Bhairav in Kasipura
292	Ranisati	In front of Tulsi Manas
293	Hrid Kunda	Over it Anadmai Hospital is constructed
294	Tulsi Manas	Tulsi Manas Popular
295	Asankhyat Tirthalinga	At Varna
296	Padodak	Varna Sangam
297	Rajputra Vinayak	Feetahi Court in the Rajghat Kila; on the north of the road
298	Kshirod	Near Adikeshaw.
299	Sankha	Near Adikeshaw
300	Chakra	
301	Gadda	Near Adikeshaw
302	Padma	—do—
303	Laxmi	—do—
304	Waman	—do—
305	Nar-Narayan	—do—
306	Narsingh	—do—
307	Gopi	—do—
308	Govinda	—do—
309	Madhaw	—do—

Sl. No.	*Name of the Tirtha*	*Location Present*
310	Haygriva	Near Adikeshaw
311	Garur	—do—
312	Purana Vishwanath Temple	Banstatak
313	B.H.U. Vishwanath	Banaras Hindu University
314	Naya Vishwanath	Vishwanath Gali
315	Varad Vinayak	Ghasiary Tola House No. 13/18 between Prahalad Ghat and Rajghat
316	Swarlineshwar Swargalingeshwar	All/29 Adampura between Rajghat and Prahalād Ghat
317	Narad Keshaw	Nayaghat, Previously known as Naradghat
318	Prahalad Keshaw	In the Prahaladeshwar Temple
319	Pichandil Vinayak	Prahalad Ghat
320	Arunaditya	Under the big idol of Hanuman behind the Trilochan Temple
321	Pipala	Near Trilochan in the Ganga
322	Manas	Near Harpap
323	Harpap	Harpap
324	Chitrangleshwar	In the north of Kedar
325	Nilkantheshwar	In the south of Kedar
326	Amrisheshwar	In Vayabya Kon of Kedar
327	Indrabhuneshwar	Near Kedar
328	Kalandereshwar	Near Kedar
329	Kama Kuṇda	Near Kameshwar Trilochan Ghat
330	Bhuwaneshwar	Near Bhelupura H. No. 19/47
331	Bhuwaneshwar Kund	Near Bhelupura H. No. 19/47
332	Nilkantha	B20/15 Bhelupura
333	Tillbhandeshwar	Tileshandeshwar popular in Bhelupura
334	Pranaw Vinayak	Trilochan Ghat, in the Manki of Hiranyagarbheshwar.
335	Hinyayagarbheshwar	Trilochan Ghat (in the north of Marhi of Trilochan Ghat)
336	Parwatishwar	In the Trilochan Temple
337	Munda Vinayak	In the Trilochan Temple

Sl. No.	*Name of the Tirtha*	*Location Present*
338	Balmiki Mandir Shivalingam	Trilochan Temple
339	Narmadeshwar Shivalingam	Near Trilochan Temple
340	Narmada Koop	Near Narmeshwar Shivalingam
341	Adi Mahadeo	Near Trilochan Temple
342	Madak Priya Vinayak	In Adi Mahadeo Temple
343	Sruvalingam Durwasa Muni	In the Kameshwar Temple near Trilochan Temple
344	Srutishwar	In the Adi Mahadeo Temple
345	Sankar Bhairaw	Near A1/84 near Trilochan Ghat
346	Kameshwar Shivalingam	Near Trilochan Temple
347	Kholkaaditya	In the Kameshwar Temple, near Trilochan Temple
348	Tarkeshwar	At Manikarnika
349	Bhimchandi Kunda	Bhimchandi
350	Kapildhara Kunda	Kapildhara
351	Wamdeshwar	Sankatha Ghat
352	Agastakunda	Agasta Kunda
353	Laxmi Koopa	Laxmi Temple Laxmi Kund
354	Dasashwamedheshwar	Dasashwamedh Ghat
355	Vishwanar	CK2/4
356	Mansarowar Kunda	Mansarovar Ghat
357	Lolarak Kunda	At Bhadaini
358	Tarkeshwar	In Gankeshwar Temple, at Manikarnika
359	Chausatti Temple	At Chausatti Ghat
360	Draupadi Kunda	At Sheopur
361	Artha Vinayak	Near Larak Kunda Bhadaini
362	Arka Vinayak	—do—
363	Lolarak Temple	—do—
364	Parashareshwar Mahadeo	Near Tulsi Mandir Tulsi Ghat
365	Tulsi Mandir	At Tulsi Ghat
366	Sangmeshwar	Near Assi Sangam
367	Assi Sangam	—do—
368	Jagannath	—do—
369	Chatpati Devi	Near Durga Kunda
370	Sankatha Mai	Sankatha Ghat.

APPENDIX-III

LIST OF 71 GHATS ON THE BANK OF GANGES AT KASHI

Sl. No.	*Name of the Ghat*	*Nature of the Ghat*	*Castes dominating*	*Linguistic group*
1	Assi ghat	Kacha	Br.	Banarasi (BS)
2	Ganga Mahal ghat	Pucca	Br.	B.S.
3	Reewan ghat	Pucca	Br.+MH	B.S.+MH
4	Tulasi ghat	Pucca	All	All
5	Bhadaimi ghat	Pucca	BS	B.S.
6	Janaki ghat	Pucca	BS	BS
7	Anandnai/Backkaraj ghat	Pucca	All	All
8	Jain ghat	Pucca	All	All
9	Buchakot ghat	Pucca	Bengali By.	Bengali
10	Prabhu ghat	Pucca	Nepali	Nepali
11	Chetsingh ghat	Pucca	Nepali	Nepali

12	Niranjani ghat	Pucca	Bengali By.	Bengali
13	Nirwani ghat	Pucca		
14	Shiwala ghat	Pucca	BG+Sr	BG+BS
15	Gularia ghat	Pucca	MH+Sr	MH+BS
16	Dandi ghat	Pucca	MH, BR.	MH+BS
17	Naya Hanuman ghat	Pucca	SJ., Br.	KN+MH+TG
18	Prachin Hanuman ghat	Pucca	SJ.+Br.	
19	Mysore ghat	Pucca	SJ.+Br.	KN
20	Harishchandra ghat	Kacha	SJ., Doml.	KN+VS
21	Wali ghat	Kacha	Sd.	VS
22	Vijayanagaram ghat	Pucca	Bengali	Bg.
23	Kedar ghat	Pucca	BG, SJ, Br.	BG
24	Chauki ghat	Kacha	BG, SJ, Br.	BG
25	Zhemeshwar ghat	Kacha	Telgu Br.	TG
26	Mansarowar ghat	Kacha	BB, MH	MH+BG
27	Narad ghat	Pucca	BG	BG
28	Raja ghat	Pucca	All	All
29	Pandey ghat	Pucca	BG	BG
30	Digapatia ghat	Pucca	BG	BG
31	Chausathi ghat	Pucca	BG	BG
32	Ranamahal ghat	Pucca	BG	BG
33	Darbhanga ghat	Pucca	Br.+BG	BG+BS
34	Munshi ghat	Pucca	Bg+S+BR	BG+BS
35	Ahalyabai ghat	Pucca	Br.+Sd	BG+BS

Sl. No.	Name of the Ghat	Name of the Ghat	Castes dominating	Linguistic group
36	Shitala ghat	Pucca	All	All
37	Dasashwamedh ghat	Pucca	All	All
38	Prayag ghat	Pucca	—	—
39	Dr. Rajendra Prasad ghat	Kacha	Sd	BS
40	Man Mandir ghat	Pucca	—	BS
41	Tripurabhairavi ghat	Pucca	Br.	BS
42	Meer ghat	Pucca	Br.+Sd	BS
43	Lolita ghat	Kacha	Dome+Khathruo	PN+BS
44	Jalasen ghat	Kacha	Br.+Sd	BS+PN
45	Manikarnika ghat	Pucca	All	—
46	Scindia ghat	Pucca	Khatree	G+MH
47	Sankata ghat	Pucca	Khatree	G+MH
48	Ganga Mahal ghat	Pucca	Guj+MH	All
49	Bhosala ghat	Pucca	Guj+MH	BS, MH, RN
50	Ram ghat		All	BS, MH
51	Jatar Raja Gwalior ghat	Pucca	Khatree	MH+RS Nep.
52	Balajee ghat	Pucca	MH+BR	MH
53	Ganesh ghat	Pucca	All	MH
54	Pancha Ganga ghat	Pucca	Br.+MH, Nep.	MH
55	Durga ghat	Pucca	MH	
56	Brahma ghat	Pucca	MH	MH
57	Bundiperkota ghat	Kacha	All	All

58	Adi Shitala ghat	Pucca	Sd	BS
59	Wal ghat	Pucca	Vaishya	BS
60	Gai ghat	Pucca	All	All
61	Badri Narayan ghat	Pucca	Khatree, Sr. Br., Br.	VS+PN
62	Trilochan ghat	Pucca	Vaishya	BS
63	Nandeshwar ghat	Kacha	Br.+Sd	BS
64	Gola ghat	Pucca	Sd	BS
65	Telialala ghat	Kacha	Vaisya+Md+Sd	BS
66	Naya ghat	Kacha	Br.+Vaishya, Sd	BS
67	Prahlad ghat	Kacha	Br.+Vaishya, Sd	BS
68	Rani ghat	Kacha	Khatria	BS
69	Bhaisasoor ghat	Kacha	VS+Sd+Md.	BS
70	Raj ghat	Kacha	Railway	Staff
71	Adikeshava ghat (Varuna)	Pucca	Br.	BS

APPENDIX IV

LIST OF THE DONORS TO THE VISHWANATH TEMPLE AT THE B.H.U.

(*Arranged State-wise*)

Sl. No.	*Name of the Donor*	*Amount in Rs.*
	UTTAR PRADESH	
1	Maharaja of Kashi	1,00,000
2	Indrachano Kejriwal (Gorakhpur)	5,000
3	Pujaya Malviyajee	1,832
4	Rameshwar Prasad Jaiswal	2,101
5	Rajeshwar Ram Tiwari (Gorakhpur)	1,100
6	Pt. Baldeo Upadyay (Kashi)	1,100
7	Amar Nath Mehrotra (Kanpur)	1,101
8	Sambhu Narayan Ram (Gazipur)	1,101
9	Srimati Padmabati Devi (Ajamgarh)	501
10	Sri Ram Kanhaiyalal (Farukhabad)	511
11	Ramesh Chandra (Lucknow)	577
12	Lalmani Devi (Ajamgarh)	50
13	Panna Lal (Lucknow)	50
14	Ganesh Prasad (Kashi)	100
15	Kadevan Ram (Kashi)	501
16	Ram Niwas (Meerut)	501
17	Gangasaran Bhargava (Kashi)	501
18	Gulgodi Devi (Agra)	1,001
19	Tulsi Ram Gupta (Kanpur)	2,100
20	Babu Vishwanath Singh (Balia)	501
21	Badilal (Kashi)	1,101
22	Bhagawan Das (Kashi)	1,101
23	Kanjee Karsan Das (Kashi)	1,101
24	Heeralal Mathura Das (Kashi)	1,101
25	Swarupjee Deo (Kashi)	1,101

Sl. No.	Name of the donor	Amount in Rs.
26	Mararjee Beljee Deo (Kashi)	1,101
27	Manganalal Nand Lal (Kashi)	1,101
28	Pakher Das Meghraj (Kashi)	1,101
29	Ram Kumar Bhusalka (Kashi)	1,101
30	Dilrukh Rai Jaidlal (Kashi)	501
31	Raghunath Pd. Satyanarain Pd. (Kashi)	501
32	Kishan Lal Rishikesh (Kashi)	501
33	Phatehchand Kuluram (Kashi)	501
34	Savitree Devi (Kanpur)	501
35	Benarsi Das Tisdiwala (Kashi)	501
36	Satyan Dhodhaniya (Kashi)	1,101
37	Srimati Kaushalya (Kashi)	501
38	R.C. Nagina (Kashi)	501
39	Srimati Maharaja Kunwar (Kashi)	501
40	Hanuman Das Mohal Lal (Kashi)	501
41	Ram Niwas Ramlal Rangwata (Khalilabad)	501
42	Babulal Kediya (Deoria)	1,001
43	Anant Pd. Burman (Kashi)	501
44	Pandey Ranjeet Shoshtri (Kashi)	501

BIHAR

Sl. No.	Name of the donor	Amount in Rs.
1	Maharaja of Darbhanga	1,00,000
2	Shiva Narain Gupta (Sahabad)	2,101
3	J.H. Bora (Dhanbad)	1,26,562
4	Srimati Rajmani Kunwar (Arrah)	501
5	Baidyanath Ram Jagannath Teli (Arrah)	501
6	Rajeshwari Devi (Arrah)	1,011
7	Ramsaran Kesari (Arrah)	521
8	Ambikadutta Mishra (Arrah)	515
9	Mahadeo Sah (Arrah)	511
10	Durga Ram Fram (Arrah)	501
11	Kausalya Devi (Arrah)	501
12	Sombar Devi (Saran)	501
13	R.N. Singh (Arrah)	501
14	Munri Devi (Saran)	501
15	Lakshmi Prasad (Muzaffarpur)	1,001
16	Srimati Tara Devi	501
17	Jangadayal Roy (Saran)	1,001
18	Chetan Das Mehra (Dalmiyanagar)	551

Sl. No.	*Name of the Donor*	*Amount in Rs.*
19	Maheshwar Singh (Sahabad)	501
20	Ganesh Ram Halwai (Arrah)	501
21	Mahadar Sarma (Palamau)	501
22	Rameshwar Prasad Singh (Patna)	501
23	Chandan Sah (Patna)	1,001
24	Laxmi Narayan Ram Narayan (Ranchi)	11,001
25	Gangaram Bajaj (Saran)	501
26	Baidyanath Jalan (Ranchi)	1,101
27	Tarabati Ranjan (Monghyr)	1,200
28	Ram Lakhan Sah (Sahabad)	501
29	Maheshwari Devi (Darbhanga)	1,101
30	Heera Sah (Arrah)	501
31	Benarsi Devi (Darbhanga)	505
32	Rambilas, Ramsanker (Arrah)	501
33	Chhati Devi (Darbhanga)	501
34	Ramkumar Malhotra (Darbhanga)	501
35	Laxmi Devi (Darbhanga)	501
	BENGAL	
1	Seth Sabharam Nagammal Bhulakka (Calcutta)	26,000
2	Seth Surajmal Nagarmal (Calcutta)	25,000
3	Seth Nangniram Ramkumar Bangar (Calcutta)	25,000
4	Seth Tarachand Ghanshyam (Calcutta)	21,000
5	Seth Mangturam Jaipuria (Calcutta)	21,000
6	Sri Ram Amarchand Bhojnagarwala (Calcutta)	11,101
7	Champa Lal Jatia (Calcutta)	11,000
8	Pratapmal Rameshwar (Calcutta)	11,000
9	Gangubaks Kanoria (Calcutta)	11,000
10	Gopiram Govindram (Calcutta)	11,000
11	Karamchand Thapar (Calcutta)	11,000
12	Sarajmal's mother Bhagawan Devi (Calcutta)	11,000
13	Daulatram Rawatmal (Calcutta)	7,500
14	Radha Krishna Santhalia (Calcutta)	7,500
15	Narsingh Das Kathari (Calcutta)	7,500
16	Ramanand Ram (Calcutta)	5,101

Sl. No.	*Name of the Donor*	*Amount in Rs.*
17	Bishwambhar Lal Braj Lal (Calcutta)	5,101
18	Ram Arjun Das (Calcutta)	5,101
19	Rai Bahadur Baldeo Nathani (Calcutta)	5,101
20	Hajarimal Somani (Calcutta)	5,101
21	Prayagdas Jagannath Agrawal (Calcutta)	5,101
22	Ram Sahay Lal Mor (Calcutta)	5,100
23	Deepchand Anandilal (Calcutta)	5,000
24	Ram Bilas Nandalal (Calcutta)	5,000
25	Ram Pratap Ratulal (Calcutta)	5,000
26	Basant Lal Dwara (Calcutta)	5,000
27	Jagnnath Hanuman Bux (Calcutta)	3,101
28	Radha Krishna Mehta (Calcutta)	3,101
29	Lakhchand Ratan Chand (Calcutta)	3,101
30	Ram Ratan Banarsiya (Calcutta)	3,000
31	Seth Jwda Prasad (Calcutta)	2,501
32	P.C. Mehta (Calcutta)	2,501
33	Bilasrai Ram Kumar (Calcutta)	2,500
34	Kishanlal Bhagwan Das Bajoria (Calcutta)	2,500
35	Calcutta Bullion Association (Calcutta)	2,500
36	Daulatram Ramdeo (Calcutta)	2,101
37	Jagannath Jutumal (Calcutta)	2,101
38	Ram Deo Laxminarain (Calcutta)	2,101
39	Jailal Hargulal (Calcutta)	2,101
40	Ram Dayal Ramkrishan (Calcutta)	1,500
41	Matilal Madan Lal Biyani (Calcutta)	1,500
42	Calcutta Wheat and Seed Association (Calcutta)	1,500
43	Beniram Benishanker (Calcutta)	1,111
44	Gyanmal Pannalal (Calcutta)	1,101
45	Lalchand Subykram (Calcutta)	1,101
46	Juharmal Srinarayan (Calcutta)	1,101
47	Jeevanram Ganguram (Calcutta)	1,101
48	Chimanalal Barilal (Calcutta)	1,101
49	Jaisingh Daga (Calcutta)	1,101
50	Harinand Savaram (Calcutta)	1,101
51	Shankerlal Ambalal (Calcutta)	1,101
52	Bhagaram Nagarmal (Calcutta)	1,101
53	Sukhdeo Das (Calcutta)	1,101
54	Pratapchand (Calcutta)	1,101

Sl. No.	Name of the Donor	Amount in Rs.
55	Gummukh Rai (Calcutta)	1,101
56	Sitaram Hariram (Calcutta)	1,101
57	Sukh Dayal (Calcutta)	1,101
58	Amarchand Murlidhar (Calcutta)	1,101
59	Balkishan Nagina Das (Calcutta)	1,101
60	Harikishan Nagar Das (Calcutta)	1,101
61	Rauthmal Beru Das (Calcutta)	1,101
62	Gulalrai Mahadeo (Calcutta)	1,101
63	Chimanlal Rameshwar (Calcutta)	1,101
64	Kanahaiyalal Pukhram (Calcutta)	1,101
65	Chhabilal Das (Calcutta)	1,101
66	Ram Narain Bhojnagarwala (Calcutta)	1,101
67	Seth J. Gopal Das (Calcutta)	1,101
68	Seth J. Bhai Katandeo (Calcutta)	1,101
69	Seth P.K. Kisan (Calcutta)	1,101
70	Bisanjee Tapan Madhajee (Calcutta)	1,101
71	Wheat and Seed Association (Calcutta)	1,101
72	Lakhi Prasad (Calcutta)	1,101
73	Rameshwar Nath (Calcutta)	1,101
74	Lakhmanilal (Calcutta)	1,101
75	Chandrakala Devi Gupta (Calcutta)	1,101
76	Thakur Das Sanka (Calcutta)	1,100
77	Srinivas Kishan Das (Calcutta)	501
	MAHARASHTRA	
1	Seth Salyanavain Sagavmal Modi (Bombay)	50,000
2	Seth Govindram Seksariya (Bombay)	25,000
3	Seth Mafat Lal Goyal Bhaideo (Bombay)	11,001
4	Ganesh Narain Onkarmal (Bombay)	11,001
5	Banarsidas Prahlad Rai (Bombay)	11,001
6	Mathura Dasjee Bisarjee (Bombay)	11,001
7	Shivaram Bansidhar Bhagat (Bombay)	11,000
8	Anandilal Ramdeo Poddar (Bombay)	11,000
9	Radha Krishan Khetan (Bombay)	11,000
10	Bishwambhar Lal Maheshwari (Bombay)	7,501
11	Ghanshyamdas Poddar (Bombay)	5,100
12	Swarupachand Prithibiraj (Bombay)	3,101
13	R.R. Purarka (Bombay)	2,500

Sl. No.	Name of the Donor	Amount in Rs.
14	Mukundlal Benarsialal (Bombay)	1,500
15	Sundar Bai (Bombay)	1,001
16	Shiva Pujan Dikshit (Nagpur)	501
17	Ramlal Ganpati Rai (Bombay)	1,101
18	Chiranjalal Annraj (Bombay)	1,101
19	Kamla Devi (Nagpur)	501
20	Parmeshvari Bai (Nagpur)	601
	RAJASTHAN	
1	Maharaja of Bikaner (Bikaner)	75,000
	Maharaja of Kata (Kata)	25,000
3	Sri Ramlal Bhimraj Tondi (Sikker)	501
4	Lukshmi Newar (Naher)	1,101
	Ramkunwar Mahabir Prasad (Sardarcity)	501
6	Visheswar Lal Hanuman Prasad	1,101
	JAMMU & KASHMIR	
1	Maharaja Karan Singh	5,000
	MADHYA PRADESH	
1	Lakshmi Prasad K.K. Gupta (Jabalpur)	501
2	Dulichand (Raigarh)	501
3	Ambika Pd. Kedarnath Dube (Manikpur)	1,101
4	Pingala Soner (Bilashpur)	501
	DELHI	
1	Gulab Rai Mahadeo (Delhi)	1,101
	Nihal Chand	1,101
	Rularamjee Mittal	501
	PUNJAB	
1	Lala Mulchand Tandon (Amritsar)	1,001
	GUJARAT	
1	Patel Khubchand Jait (Birnagar)	1,101
	MADRAS	
1	Ram Kumar Jalan (Madras)	1,101

Sl. No.	*Name of the Donor*	*Amount in Rs.*
	SOUTH AFRICA	
1	Soni Maljee Harjee (S. Africa)	1,125

Besides these aforesaid persons there are about 25 devotees hailing from businessmen community, Agriculturists, intellectuals and service holders.

APPENDIX V

LIFE HISTORIES

Life-history No. 1

Name :	K.S.T.
Age :	52
Sex :	Male
Sect :	Shaiva
Caste :	Saryuparin Brahmin
Education :	High School and Madhyama
Occupation :	Organising Temple-Management *(mahanta)*

Birth and early Childhood

I was born in a Saryuparin Brahmin family in Kashi in Vishwanath Gali Mohalla in the year 1921. My father Pt. Sri Laxmi Shankar Tripathi was simply a share holder of the Vishwanath temple at that time. But he was very religious-minded. So he used to spend most of his time in the temple in looking after the management of the temple organized by Pt. Mahabir Prasad Tripathi, my father's uncle.

Being the eldest son in my family, I was very much loved by all. There is an interesting story regarding my birth. Even after many years of her marriage, my mother had not had any child. Once she kept a sacred vow before the Lolark Deota near Lolark kund for begetting a son and fortunately after sometime I was born.

When I was 5 years old, my *mundan* ceremony (first hair shave of the head) was performed at Lolark kund. My mother and the other women of my uncle's family took me there. There were many *dholakiyas* and musical instrument players with us. After my head was shaved off I was provided with new clothes and I offered a *dhoti*, some *sindur*, *akshat* (rice) and *paisa*, etc., upon the diety Lolark. As soon as I arrived home I went to the golden temple of Vishwanath with my father and uncle and offered *gangajal*, flower, *belapatra* and *rori*, etc., upon the *linga* of Vishwanath. Thereafter I bowed upon the feet of the elders of our lineage for getting their *ashirvad* (blessings). They blessed me and each gave me some rupees

In the same year I was admitted in a Primary School named Gyanodaya Vidyalaya near Aparanath Math. From class I to class III, I read in that school under the guardianship of Pt. Chandrika Prasad, a local Saryuparin Brahmín. There I was taught Hindi, Sanskrit and Arithmetic.

During this period my uncle Vijaishankar Tripathi, K. Tripathi and a few others, who are nowadays engaged in business in the Vishwanath Gali, were my best friends. With them I used to move in my street and the adjoining areas. Sometimes we used to go to the Ganges to take bath and swim.

Education and Other Sacraments

At the age of 9, I fell very ill and it affected me so much that I had to give up my study for a year. Though I was very eager to go to school, my father did not permit that. But he appointed a private tutor for me and I was coached at my residence. Whenever I could get some leisure at home I went into the golden Vishwanath temple to collect money from various sacred shrines located therein.

When I regained my health after a year i.e. at the age of 10, I was again admitted in Harishchandra Inter College in Class IV. At that time Sri Badri Prasad Agarwal, Mohanlal Kedia and Girdhari Choube were my very close friends with whom I used to play football and *kabbadi*. I was a good footballer and I won three prizes in football matches. I used to play football till evening daily and for that my father started scolding me and ultimately I decided to give up playing football.

When I was of 11 years, my grand-mother died of Cholera and we became very anxious about our life too. My grandfather, Pt. Mahabir Prasad was the eldest man in our lineage and he appointed 11 *Karmkandis* to worship Lord Vishwanath especially for obtaining divine blessings and protection from Lord Shiva for us.

At the age of 12 my sacred thread ceremony was performed. Pt. Sitaram Tiwari, my *kulaguru*, became my Acharya and he initiated me. My relatives were invited and they came to participate in it with clothes and various other presents. Some of the local pundits and other official administrators of Varanasi had also been invited to bless me. But I do not exactly remember their names.

After this ceremony was over, my father instructed me not to eat at all in the morning every day till I had performed *puja* of Lord Vishwanath. For six months he took me along with him to the temple to perform daily sacred performance. For three months, my guru Pt. Sitaram Tiwari taught me how to recite and perform the Brahmanic daily rites. He also taught me some of the relevant stanzas of the Shukla Yajurveda and asked me to learn them by heart.

Before my sacred thread ceremony I had the freedom to move in and around any shrine in the temple precincts to collect money from the priests sitting there, but after I had worn the thread, my father imposed restriction on me from doing so. He made me understand that I was the son of a Mahanta of the temple, so I should not accept money from the *pujaris*. He further told me that since I was the eldest son in my family, after his death I would become the Mahanta. Therefore I must keep up his prestige. I took this instruction very seriously and since then I never went to temple precincts unless I had any necessary work there.

When I attained the age of fourteen I began to participate in the distribution of articles and money offered by the worshippers in the Vishwanath temple. Then I came to know the matters of dispute among my uncles who were the share holders in the temple. I often observed that each share holder tried to get more than his share without any consideration for the others.

Once, when I was about 15 years old the Maharaja of Gwalior came to worship Lord Vishwanath and he had to offer a big sum and other materials. All the Mahantas wanted to get him (the Maharaja) to stay at their own residence. The situation became so bothersome that the Maharaja could not stay anywhere at all. The real intention or objective behind the struggle to have the Maharaja as the guest was simply to induce him to give a large *dakshina*.

Since then I started taking an active interest in the matters of dispute among us regarding the temple management. In 1938 my father's uncle Pt. Shri Mahabir Prasad died. Again there was a skirmish among us for his vacant *gaddi* of the Chief Mahanta. The case was filed in the court of the District Judge and consequently S.M. Birappa, Manager of the Nagar Chhatram was appointed as a Receiver of the temple and he started looking after the management of the temple.

When I attained the age of 16, my father fixed my marriage at a village named Miltiuchha in the District of Jaunpur, about 58 kms. from Kashi. My father-in-law was a landlord (agricul-turist). Some of our relatives, friends, pundits, etc., partici-pated in the marriage party. I could not get any dowry. An obvious reason of my marriage in this family was that my father-in-law had a good reputation with the English Rulers. Through him my father desired to get a favourable decision in the family dispute for the *gaddi*. Later on I also felt interested in this marriage.

During this period I appeared at the High School exami-nation and did fairly well. Then my father suggested to me to try to pass the Madhyama examination as well in order to acquire Sanskrit learning. I did accordingly and passed Madhyama in the second division.

Two years after my marriage my father advised me to dis-continue study and take care of the domestic work as he had no time left to do that after attending to the litigation and other chores of the temple management.

Temple Management and Mahantaship

In 1944 all the share holders of the temple struck a com-promise on the formula that from each family there would be a single Mahanta who would look after the whole temple management for a year and as my father Laxmi Shankar Tripathi was the oldest among all the share holders, so he got the first chance to look after the temple management.

For a year my father looked after the temple management as the Chief Mahanta of the temple. As per the agreement held earlier, he was to hand over the charge to my uncle Sri Ramashanker Tripathi. But since my uncle had, it seems, talked to some local people against my father's efficiency, my father refused to hand over the charge of the temple to him in defiance of all the pressures put on him to do so. Finally, a case was lodged against my father by the rest of the share holders. But then my father had continued as the Chief Mahanta for near about four and a half years. The suit could not be decided and S. Birappa was again appointed as a Receiver in 1948. The management of the temple was handled by him for four years. In the meantime all the share holders gathered again to make a compromise. And in 1952 a compromise was held and it was decided that from each family there would be a Mahanta and the temple management would be looked after by the four Mahantas from all the four contesting families. Pt. Laxmishanker Tripathi, my father, Pt. Ramashanker Tripathi and Pt. Vijaishanker Tripathi all my uncles became the Mahantas of the temple.

In 1956 my father suddenly died, leaving behind his three married sons and a grand son and a grand daughter. Being the eldest son I had to perform his *antyeshti samskar*. I spent nearly ten thousand rupees on his last rites. This included the gifting of bighas of land to the Mahapatra of my family.

By now I had a son and a daughter. My two younger brothers, studying in a Middle School, had also grown up and attained the age of maturity.

After the death of my father, I, as the eldest in the family, took over the position of the head of the family and, was also therefore assigned the post of Mahanta to look after the management of the temple immediately after the last rites were over.

Harijan's entry into Vishwanath temple

In the same year the movement of Harijan entry in the temple of golden Vishwanath came up. All of us share holders, who had the authority over the temple affairs, met together to decide this issue. Should the Harijans be allowed entry in the temple ? We decided to wait and watch for the time being and play a convenient role towards both the views. However as the demand intensified, the orthodox Brahmins and the supporters of Harijans started fighting with each other. The leaders of orthodox Brahmins such as Swami Karpatriji, Swami S.N. Saraswati, Pt.V.N. Datar, Pt. Rayeshwar Shastri, Vaikunth Nath Upadhyaya and a few others came before us and told to warn the Harijans not to enter the temple.

Though from the core of our heart we were not willing to break an old tradition and allow the Harijans' entry but we had to acquiesce in view of the government rules and amendment to the Indian Constitution. But this has turned out well. With the Harijan entry, the number of worshippers has exceeded. The amount of offering to Lord Vishwanath has also increased. However due to the abolition of Zamindari and Privy Purses of the erstwhile rulers of the Princely States the amount of offering made by the Zamindars and ex-rulers has decreased. Therefore our income from the temple has remained nearly the same as before. But, however, the expenditure has increased by several times.

People's religious outlook

I feel that the religious outlook of the people is changing but they are not neglecting the Hindu religion. For example, in my temple (golden Vishwanath) I see that about 20% of the worshippers come putting a pant and shirt, a western dress, but also offer pranam as well as flower, belapatra, etc. I think that only the rigid orthodoxy of religious matters is decreasing, but the people are still quite religion-minded.

As regards the conception of sacred and profane is concerned I feel that 'sacred' is only to feel or belief, and all not sacred is profane. For example, if I believe that an ordinary rock is an emblem of a deity, certainly it would be sacred for me, but another may call it a profane.

Though I am a Mahanta of the temple but I do not differ from an ordinary man as regards the movement of society; the impact of westernization has also affected me and my family. For example, during the period of my father and grand-father we never used dining tables, cups, plates and crockery made of china, and our way of life was also somewhat different, i.e. all the daily prescribed rituals of the temple were performed by us. But since the death of my father and appointment of four joint Mahantas, it was stopped and many new things have come up which we have embraced in our lives.

I want to educate my children so that they can get better assignment in government services. The members in the family have increased greatly over the years but the income of the temple is almost the same as in the days of my grand-father. Therefore, to maintain ourselves I wish to give proper education to my children so that they can get better jobs elsewhere.

My father did not provide me with higher education because we had then enough wealth at our disposal. I have totally followed in the footsteps of my father and thus also acquired all his bad habits. For instance, like my father I also remain idle for the whole day at my residence; like him I also drink *bhang* three times a day, viz. *kagabasi*, in the morning, *satyanasi* in the afternoon and *bhogabilasi* in the evening. I prepare *bhang* with a variety of spices, sugar and milk. Daily in the evening my colleagues and priests of the temple give me company in taking *bhang*. Besides *bhang*, sometimes I also offer them sweets, fruits, etc. which I get from Baba Vishwanath (articles offered by the worshippers to the Lord).

Life-history No. 2

Name :	G.N.D.
Age :	40
Sex :	Male
Caste :	Kanyakubja Brahmin
Profession :	*Tirthapurohit*

Birth and early childhood

I was born on 18th December 1928 in Kashi in a Kanyakubja Brahmin Tirtha Purshila family. Before my birth I had an elder brother who was five years elder to me. My grandfather had died three years before my birth.

Upto seven years of age I was extremely loved by my grandmother and she used to take me with her when she went to Manikarnika ghat for taking bath and golden Vishwanath temple for performing sacred performances to Lord Vishwanath.

At the age of seven my *mundan* ceremony was performed at my own residence in CK11/8 Brahmal. After *mundan* I was brought to Chakrapushkarani Tirtha at Manikarnika ghat to take bath in the *kunda*. It is believed that Chakrapushkarani is our ancestoral property which must be shown proper respect. My relatives and other neighbours, particularly the women, accompanied me to the golden Vishwanath temple, where I had gone to bow before Lord Vishwanath.

During this period my best friends, with whom I used to play in the streets of my Mohalla as well as in the city, were Sri Ramji Kapoor, Adihy Narayan Sukla and a few others who are now no more on this earth. From my childhood I had an aptitude towards wrestling as my father was also interested in it. With him I had often visited my own Akhara Baba Naganath which even today is believed to be the oldest *akhara* of Kashi. We believed this *akhara* to be our ancestoral property. It is said that long long ago one of my forefathers was walking along the bank of the Ganges where he saw two snakes playing beside Manikarnika. When he returned home, in the night he dreamed that Baba Naganath was telling him to establish an *akhara* at the site where the snakes were playing. Since then that place became an *akhara.* So I and my close friends used to visit the games played by the Ahirs and others.

Yajnopavit

Three months after my Mundan I was admitted in Saraswat Khatri Vidyalaya at Surya Mohalla. In addition, my father also coached me to write Hindi alphabets and primary arithmetics.

When I attained the age of nine, my *Yajnopavit* (sacred thread ceremony) was performed. Pt. Shri Bholanathjee Maharaj, a local *karmakandi* Saryuparin Brahmin, became my *guru*, and gave me *guru mantra.* He taught me the Brahmanic rites such as Sandhya Sandhan, Gayatri mantra and Rudra ashtadhyayi for two years.

In October 1947 my father died away suddenly and I had no one left to look after us except my old mother. I had to perform the Shraddh kriya of my father in Brikhatsarg process which caused me an expense of nearly five thousand rupees.

Involvement in Jajmanika

Now I began to look after my Jajamani work in which my few *gumashatas* (functionaries) also assisted me. There were *gumashatas* of many sub-castes such as Maithils, Saryuparin, Joshi, etc.

At the age of 16 I was transferred to Harishchandra Inter College to study in the eighth class. I studied there for three years but owing to my engagement in hereditary profession of Tirtha-purohita I could not appear at the final examination of High School and I discontinued my studies.

Many of my friends and relatives pressed me for marriage but as I was considered rather a rude youngman, none of the Kanyakubja Brahmins would accept me as a son-in-law. Finally I decided to remain unmarried for leading a saintly life. When my mother became too old to do any domestic work I got my younger brother married in Gaya in an agriculturist Kanya-kubja Brahmin family.

As regards the rise and fall of my profession of *tirthapuro-hitai* is concerned it has taken many trends. But the present period is the worst of all. Though we are the descendants of those persons who were the first settlers, who cleared the forests and made this place habitable, but we are of no importance now.

My forefathers were Raj Purohit gurus of Rajasthan, Malwa, Mithila and other States of India. In those days my *jajamanika* activities spread over Kala, Bundi, Jodhpur, Bikaner, Sirahi, Idar, Thal bara, Ajamer, Kekari, Kisangarh, Kharwa, Pisagarh, Bharatpur, Masunda, Ratlam, Jhambua, Sitaman, Khilchipur, Raghogarh, Bara, Kachhi, Baroda, Nagod, Uchhara Jaudhri, Sarang garh, Jaitpur, Jabra, Simli, Kasanda, Padriya, Chakhari and Mithila. All the castes within these regions were my *jajamans*. The records and other evidences of all the aforesaid localities are still with me. But owing to our carelessness and mismanagement only a few of these are now handled by us. It is due to the freedom of *Panda* profession that the family members of *gumashatas*, whom our forefathers employed are claiming to be old Tirthapurohita and we are helpless to check them. Though we have lodged several suits against them for prevention but the decision of the court has always gone in their favour. As a consequence of their adopting our profession it is now considered an avocation of lower social scale.

My father was not only a Tirthapurohita but was also a renowned *sangitigya* (musician) of Varanasi. He had a good deal of skill with sitar, bela, harmonium, tabla, veena, sarangi, sarod, satranga, jalataranga, pakhavaj, bansuri, etc.

He had great friendship with Maharaja Kameshwar Singh of Mithila. Maharaja Kameshwar Singh built a *Dharamashala* 'Mithila grihi' for the lodging of pilgrims from Mithila. The Maharaja also donated a large number of flower plants to my father to plant a garden.

My father taught sitar to Shri Lakshman Singh the then Prince of Gangabar state of Bharaich in U.P. Maharaja saheb of M.P., Sri Dilip Singh, was one of the sitar pupils of my father. Sri Harishchandra Srivastava the late judge of Varanasi appointed my father as a guru for teaching sitar to his daughter. Maharaja Bibhuti Singh of Kashi also learnt sitar from my father. Besides that my father taught several musical instruments to the princes and princesses of many states of India and received valuable presentations and honour.

As my ancestors were the Tirthapurohita of various princely states of India he was called Rajaguru Tirthapurohita.

Because the temple of Vishwanath was at first managed by the *sadhus*, my ancestors did not accept to take *Shiva Nirman* for, it is believed that the *dan* offered upon the Shiva is not auspicious for a *grihastha*. Another reason was that, unlike today, we had sufficient income, hence there was no pressing need to acquire the offerings of Shiva also.

It is said that the land falling in the area (with Kachauri gali towards the west, Sidheshwari to the North, and the river Ganges in the east) was in the possession of my great grandfather. I have enough evidence to prove it and on 12 June 1803 a decision regarding this was made. But the time changed and it began to decrease day by day. Just after the death of my father four plots of land were claimed by some of the neighbours of mine. He produced a forged paper of loan in the court and I lost the land and building of Brahmal where at present there is a vegetable market of local Khalri families. I have become considerably poorer now than my late ancestors.

Religious Belief

I believe that the religious fervour among the Hindus is decreasing day by day owing to certain factors. I may mention but a few factors which I believe are the most obvious, viz., westernization has affected the dress, living pattern, way of education and the mind of the Indians. Therefore, pilgrims coming to Kashi do not confine themselves to *puja patha*, but also take interest in visiting the modern things like Sarnath Museum, B.H.U. Vishwanath, Bharat Mata Mandir, and so on. The Indian mentality has changed so much that they do not obey their parents without argument so less they would follow the *tirthapurohitas*.

When I was a child I always saw a large number of pilgrims and devotees at my *tirtha*, Manikarnika ghat, but nowadays a few people come and take bath in the Ganges. However, even if the traditional mode of religion is changing I feel proud of my profession that I have such a beautiful and glorious *tirtha*, Manikarnika, where both security of long life and security for best death are simultaneously attainable. The reality of life is seen here in its many facets. For instance, you may see the mother of a dead son weeping for her son while another mother prays for the long life of her son and performs Ganga *puja*, etc.

I believe that Manikarnika is the daughter of Vishnu and the Lord Vishwanath has honoured her giving the name of Mokshadayani (giver of salvation).

Besides my daily sacred performances I observe an annual sacred performance to goddess Manikarnika at Chakra Push-karni *tirtha* where all the *tirthapurohitas* of Kashi gather together and bring the idol of the deity from my house to the *kunda*. It is performed on Vaisakh *shudi akshaya dwitiya* (second day of the light fortnight of Hindu month Vaisakh).

Life-history No. 3

Name :	K.
Age :	58
Sex :	Male
Caste :	Joshi Brahmin
Sect :	Shaiva
Occupation :	*Pujari*

Birth and Early Childhood

I was born in Kashi in a *yatrawal pandu* family. My father was one of the prominent *yatrawals* of Kashi. I have been told by my elders that I often used to weep at the time of my father's departure from home to the golden Vishwanath temple. Though

I had not any knowledge as to where my father was going but owing to my close association with him I never liked to be separated from him even for a short time. At that time we lived in a joint family.

I still remember very clearly an instance of an obstinancy of my boyhood. At that time I was of 8 years. A rich *jajman* of my father came from Calcutta to our house. He had a basket of fruits and sweets and several new articles like clothes, stationery, etc. Actually he had to undertake the pilgrimage of *panchakosi* with the help of my father. I began to weep that I must accompany them. My father was annoyed and rebuked me. In sullen anger I decided to go away from house. But my grandmother was very gentle and she assured me to undertake the pilgrimage with her. Ultimately I undertook the pilgrimage of *panchakosi* with her but I do not remember now any significant detail of that pilgrimage.

Till the age of six, I studied in a primary school and after that at the age of 8 I was admitted in class IV in Harishchandra School. While I was a student of class V my sacred thread ceremony was performed. My guru Pt. Sri Puroshottam Maharaja, who was a noted Sanskrit scholar of Kashi in those days, started to coach me Brahmanic rites, viz. *sandhyopasana*, Gayatri *mantra*, etc. after finishing the *darshan*, *puja* of the lord Vishwanath. He coached me the said mantra for six months continuously. He was the oldest person of my locality. He was a Joshi Brahmin of 75 years age.

During my school days most of my friends came from well-to-do families of Kashi; some of them were even from the house of princes of different states of India. In their company I learnt to play cricket, volley ball, hockey, etc.

At the age of 15, I was married at Chokraghat in Banaras in a *yatrawal* family. That day was perhaps the most pleasant in my life when I started with the *barat* party being seated in a silver palanquin and several elephants, horses and other vehicles following me.

Just after a year after my marriage my mother took seriously ill and died. My father, though, an old man at that time, wanted to marry another lady. I opposed him and as a result there were serious differences between him and me which ultimately led me to leave his house and take shelter at the residence

(Chhatiyai in Kashi) of my maternal grandmother. As she had no son, she loved me very much. She was not a rich lady but a courageous one. She encouraged me to continue my education. I was 16 years of age at that time. Just after six months of my stay at her residence, she fell ill and there were some financial difficulties. So I decided to discontinue my study. My friends advised me against it but my circumstances compelled me to take the step. In all this trouble, my brother and father never helped me; I too was not in a mood to ask for any help from them.

I did not like to become a *yatrawal* in spite of my adverse financial circumstances and many suggestions from my well-wishers. So my uncle got me an assignment to ring bell at the *nobatkhana* of the golden Vishwanath temple daily for two hours. I remained in this job for two years. At that time I was getting only Rs. 15 per month. I had by now started taking betels, drinking *bhang* etc. and was lured by the good income of the *yatrawals*. So I gave up the job of ringing bell at the *nobatkhana* and joined *yatrawal pandagiri* profession.

I started first day of yatrawal profession from Dasashwamedh ghat. I escorted a pilgrim (male) to the golden temple of Vishwanath and other smaller shrines of this locality to assist him in *darshan pujan*. I simply guided him indicating the identity of the deities. That day I realised that if I had known how to perform *puja* and other rituals, I might have received more amount than what I had got in such a simple service of guide. I made up my mind to learn *karmakanda*. One day I requested a pundit of Kashi who was a teacher in Gauri Shanker Pathshala, Lalitaghat, to train me in *karmakanda*. He was very pleased and asked me to come to his residence twice every day, in the morning and evening. After having done that for 16 month I had learnt to perform *abhisheka*, marriage rites, yajnopavit and other sacramental rites.

As soon as I acquired knowledge of *karmakanda* I behaved like a pundit. As none of the *yatrawal pandas* had the knowledge of all the sacramental rites of the Hindus, they respected me. At the same time my earning grew. And owing to my versatile knowledge I used to assist the pilgrims and devotees in all types of sacred performances.

My financial condition improved gradually and my

daughter, the only issue of mine, now attained the age of 9. One of my friends suggested me to get my daughter married with his son. I hesitated but he insisted that this sort of marriage is believed to be *Vijayagami vivah*, an auspicious connection. I did not have much money at that time. Therefore I went to Kanpur and I acquired the help of Rs. 5,000 from a *jajman*, the widow of a Marwari who had no issue. I performed the marriage of my daughter with great pomp and show.

Dr. Sampoornanand, the then Chief Minister of U.P., gave me an offer to join as a priest in the Shiva temple near his house. He also assured me that he would provide a good building to me. Tempted by his offer I joined that temple. But after my 10 years service in that temple he did not pay any attention towards me and ultimately I had to leave that service.

Again I returned to the *yatrawal pandagiri* profession at the golden temple of Vishwanath. But this time I requested my friend Bansropan Mishra, who was then the Manager of the temple to get me fixed up as a temple priest. He requested the *mahantas* of the temple and the same day I was appointed as a priest at the Abimukteshwar shrine in the precincts of the golden temple of Vishwanath.

For three years continuously I faithfully and punctually served at Abimukteshwar shrine. All the *mahantas* were pleased with my diligence and they assigned me the service of Satyanarayan shrine which is believed to be the most responsible job in the golden temple of Vishwanath because all the golden ornaments as well as the costly materials of the temple are kept inside this temple.

Complimentary questions

Q. Did you enter politics any time in your life ?

A. I had never any taste for politics, because when I was in class VIII in school, two friends of mine fell in enmity owing to their allegiance to separate political parties. This led to all the students of my class to divide themselves in two groups and ultimately one day there was a fight between the two groups and two boys from each group were seriously hurt. Since then I have made up my mind not to get into politics in my life.

Q. Do you think that better economy is the best measuring rod of one's life ?

A. I think material comforts are necessary for maintaining the physical health of a person on the one hand but on the other hand to satisfy the hunger of soul it demands some communications which may be practised through interaction with the whole social settings, viz. man, woman, deities, animals, environment, etc. But as a whole what is the most important in all in practical these days is only the money by which every thing in life can be had even for some time.

Life-history No. 4.

Name :	M.M.
Age :	50
Sex :	Male
Caste :	Joshi Brahmin
Profession :	*Yatrawal.*

I was born in a Joshi Brahmin family on July 17, 1922 in Kashi. My father was a *Yatrawal panda* of Kashi and owing to his knowledge of Sanskrit he had a good reputation. We lived in a joint family and my two younger uncles were also engaged in the same profession.

I was the eldest child in the family and was very much loved by all the family members. Specially my grandfather was very fond of me and brought for me a lot of toys and sweets.

At the age of six in 1928 my *mundan* ceremony was performed at Vindhyachal, because my mother, when she was carrying me, had taken such a sacred vow before Vindhyachal Mai. After completing a year I was admitted in a primary school in my own *mohalla.*

At the age of 12 in 1934 my *yajnopavit* (sacred thread ceremony) was performed at Vindhyachal, because my *mausi* (aunt) had taken a vow before Vindhyachal Mai that I would be again brought there for that ceremony if I remained alive till then. In fact in my childhood, I always maintained bad health, hence the vow. My sacred thread ceremony was performed under the guardianship of Pt. Kunwaji Maharaj who was my *kulaguru.*

After my *yajnopavit* my father made me follow a strict daily routine. I had to leave bed early in the morning at 5.30. After attending to the call of nature I used to sit with my father to recite the sacred *mantras*, viz. the gayatri *mantra*, *sandhya vandana* and other sacred *mantras* related with the *yatrawal* profession, like the *yatra mantra* to appease 56 Vinayaks, for the *panchakosi yatra*, and so on. Thus he taught me for about a year.

I had passed the sixth class from the Middle School in Payari Mohalla. Since my school days I had a liking for visiting the various sacred shrines of Kashi. Just after a year I was transferred to Kabirchaura Middle School to study in the eighth class. I learnt there Hindi, English and Sanskrit.

In the meantime my father fell seriously ill and was afflicted with cancer. Due to ill health of father the financial condition of our family deteriorated day by day. As a result my uncles separated from us. I tried to get my father treated at a number of places, but his condition grew from bad to worse till one day finally he breathed his last.

At that time I was touching 20 and my mother felt the need for getting me married. One of my friends Maksudan Maharaj, belonging to a *yatrawal* family, negotiated my marriage at Harha Mohalla. I was soon married. At that time I was of 20 years and my wife was of 16. My father-in-law was a *jyotishi* (astrologer). On the eve of my marriage I was given new sets of shirts and *dhoti*, utensils and some money by my father-in-law and his relatives.

After a year of my marriage, my father-in-law too passed away. I participated in his *antyeshti sanskar* (last rites). As my wife's brother was younger than his sister and I was the eldest of his brothers-in-law, I had to conduct the *shraddh* management. Also I helped him financially. My continued adversity compelled me to discontinue my studies. As a result I was now not eligible for any educated employment. So I decided to follow my hereditary profession of *yatrawals*.

On my first day in this profession, I stationed myself near a big image of the Nandi close to Gyanvapi. I waited there for two hours but could not get any *jajman*. I was about to go back home, when I saw a resident of Banaras, and solicited him for *darshan* and *puja*. He agreed. I purchased flowers and garland and got Gangajal on his behalf and escorted him to the main shrine of Vishwanath. I recited some *mantras* to perform *puja* and offer flower, Gangajal, etc., upon the *linga*. On the completion of the *puja* he gave me *dakshina* of five annas and asked my name. This was my initiation into the profession for the maintenance of my family members.

My bad financial condition compelled me also to discontinue the education of my two younger brothers (aged 18 and 16) who were studying in Middle School. I got them married at Allahabad and Harha (Kashi) respectively.

In spite of our adversity I was not unhappy. But the lack of an issue made me sad. Even after several years of marriage, my wife could not conceive. I got her examined by doctors. We also took several sacred vows before the deities like Lord Vishwanath, Mata Annapurna, Lolark kund, Vindhyachal Mai and others for begetting an issue but as ill luck would have it, she remained without a child.

Many friends and relatives advised me to marry another girl. But my conscience did not permit me to do so. Thus till today I am without an issue. Most of what I earned I spent on my own maintenance and the rest of my earning was spent on my nephew (sister's son).

During the period I worked as a *yatrawal panda*, I faced a lot of ups and downs in my life. The Harijan entry into the Golden Vishwanath temple was one of the major incidents which very much disturbed the citizens of Varanasi. Like all of them I too believe that it was totally a political issue, motivated by the political parties, against the Ram Rajya Samiti of Swami Karpatri.

The idea of allowing the Harijans into the golden temple of Vishwanath had been in the minds of the political leaders for a long time. But it took a practical shape only in September 1956 when at 7.30 p.m., some political leaders gathered a large number of Harijans outside the temple gate and rushed in to join the *shringar arati*. The orthodox Brahmins agitated by laying themselves at the gate but could not check their entry.

On this day a good number of citizens gathered in front of the temple gate to see this historic event. I saw that the orthodox Hindus were crying '*Har, Har!* Vishwanath!' The Harijan entry became a controversial matter among the citizens of Kashi. So far as my attitude towards this incident is concerned, I did not take it seriously, because it was known to us that the Harijans had access to the temple even before. but it was a somewhat unpublicized practice.

I believe all that as 'sacred' that had been directed or shown in our Vedic text, i.e. the permitted modes of behaviour or action practised in societies are believed to be 'sacred' while the acts or things not socially sanctioned are 'profane'.

I believe that the traditional modes of handling the religious life of our Hindu society are changing very rapidly nowadays owing to our modern education. For I find that the people today have no feeling for the *yatra.* They have little affection for taking *darshan*, nor much inclination towards performing *puja path.* But the pilgrims in the ancient times took great care in doing all the said religious activities

I also believe that the political agitations, a bad social order and loose administration have also affected the institution of pilgrimage. The pilgrims, most of whom are peasants from villages feel insecure on account of the increasing rowdyism and goondaism in the places of pilgrimage. The strikes by transport employees have also affected the pilgrimage.

About 30 or 40 years back, most of the pilgrims used to stay with their respective *pandas*, *tirtha purohitas* or at *dharmashalas.* In the olden days, the rules and regulations of pilgrimage were strictly maintained, the rituals were performed elaborately, and the pilgrims were bound to stay for at least three nights in the place of pilgrimage. They had great affection in paying *dakshina* and *dan.* But the situation is quite different today. The pilgrims travel in their cars, stay at hotels and do not like to stay here for more than a few hours.

It has also affected the management and organisation of temples. For example, the management of the golden Vishwanath temple does not take any interest in the daily *puja path*, *bhog rag* of the temple.

The example may be cited of the Golden Vishwanath temple. The late Mahanta Pt. Mahabir Prasad had a keen sense of devotion towards the temple service. He daily used to perform two *araties* and extra puja for an hour. But the *mahantas* of today do not take any interest in daily *puja path* of the temple. Consequently the priests employed for looking after and performing the daily rituals of the deities are not qualified enough. The temple in the old days was under such a good management that more than 50 Brahmins, Sadhus and beggars were fed daily but today the situation is quite the reverse. The priests and *mahantas* are interested only in their own income.

Life-history No. 5

Name :	D.S.M.
Age :	71
Sex :	Male
Caste :	Saryuparin Brahmin
Sect :	Shaiva
Profession :	Temple Priest (G.V.T.)

I was born in 1902 in Rani Mahal of Kashi, the then palace of the Raja of Udaipur. My father at that time was a priest at the golden temple of Vishwanath, appointed by Udaipur State. I was the only child in my family with not even a cousin.

My father's sister, who was the eldest lady in my family, often told me fairy tales of the deity Indra and his *upsaras.*

My best friend at that time was Kanhaiyaji, son of a businessman. His father used to discuss religious topics with my father. I often brought betel from the shop and arranged their *bhang* drinks. I remember an instance when I was only 7 years old. It was the day of Shivaratri. My father gave me a glass of *bhang* to drink. After half an hour I started vomiting and it continued for so long that my father had to attend to me leaving the *puja path* in the temple. Everybody in my family began to cry. When I was cured my father took a vow never to give me any such drug.

I was admitted in a primary school in Jangambari at the age of seven in 1909. The school was under a private management aided by the local affluent Marwaris. Most of the students were Brahmins and the medium of teaching was Sanskrit. Pt. Diwakar Sharma was our teacher; he was also a *karmakandi.* I studied there for four years. When I was in the fourth class in the year 1913, I wore *yajnopavit* (sacred thread ceremony was performed). Pt. Diwakar Sharma became my *guru* and he taught me *sandhya vandana*, Gayatri *mantra, surya puja*, ganga *puja* and other Brahmanic rites.

After passing the fourth class I went to my mother's parental village (Chandauli in Mirzapur District, U.P.) and engaged there in agricultural operation. My grandfather, who lived there alone loved me very much. I remained there for two years but I did not like living in a village and ultimately returned to Kashi.

My father was very much annoyed by my returning as he wanted me to inherit the property of my grandfather who had no issue except my mother. My father had hoped that I should become the heir to my grandfather's property. He now asked me to come to the temple of Vishwanath to earn money by assisting the pilgrims and local devotees in performing *puja* and *darshan* of Lord Vishwanath.

At times when my father was absent, I performed *shringar arati* at the Golden Vishwanath temple. I had learnt by heart the *arati* songs as well as the *puja* performance from the elderly priests. At that time Pt. Mahabir Prasad was the chief priest of the *shringar arati*.

My father died in 1921 when I was only 19 years old. As I was the eldest son of my parents I had to perform the *antyeshti sanskar* (death rites). I spent about Rs. 500 in performing *shraddh karma* of my father. I got Rs. 200 from the Raja of Udaipur and Rs. 300 by selling off my maternal grandfather's lands and property.

During my bereavement period, the chief priest's son Shri Rudranath performed *shringar arati* as a substitute for my father. After the completion of *shraddh karma* I took permission of the Raja of Udaipur to perform *shringar arati* at the Golden Vishwanath temple in place of my father. Since then I became a priest of the temple.

At the age of 21 my mother thought of getting me married because she was the only woman in the family. My brother-in-law (sister's husband) who lived in Sultanpur, brought some marriage brokers to my house. My mother asked him to carry out the negotiations and arrange the matter. Accordingly I was married to an illiterate girl of 13, from a cultivator's family. There were about 50 persons among the *barat* (marriage party).

Most of them were my relatives and friends. I rode a mare and other kinsmen were on bullock carts. I got two pairs of *dhoti*, a *kurta*, a pair of shoes and a shawl in *bidai* (gift) from my 'in-laws. After five years of my marriage a daughter was born to me, but she did not survive for long and died at the age of five.

After 14 years of service as a state priest in the temple, in 1935 I was appointed as a full-time priest of the temple, under the *mahanta*. I carried out both the duties of a state priest and temple priest for the next 12 years. Two months after I joined the temple as a full-timer, a son was born to me. After my appointment, the Bachcha priest died. Since the then Mahanta, Pt. Mahabir Prasad, was very fond of me he asked me also to carry out the duties of Bachcha Pujari.

At that time I was getting Rs. 12 p.m. from the Raja of Udaipur. I also got some money from the local devotees—generally the affluent businessmen. My financial position was comparatively better than it is today.

At that time the rules of the temple were strictly followed. Temple priests were not allowed to enter the *sanctum* without taking a bath, also not after taking betel or tobacco. But now-a-days the priests do not observe any such restrictions.

Pt. Mahabir Prasad was the chief organizer of the temple and he participated in the *puja seva* of Lord Vishwanath. All the daily sacred performances, viz., *mangal arati*, *bhoga arati*, *shringar arati* and *shyana arati*, were performed by him, assisted by the other priests of the temple. But since his death every thing in the temple has become disorganized. The *mahantas* (shareholders of the temple) began to quarrel among themselves for taking charge of the temple management, and have started litigation.

By then my son also matured and I handed over the duty of state priest (performance of *shringar arati*) to him. At that time he was studying in a school. I myself coached him in the way of the sacred performance and taught him the *mantras* of the *Vedas* to be pronounced in the *shringar arati*.

When I was a youth of 19, political consciousness developed in me and I began to participate in the freedom strug- of our country.

In 1921 a meeting was held at Gyanvapi. The chief

participants were Shiva Prasad Gupta, Dr. Tara Chand and Mohammed Ali. There was a huge gathering there of the youth of Kashi ; I also attended it. Police came to arrest the leaders there. Knowing me to be one of the priests of the golden Vishwanath temple they did not arrest me. But I courted arrest and remained in jail for a week. There in the jail I continuously thought that if Lord Vishwanath had the power, the English people would have to leave India. Even in jail I used to perform *sandhya vandana*, gayatri *mantra*, etc. to maintain personal purity and sanctity.

I used to carry secret messages regarding our party programme to the freedom fighters because, since I was a priest, no one would doubt that I had any political connection. In fact the English people were very religious minded and always showed full regard to the temple and *puja path*. Contrary to the English rule, our Indian rule has attempted to destroy the sanctity of our Hindu religion by challenging the very beliefs in the *Vedas* and *Puranas*. The Harijan entry in the golden Vishwanath temple brought a new era of decline to the Hindu way of life and since then the sanctity of the temple is decreasing day-by-day.

During my service period in the golden Vishwanath temple, there have been several cases of theft but the most serious case happened in 1964. I was then away from the temple. In the night, the jewelled crown of Lord Vishwanath was stolen. Though obviously I had no connection with this occurrence, but being a temple employee I had to appearbefore the Court and stand in the dock to answer questions. I felt much ashamed.

In contrast with the treatment meted out to the priests by late Mahanta Pt. Mahabir Prasad, the present *mahantas* treat them very shabbily. The priests are even made to do domestic service. I have often thought of leaving this job but the fear of unemployment has held my hand.

I believe anything touched with the *linga* of Vishwanath or any dominant deity becomes sacred. For example, the *prasad*, when it is at the shop, is not at all sacred, but when it is brought before the *linga* and touched with it, it becomes sacred.

Life-history No. 6

Name :	B.P.T.
Age :	55
Sex :	Male
Caste :	Saryuparin Brahmin
Profession :	Associated with the B.H.U. Vishwanath Temple

I was born in a Saryuparin Brahmin family in 1918 in a village named Simarana in Gorakhpur District of U.P. My father was an agriculturist. I was the second son of my parents, five years younger than my elder brother. I was considered quite handsome as a child and so was fauned upon by my grandfather.

Just after three years of my birth my grandfather died. I was a sickly child till the age of five, but after *mundan* ceremony (first hair-cropping) I grew strong. During this period my elder brother and three cousins were my pet friends and with them I used to play football and other small games. I did not have close intimacy with my own brother because he always tried to impose his will upon me and scolded me when I did not do his bidding.

At the age of five I was admitted to the first standard in a L.P. School. This school was about a kilometre at Bartee village. Before my admission I had been taught Hindi alphabets and counting by my father. I studied in this school for four years. By then my elder brother was admitted to a middle school in Jagdishpur village about five miles from my native place. As soon as I passed the fourth class my *yajnopavit sanskar* (sacred thread ceremony) was performed. Pt. Vijai Datta Sukla, a teacher at my school, became my *guru* and gave me *guru mantra*. He was also a Saryuparin Brahmin but was not my kinsman. He taught me all the Brahmanical rites, viz., *sandhya vandana*, gayatri *mantra*, *Savitri*, *Pranayam*, etc. for about six months.

A few months after my *yajnopavit* ceremony, my mother died of fever. Now left alone, my father desired that I should give up my studies and look after my younger brother and sister. Accordingly, I left school and remained at home with the younger ones in the family. After about six months, however my elder brother advised my father to continue my studies and rather find some alternative to look after my younger brother and sister.

During this time my uncle (father's brother-in-law) visited us. He agreed to send his wife (my father's sister) for at least a year to look after our family. This perfectly suited my father and I started going with my elder brother to Jagdishpur High School. Though my father was not very well off at that time, he had a keen desire to get his sons proper education. My education could have become a financial problem, but fortunately I was selected in the merit competition at my school, and was able to secure a stipend covering my food and lodging.

I studied for the next six years at Jagdishpur Sanskrit Vidyalaya and passed the Madhyama examination. Life at Jagdishpur was quite peaceful and carefree. Food and lodging provided were good. The school management even provided some stationery. Till I remained in the school, my father had not to worry for me. After passing Madhyama I followed the advice of my brother and in 1933 came to Kashi to continue my studies at the Kashi Sanskrit Vishvavidyalaya. I lived with my brother in the hostel which provided food and lodging to the students. The management was communal, consisting of local Marwari Baniya (the businessmen).

I was admitted to Ruiya Pathashala at Nayawa Mohalla. I studied there only for six months because it was far off from my residence. I left this institution to be admitted to Rambir Pathashala at Kamachha. I remained at this Pathashala for two years and attained good command of Sanskrit grammar. After that I took admission in Queen's College for the Shastri examination and passed that in the second division.

Meanwhile my father sent word to my brother that he had arranged my marriage. I expressed my disinclination to getting married but my brother disregarded that and set off for our village to help father arrange the marriage. Thus at the age of 25, I was married to a girl of 16 years, from a Saryuparin Brahmin family, at the village Rampur in Deoria District of U.P. My father-in-law also was an agriculturist. My wife was literate. My father took only two oxen and a buffalo from my father-in-law in dowry.

After my marriage I returned to Varanasi to coutinue my

studies. But now I felt a sense of responsibility to earn and help the family. So, I took a part time job in a Sanskrit Vidyalaya, founded by the late Swami Karpatri in Bari Gaibi Mohalla.

To get a better knowledge of Sanskrit I again took admission to the Acharya level in the Banaras Hindu University and studied there for nearly five years. I passed from the University in 1946 with the degrees of Vedantacharya and Darshanacharya.

In 1948 I was appointed lecturer in the Sanskrit College founded by Marwari Seva Sadan at Assi Mohalla. I was paid there only Rs. 48 per month as monthly salary, besides two meals and clothings, etc. With such meagre salary I could not stick to that job for long and next year joined Rambir Pathashala as its *upadhyaksha*. I remained in that post for four years for the teacher whom I was temporarily substituting was on leave.

During the period Raja Baldeo Dass Birla came to Kashi to lay the foundation stone of B.H.U. Vishwanath temple. I knew his manager and through him was introduced to Shri Birla, who gave me an offer to join temple service at B.H.U. at whatever the amount I wanted. I at once agreed to the proposal and started serving at B.H.U. Vishwanath temple from the day of its foundation. At the same time I took the degree of 'Dharamashastracharya' from Bharat Maha Mandal and acquired the degree of M.B.B. from Gorakhpur University. I have spent nearly 14 years in serving the Vishwanath temple of B.H.U.

I believe that our social values have not fully changed by westernization or modernization. They are still mostly the same; only their modes are changing.

I believe in the theory of the realization of the soul. I further believe that all the temples of Vishwanath have the same merit. It depends upon the feeling of the worshippers as to what extent he or she believes in it.

The temple of B.H.U. Vishwanath has its merit and it follows the rules and regulations for the mass, viz. untouchability, feeling of caste, creed, religion and nationality are not its aim rather that allows everyone to come and share in Hindu religion and religious ideas.

I have often seen that the Muslim, Christian, Sikh and

followers of many other faiths come here and bow before the *linga* of *Vishwanath*.

Life-history No. 7

Name :	D.N.U.
Age :	63
Sex :	Male
Caste :	Saryuparin Brahmin
Profession :	*Karmakandi*

I was born in a Saryuparin Brahmin family in the Vikrami Samvata 1977 in village Bibikhurda, District Arrah (Rohtash). My grandfather had 1,000 bighas of land under cultivation and was considered one of the richest Zamindars (landlord) of the locality. He had four brothers. On account of our wealth and property, our family wielded great influence among the people of the locality.

I was the second son. While I was only 8 years old, my mother died. My grandmother and grandfather loved me very much and at the age of nine, my *mundan* (hair cropping) and *yajnopavit* (sacred thread) ceremonies were performed.

On the occasion of my *yajnopavit*, Pundit Devanath our *kulaguru* became my Acharya *guru*. For five months he taught me the recitation of Gayatri *mantra*, *sandhya vandana*, *pranayam*, *Savitri* and other Brahmanic rites. Then I was sent away to a Brahmacharya Ashram in Kashi to be trained as an orthodox Brahmin in the Brahmanic codes.

At the Ashram, we were about 30 students. We got up at 4 a.m. and went out to take our bath in the Ganges. The management of the Ashram had appointed a wrestler named Kamta Prasad Mishra, who used to accompany us to the *ghat*. Before taking bath we did exercises and were trained in wrestling by *guru* Kamta Prasad Mishra. At the time of bathing we regularly performed Surya *puja* and Ganga *puja*. Then we would go to Vishwanath temple and other small shrines to perform *puja* and *darshan*. As a routine, we recited the Gayatri *mantra* and *Shivastotra* for two hours continuously at the Golden Vishwanath temple. Again at the Annapurna temple we used to participate in *puja arati*.

From 8 a.m. to 10 a.m. we had to sit in our class room with our *guru*, Pt. Ganga Prasad Tripathi, who was a noted Vedic of Kashi in those days. There was no wooden furniture for the students; every one of us had a mat made of *kusha*, believed to be sacred grass. Our *guru* sat on a lion-skin.

After that we had to participate in the *Bhoga arati* in the Rama temple just beside the Annapurna temple, where we were provided food. Though we were sent there simply to watch the performance but at times we also assisted the priests in managing the *puja* articles, by ringing the *jharighanta*, blowing the *shankha*, making *arati* and so on. Just after finishing the Bhoga arati of Lord Rama we sat in a queue on the mats in the varandah of the kitchen to get Balabhog (meal). But before taking meals all of us had to perform *sandhya vandana* nearly for half an hour.

Again in the evening we had to perform *sandhya vandana* after taking bath in the Ganges and sit to study with our *guru* in the same way.

I studied in Kashi for about 12 years. Of this period, I was in the Brahmacharya Ashram for five years continuously. During my five years' stay at Kashi two of my grandfathers passed away. However I was not allowed to leave the Ashram and visit home owing to the strict rules and regulations of the Ashrama.

After completing the Prathama course I gave *dakshina* to my *guru* and returned home with my father. I was then 15. In the meantime, my real grandfather also died of cholera. On account of his death, the whole family affairs were upset. The property was divided among all the sons of my grandfathers.

For two years I remained at home and assisted my father and brother in agriculture. At the age of 18 I was married to a girl of 13, from village Morahaviya, in district Arrah. My wife was illiterate. Though I could not get any cash in dowry but in kind I got brass utensils, ox, buffalow, etc. As I showed no interest at all in agriculture, two years after my marriage I was asked by my father to continue further studies. I again went to Kashi and was admitted in part one of the Shastriya course.

Along with my study I started my career as a *karmakandi* and it became a source of income. Just after the completion of my Shastriya examination in two years I again returned to my native village owing to the illness of my father. After three years of prolonged illness he died. Within a yeaı after the death of my father, there were quarrels between my wife and *Bhabhi.* And finally I got myself separated dividing all the ancestoral properties. I had no interest in agriculture so I again returned to Kashi for engaging myself in *Karmakandi* profession.

Meanwhile in 1956 the Harijan entry into the golden temple of Vishwanath took place and a new Vishwanath temple was built by the orthodox Hindus led by Karpatri, a recorded Sanskritist in Banaras.

In October 1961 Swami Karpatri listened to my clear pronunciation of the *Vedas*. He was pleased with me and offered me the opportunity to serve as a priest in the Naya temple of Vishwanath on the fixed salary of Rs. 40 per month, including fooding and lodging. And since then I stopped going to other sacred shrines of Kashi to perform sacred performance either for myself or for others.

As regards the Harijan entry into the Golden Vishwanath temple, I believe that it was not a good thing on the part of our Hindu society. Though before the construction and joining there as a priest in Naya temple of Vishwanath I had to go into the golden temple for my professional work but I was not doing that whole-heartedly. I had always in my mind that the scared *linga* of Vishwanath was polluted. Since my appointment in the Naya temple of Vishwanath I had never gone there till now, for I believe it polluted.

I believe that 'sacred' is such a thing which has got its significance in our Vedic codes and *suchiachar* and the 'profane' is whatever is contrary to the 'sacred'. For example, the *Vedas* have not left room for the accommodation of the *Shudra* to participate in any *yajna* and that is why it would be profane if it is done like that. Similarly our *suchiachar* is also the traditional mode of handling all the spheres of life.

I believe that our traditional religious outlook is fast changing. For example, even the Brahmin community is adopting modern dress, food habits, etc., as is done by other castes. The prevailing calamities, viz. earthquakes, famines, droughts, etc., are the result of our Brahmanic social disorder.

I believe that every living being is reborn again and again, and this cycle does not end till the being gains *moksha* (salvation).

I believe that modernization has mostly affected the religious sanctity, purity and fervour of Hindu religion. For instance, our Naya Vishwanath temple is the most sacred where *puja* is performed in the puıe shastric *paddhati* but it has usually a small gathering of the worshippers. But the Golden Vishwanath temple without having Shastric purity attracts a lot of people.

Life-history No. 8

Name :	A.S.D.
Age :	25
Sex :	Male
Caste :	Gujarati Brahmin
Sect :	Shaiva
Education :	Student of M.A. (Philosophy)
Profession	Part time priest in Adi Vishwanath Temple.

I was born in Kashi in a Gujarati Brahmin family. My father Shiva Shankar Dase had a printing press at Lusau. As I was the first issue of my parents, and therefore was very much loved by all the family membeıs. Later on I had two brothers and a sister younger to me. I often quarrelled with my brothers because they teased our sister. My grandfather S.N. Dase was a priest in the Adi Vishwanath temple and so lived in a house within the temple precincts, provided by the temple-owner, Maharaja of Jaipur. Though Lord Vishwanath was the cheif deity at my house, I was more attracted towards Lord Krishna's image with flute in his hands.

At the age of six, I was admitted in Saraswat Khatri Vidyalaya of Varanasi and after studying there for a year I was transferred to a school managed by Nagar Mahapalika. In the school I was considered one of the best students of my class. At home my father coached me in Sanskrit and Mathematics. He often tried to teach me Sanskrit songs from the *Ramayana* and the *Gita*. I liked this rhythmic poetry and sung them and other devotional songs in sad tunes.

After getting through my fifth class in first division, I was admitted to a Junior School at Dasashwamedha. There in my eighth class I took distinction in Mathematics, English and Sanskrit and got the fourth position in the Banaras District. However, it was sad that only a week after these results were published, i.e. on August 10, 1962 my father expired from cancer. The whole family was shocked with grief ; particularly my grandfather who almost went mad.

After the expiry of my father the financial condition of my family became adverse. Things got from bad to worse and I developed such inferiority that I began to avoid my friends. We had another great shock just two months after father's death; my grandfather also expired from a heart attack. That left the family dependent upon my widowed mother, who could neither earn nor go out begging. That left the whole burden on my young shoulders as I was the eldest male member of the family.

I thought of selling my printing press so that with the money so received I could run my household for some time. But in that also I was cheated by my relatives and got a meagre amount. Another trouble faced us when the Devasthan Vibhaga of Rajasthan Government appointed a priest in the temple of Adi Vishwanath to fill in the vacancy caused by my grand-father's death. After my grand-father's death I had been performing *puja path* in the temple. So now I staked my claim for the post of the priest and appealed that my family's survival depended on it. In this situation, a friend of my late father helped me and used his influence to get me the job. But the income from the temple was not sufficient to provide us sustenence, i.e. fooding, clothing, education etc.

Fortunately, I again got the first position in my class and besides my freeship, books, etc., I was granted Rs. 35 per month from the Poor Boys' Fund of my school. I was very much interested in debating, drama, dance, music and wrestling. As a student of class XI, I got several prizes and certificates of merit. Once I took part in an inter-school Sanskrit Sabha and won the first prize. I also received prizes in an essay competition on religion, and for outstanding acting in the roll of a girl in a play, *Sakuntala*. But in spite of my good results and encouragements from my teachers I was very much frustrated due to my adverse financial condition and family problems.

In 1964 I took admission in P.U.C. in the Banaras Hindu

University and passed it in the first division. But my family condition by now was so miserable that I made up my mind to give up studies. But again my teachers restrained me and got me admitted in B.Sc. I started taking tuitions of High School and Junior class students and through this income I maintained my family as well as continued the education of my younger brothers and the sister.

During this period I went through a book, *Sant Gyaneshwar* by Gyaneshwari. I was so touched by it that I renounced every thing and became a *sannyasi.* I also left my house one day. During my absence from the house my widowed mother started performing the daily rituals of the temple.

As a *sannyasi,* I travelled to Mathura. I tried many ways to obtain peace of mind but could not. So I returned to Banaras. My teachers rebuked me very much and advised to resume my studies. I had already lost one year. So I appeared for the B.Sc. examination the next year, but as ill luck would have it, I again fell into trouble. One of my younger brothers was accused in a theft case and I was also implicated along with him.

These troubles, coming one after the other, depressed and frustrated me so much that I thought of worshipping goddess Durga and seek her patronisation to get rid of bad luck. Daily I used to recite three *adhyayas* (chapters) of *Durga Saptashati.* This helped me to strengthen my will power again. It was again perhaps as a result of my Durga worship that I became free of the suit on 15 August 1971. With Her grace I also passed B.Sc. examination in the first division.

Even after I was free of troubles I could not get over my sadness. To obtain mental relief I decided to learn music. So I went to Pt. Jyotin Bhattacharya, a noted musician in Kashi with the intention of becoming his disciple and learn *sarod* from him. Punditji took pity on me and accepted me as his disciple. Since that day I became wedded to music and learned to play flute, harmonium, *sarod* and violin. I practised daily at my home as well as in the temple whenever I found time and a peaceful atmosphere.

Though I have been assigned the duty of performing daily *puja arati* of Lord Vishwanath in the Adi Vishwanath temple, but owing to my heavy preoccupation with teaching private students, learning music and attending my M.A. class, I often miss the duties.

Complimentary Questions

I have a great faith in our religious ideas, codes, customs and manners because I believe that God exists and governs all the ups and downs of life.

Professionally I am not interested a bit in the priesthood, rather wish to invest my brain in some literary or intellectual pursuit. In my opinion, priesthood is only for those who want to remain idle or have no other choice of employment. Second reason of my disinterest in priesthood lies in that I do not get same respect through it as my father and grandfather commanded.

As regards the treatment of the 'sacred' is concerned I feel it is not a substance or a thing, it is just a quality which can only be felt. For example, even though I remain in the temple precincts I do not feel that the *nirmal* (articles offered upon the *linga* of Lord Vishwanath) are sacred material and that is why I do not mind treading on it. On the other hand, for a pilgrim or devotee, these are sacred.

Life-history No. 9

Name :	S.N.P.
Age :	50
Sex :	Male
Caste :	Brahmin (Mahapatra)
Occupation :	Mrityu Sanskara performance.

I, Shri Sambhunath Pandey, working as a Mahabrahmin on both Manikarnika and Harishchandra ghats, am the son of Biharilal Pandey. My grandfather who was Jageo Maharaj had three wives. My father had five brothers, but three of them expired, and so now he has only two brothers, and two sisters. I had a sister Pritidevi who was married to Rudrakant Pandey of Lucknow. She is not alive now.

Education

I was a student of Harishchandra School. I started my

education at the age of six and continued till I was 16, and had reached my ninth class. Thereafter I was not interested in study. However I learnt from my father and other familymembers how to assist and guide pilgrims and local devotees, i.e. performing *shraddh*. Besides this I was interested in physical exercise.

Married Life

When I was 17 years old I was married to Shyamjani Devi of Barka village of Arrah District. Since then I have got four sons—Bijoy Kumar, Raj Kumar, Ram Kumar and Deo Kumar. Bijoy Kumar has been married to Urmila in District Azamgarh. Raj Kumar has also been married to Sushila of Babhua in Arrah District. Ram Kumar has recently been married in Gaya District. I also have three daughters, Laxmi, Maya and Bachi.

Professional Life and Cultural Knowledge

A person who conducts the ritual *mrityu sanskara* is known as Mahabrahmin. I do not conduct the ritual of Mrityu Sanskara for the castes like Dom, Chamar and Bhangi.

There are three types of *shraddh* mainly:

(*a*) *Panchandan*: In this *shraddh karma* shoes, umbrella, cow, bed and gold are offered.
(*b*) *Vriti*: In this type of *shraddh*, four calves, one dhenu cow, one bull, horse and elephant, etc. are offered.
(*c*) *Narayani*: This type of *shraddh* is performed for a person who has died accidently.

Pindadan

It is a kind of ritual for the dead. Articles required at the time of Pindadan are *akshat*, *dhoopbatti*, earthen lamp, *ghee*, *kusha*, wool, *bhangrorya* (leaves), etc.

A pindi is made of the following material: flour of *jau*, *kheer*, etc. A white flower is necessary at the time of *pind* offering.

Upto *das karma* one pind is offered every day but on the day of *das karma* ten *pindis* are offered. On the day of *ekadasa*, one pind is offered.

When any one dies on the day of panchak, five pindas are

offered to the dead to relieve the dead from *ashauch*. The performer gifts us things like a cot, *chadar*, utensils, food-grains, etc., in accordance with his financial position. Unless such a donation is made, the *shraddh karma* is considered incomplete.

Religious Life and Knowledge

I regularly take bath in the Ganges, I do Ganga *puja* by offering *arghya* to mother Ganga. I visit other temples such as Vishwanath, Annapurna, etc. irregularly and offer flowers and Gangajal.

It is said that if pindis are offered in Kashi for any dead, he gets *moksha*. I consider *shmashan* pure where Lord Shankar resides and smears his body with the ashes of the dead. Kashi is situated on his *trishul*.

The people of different linguistic groups have their different *mahapatra* such as the Bengali, the Gujarati and so on, have their respective *mahapatras*.

Miscellaneous Questions

Pap : To oppress is *pap*.
Punya : To help is *punya*.
Sacred wood : *Bel*, *chandan*, *tulsi* are all sacred wood.

Life-history No. 10

Name :	R.N.S.
Age :	48
Sex :	Male
Caste :	Brahmin
Place :	Malda district (Bengal)
Profession :	*aughar* (Ascetic)

Personal Observations

Sri Rabindranath Sharma is an *aughar* who resides at Manikarnika ghat. Actually he may be called a semi-*aughar* because he lives with his wife. She herself is an *augharni*. Thus he leads both the *garhasthys* (family life) as well as *aughori*.

He wears *gerua* (ochre) *vastra* (clothes) and the garland of

Rudraksh on his neck. He has long hair, beard and moustache. He wears *kara* (iron bangle) on his wrist.

He was sitting on a pavement and weaving broad and thick *par* with silken threads which helps him in earning money for subsistence. When I approached him, he seemed under the influence of *ganja*. His eyes were rolling and red.

During the course of conversation he used many English words and he understood English words well. He also knew Urdu and Bangla languages.

He did not like to reveal the secrets of the knowledge and methods of performing *shmashan puja* to revitalize his *aughar kritya*, which he does on every amavasya.

I, Shri Rabindranath Sharma, am an ordinary man, was born in the Malda district of West Bengal. When I was six, I was sent to school. After completing my study, I joined service in P.W.D. and worked there for 20 years.

During my service period I came in contact with a *siddha purush* Shri Haran Chandra Mukherjee of Malda district. He is 80 years old now. He has many disciples like me. Twenty years ago I became his disciple. At that time I heard that a king of Bengal was himself a *siddha purush* who used to worship Bhagvati in an underground house covered with a slab of stone. After sometime the king had a son. It is said that the slate had a mystic power and could be lifted only by the king's relatives. Once the king's son, when he was travelling in a train, saw a dream in which he saw an *aughar* who was ahead of him while he was following him. By chance my Guru was travelling in a first class compartment and that king's son saw him in the compartment. He was surprised to see my Guru as his face tallied with the *aughar* he had seen in the dream. Seeing him, my guru smiled and said, "Do you remember me. I had met you in the dream."

The very young lad knew that he was to follow the guru. He became a disciple of my guru. My Guru told him to bring him the slab and accompanied him to that place. A truck was arranged to bring that slab. The very boy lifted the slab easily and loaded it in the truck but the truck was broken. Again a tractor was arranged and thus the very slab was brought to my guru's ashram, named as "Shree Shree Satyapitha Ashram". This story I came to know from other disciples. I have also seen the slab guruji had brought because of its mystic power.

Before becoming a disciple I was married. My wife is still alive. My wife is also with me and she is also the disciple of Haran Chandra Mukherjee. (She is of dark complexion, wearing red cloth and Rudraksh on her neck. She has been seen begging.) I have no issue from her.

I had developed my interest in *aughari* because of my contact with persons of similar interest. The world of *aughari* is full of mystries. It is the way to know the mystry of *Abadikhana*.

I have visited many *siddha pithas* such as Gangasagar, Badrinath, Dwarka, Prayag, Vindhyachal, Kamru-Kamachchha Calcutta, Tarasiddha pitha (Bengal) and so on. I am a flying bird and thus do not remain very long at one place.

Religious Activities

Whenever I get time I visit temples, *kunds*, and *ghats* of Varanasi, such as Vishwanath (B.H.U.), Naya and Adi. Besides these, I have visited Laxmi kund, Durga kund, Sarnath, Dasashwamedh ghat, Manikarnika ghat.

I take bath in the Ganges. I daily worship Kali for three hours: One and a half hours in the morning and one and a half hours at night. In the day hours I weave bags to earn money.

CULTURAL KNOWLEDGE

Manikarnika Shmashan

This *shmashan* is an Akhand *shmashan*. I mean to say that dead bodies are cremated there for all around twenty-four hours. It never remains idle without dead bodies. That is why it is said as *Mahashmashan*.

The characteristic of this *shmashan* is that *samadhi* can be achieved here soon and easily. Once it happened that Swami Ramkrishna with his disciple Mathur was passing by boat through Manikarnika. He was surprised that he could easily achieve *samadhi* here. He saw with insight that the *Mahakala* recites *tarak mantra* in the ears of the dead and that is why the dead get *moksha* after being cremated here.

Shmashan

Shmashan may be conceived in terms of *Abadikhana* and

Barbadi-khana as used in Urdu language. By Barbadikhana I mean the world where men fulfil their worldly desires and suffer from worries, diseases, temptation. Actually they are gradually destroyed. They are not engaged in searching for the ultimate reality.

By *Abadikhana* I mean *shmashan*. Men can cremate their dead but not their shape of souls. Buddhist, Muslim and Christians—all believe in the formless soul but not the sanatani.

Shmashan is the most suitable place for *aghoris* where they can get *samadhi* well and vitalise the *shmashan*. The *aghoris* want to keep aloof from worldly desires and the *shmashan* is the place where they can do so as well as feel the reality and truth of life. For example, whenever you come with a dead body to cremate, you feel yourself vacuum i.e. everything of the world seems useless and meaningless to you and to retain the sense of meaninglessness the *aghoris* take the help of *shmashan* for acquiring *Siddhi*.

Siddhi

Truly speaking I have not acquired a single *siddhi* because of the lack of economic help. To do *puja* for getting *siddhi* requires a number of things, i.e. articles used in puja which I cannot afford.

I visit the *shmashan* on each *amavasya* and use *agurbatti* and *dhoop*. I cannot tell you the methods of puja because it is secret. To do any *kriya* depends on the mood of the performer.

As I can hardly mention my food and other things I weave silken *par* to earn money. You must have come to know that in *aghori kriya* it requires wine, meat and cooked food which I cannot get. Food is also an important factor for *aghoris*. There are eight type of *siddhis* but any man has not acquired *ashtasiddhi*.

Ghost

Those souls who do not get *gati* move in the sky (air world) for getting proper place and they disturb the human beings. Those souls are known as ghosts. They are formalities and are regarded as *Updevta*. To pacify and to control those devil souls the Aghorism has been developed. The Lord of those ghosts is Bhootnath (i.e. the master of the ghosts) who resides on the Shmashanghat.

Moksha

By moksha I mean dhruv i.e. neither death nor life. It is said that when a person dies with his will, he gets *Moksha*. To die when any one is in *samadhi* also provides *moksha*. Actually *moksha* means to vanish into this infinity or attachment with the ultimate reality.

It is true that a number of pilgrims come to die in Kashi for attaining *moksha* but it has also been seen that a person who is ill gets cured here and when he visits his own native place he dies there.

Siddhpitha Visited

Besides Kashi, I have visited Birbhum where there is a place named as Rampurhat of Bashishtha period. There is an *aughar* Bamakhepa. Bhog is not offered to Devi unless any dead is brought there. Mahatmas or *aghoris* eat flesh of the skull or use skull as pot for taking food or wine. That place is of great importance.

CULTURAL KNOWLEDGE

Miscellaneous

Pap : Ashuddh bhavna is *pap*.
Punya : Shuddh bhavna is *punya*.
Life : What we see is life.
Death : What we do not see in death.

28.8.73 : Previously there were enough facilities for *aghoris*. They were donated money by persons. Nutritious food was available. The monetary donations helped us in fulfilling our aim and thus there were many *aughars* who acquired mystic power.

Present

But these days we do not get nutritious food. Even for *agarbatti* I have to pay 5 annas and 10 p. for a good *agarbatti*. The *tapasya* requires good food because four *asanas*, *pranayam*, *nyas kumbh* and *rechak* cannot be done without nutritious food. And this is the only reason that a *siddha purush* is rarely found these days.

Next year, i.e. in the year 1974, I will join the *kumbha mela* where I will meet my Guruji. Next year I will get a certificate of my examination from my *aughar* guru.

Kapalkriya

This *kapalkriya* has an interesting story. It is said that when Britrasur wanted to capture the kingdom of God Indra, Indra and his colleagues were upset.

So all of them wanted to meet Rishi Dadhichi. Indra reached in disguise but the Muni recognised him and asked the reason of his visit. Indra told his worry to him and asked for his spine from which a weapon was to be made. Muni accepted his demand. But he said, "You rub my body with salt and a cow will lick it. And Indra did accordingly. The Muni went into samadhi, i.e. he attached himself to the Brahma. The cow licked Muni's blood and then also the flesh, leaving only the bony structure of his body. From his bone Indra made a weapon, i.e. Vajra to kill the demon. Although the flesh and spine of the Muni were removed from this body but he was not yet dead. His *prana* was in his brain. So Indra did *kapalkriya* for Muni's *sadgati*. Since then, this ritual is performed.

Tantra Vidya

The tantra vidya is not related with *shmashan*. There are two broad categories of saints and sages : (*a*) Vampanthi and (*b*) Dampanthi.

(a) *Vampanthi* : The sages who are associated with *shmashan* and who drink wine come under the Vampanthi marg, such as *aughar*.

(b) *Dampanthi* : Those sages who are not associated with *shmashan*, but have acquired mystic power, are called *Dampanthi*. They never take wine. Tantrics, Vaishnava saints, etc., are Dampanthi.

Sacred myth about Aghoris

Kharabdas

Baba Kharabdas was a *siddha purush* of Varanasi. He used

to mediate in the water. Once a British man came and asked him to come out of the water. But instead of coming out he abused him. His secretary who was an Indian jailed him.

In the jail the prisoners had to turn a *chakki* (hand grind). Kharabdas Baba told the prisoners not to do so. It happened that the wheels started turning of their own. This miraculous news reached the jailor and also the secretary. Coming to him both of them bowed before him and apologised. The *samadhi* of Kharabdas is at Ramnagar (near Bedbayas).

Keenaram

Baba Keenaram was a famous *aughar* of Varanasi. He was Rambhakt. For 20 years he served God but he could not find him. Once he thought to take wine. As soon as he lifted his arm to drink, God held his hand. Keenaram said to God, "I cannot leave it as it has brought me in contact with you and thus this wine is my Guru."

Life-History No. 11

Name :	G.P.
Age :	38
Sex :	Male
Caste :	Nai (Barber)
Profession :	Barber

Personal Observation

He wore dirty white clothes. He had failed to maintain a harmonical relationship with Dom of Manikarnika.

Even then he was a clever fellow. He shaved the heads of those persons who came there to offer fire to their dead. He took money on Saloon rates and in this way he earned Rs. 4 or 5 daily.

He was in interaction with *mahapatras* but he was called on by them whenever he was required. He believes that the money earned at Manikarnika should also be offered to God otherwise it would harm him. That was his personal attitude towards the money of the *murdaghat*. He did not think good to use all the money without offering a part to God. But he earned money at the Manikarnika ghat because customers were easily available to him.

He informed that the *antyesthi kriya* is similar in all castes of Hindus but variation is found because of the economic status.

I am a barber of Manikarnika. I shave the heads of those persons who come to cremate their dead. I sit on this pavement just in the west corner of the cremation ground because I could not adjust with the Choudhuri, the owners of the Manikarnika.

Education-Life

I was born in 1934. The name of my father was Shiv Nath Thakur from Laxmi Muhal. I was sent to school at the age of 6 years and got education only upto the first class in a school of Piyari. I can read Hindi well. I left the school because I was totally disinterested in education.

Profession

At the age of 12 I adopted the profession of barbery. It took me a year to learn this art of shaving.

On the professional level I used to visit among the Baniya, the Khatri and the Kayastha. These three castes are my *jajmans*. I do not visit the house of the Dom, the Chamar and the Dhobi because I am not in interaction with them. I accompany the *mahapatra* whenever I am required by any *jajman* whose relative has expired.

I accompany the dead of the *jajman* to the *ghat*, shave off the head of the fire-giver and help them in burning their articles required in cremation. When the cremation is finished I go to my house where I am given a lota filled with water to wash hands and feet.

In case of the Agrawals and other castes the dead is washed and is anointed with *ghee* and *til*-oil. Since man's soul is outside the body, it should be brought on the *shmashan ghat* to be cremated.

Next day, the Agrawals offer milk and black *tils* to the dead where he was cremated.

On the tenth day, *shraddh karma* is performed. *Shraddh karma* is performed either on the third, seventh or the tenth day of the death. On that day, I visit the house of the *jajman* to shave their heads and to cut their nails. The *mahapatra* is required to perform the *shraddh karma*. He is offered the following articles:

(a) *Khatia*, *dari*, *takiya*, *dhoti* (must), *chadar*
(b) *Sidha*, *Dal*, *Chawal*, *Namak*, Vegetables (green)
(c) Spices: *Jeera*, *Mirchi*, *Haldi*, *Dhaniya*, *Garam Masala*
(d) Lantern with Kerosene oil : *til*-oil, Mustard oil, Secut, Fountain-pen
(e) Utensils : *Thali*, *Batna* (kettle)-2, *Katora*, *lota* and so on including money.

It is generally believed that all these articles given to the *mahapatra* will be gained by the dead.

Since I also assist the *mahapatra* in *shraddh-karma*, I am liable to get commission at the rate of two annas per rupee from the *Mahapatra*.

The same method is followed by each caste I have visited. You may find variation in the performance of the *shraddh karma* only due to the variation in economic status.

Besides this I also visit the house of Jajmans on the occasion of other sacred performances such as on *Mundan*, *Janeo* and *Vivah*.

I have professional interaction with *mahapatras*.

Marriage-Life

I was 16 years old when I was married to a girl in the Muhalla of Laxmi Muhal of Banaras town. I have two sons and one daughter. I have settled in my wife's family.

Religious Life

There is a temple of Sankataji (Santoshimata) on the Scindia ghat. I visit there on each Friday. I believe in Her that she listens to my distress. I also worship her with a view to offer some amount of income which I earn on the Manikarnika ghat. It is my belief that the money earned on this *ghat* cannot be utilized unless first offered to Her. To take money on the *murda ghat* is not good.

I do Brahman bhoj early in the month of Ashwin when the *pinda* is offered to my parents by the *ghatia*. At that time both the *ghatia* and the *tirthapurohit* are invited for meal for the satisfaction of the *pitar's atma.*

I also visit Vishwanath (G), Annapurna, Durgaji, Sankatmochan, Rammandir (Lanka), Kalabhairava and Dhundhiraj occasionally.

I bathe in the Ganges daily. When I wake up in the morning I remember Bhole Nath, Sankatamai and Ganeshji for my good day.

Satyanarayan *puja* is also performed when any *manata* is satisfied.

Whenever I get time I visit Gyanvapi occasionally to listen the *katha.* I have also visited Panchkosi three times uptil now. I know that the area from Varuna to Assi is the sacred geography of Kashi.

I have visited the sacred places outside Kashi such as Ayodhya, Vindhyachal, Allahabad on jajman's work. I visit Vindhyachal yearly. I visit the sacred centres of Kashi with a religious point of view although I do not know the methods of the sacred performances.

Complementaries

Life : I cannot explain what life is but I know that a man lives here to sow and to reap.

Death : It is a *niyama* of the nature and every one has to die.

Birth : It is a *niyama* of the nature. A man takes birth to reap.

Pap : To trouble others and to take advantage illegally of others is *pap.*

Punya : To donate for others (other persons such as beggars) is *punya.* A man is *punyatma* (pious) who does not care for anything and what he gets he eats.

Sacred wood : The wood of *Am, Bel* and Chandan are supposed to be sacred.

Manikarnika : The *shmashan* Manikarnika is profane because the dead are cremated here. I do not understand Moksha but I know that a man gets return for his deeds.

Important events : I do not have any idea of the important events in my life.

Electric Crematorium : It is a good thing for the jajmans

but it would affect the income of other poor persons who work on this *ghat*.

Life-history No. 12

Name :	K.N.S.
Age :	25
Sex :	Male
Caste :	Rajput
Sub-caste :	Raghuvanshi
Clan :	Bharadwaj
Sect :	Shaiva
Profession :	Sells the articles of mortuary rites at Manikarnika

Family Background

I am a son of late Sri T.N.S. of Brahmanal near Manikarnika. I was born in Banaras in 1947. I have two sisters, Sitadevi and Gitadevi who have been married with Babu J.S. and F.S. I have also one younger brother whose name is R.N.S. B.N.S. is the eldest brother of my father. G.S. is his son. Really my real grandfather belonged to Daranagar of Varanasi but my fictitious grandfather N.S. was the shopkeeper of Brahmanal and my father was the adopted son of N.S.

Education

I was a student of Adarsh Seva Inter College. I have read upto the ninth class but I could not pass. I left my school in 1967. I am unmarried uptil now.

Primary Profession

My primary profession is to sell the articles for mortuary rites and my livelihood is based upon it. This profession which I have adopted is hereditary and in continuation for the last 52 years. I am doing this profession since my childhood and I like it because my father used to do it. Usually I sell the articles required for the mortuary rites but in my absence other persons of my house look after it. I bring the articles for mortuary rites from Chowk Market.

In my caste, the dead body is prepared as follows :

(*i*) If a woman is alive and her husband has died, the husband's dead body is covered with white cloth.

(*ii*) If a woman is dead and her husband is alive, the dead body of the woman is covered with *chunri* coloured in red and yellow, bangles and vermilion *(suhag)*.

(*iii*) If a widow dies, her body is covered with white cloth only.

(*iv*) If a widower dies, his body is covered with Pitambari.

The persons who come to buy the articles for mortuary rites, take—**(a)** *Chandan*, **(b)** *Ghee*, **(c)** *Raal* (a kind of thing helpful in burning the pyre), **(d)** *Dasang*, **(i)** *til* (*Sesame*), **(ii)** *Jau*, **(iii)** Rice, **(iv)** *Bhojpatra*, **(v)** *Makhana*, **(vi)** *Khaad* (Panch-meva).

All these articles are mixed with *ghee*. But these articles are purchased only when one has to perform shraddha (Devotion) for the dead. In other cases, both the poor and the rich purchase the articles which are required according to our tradition. They buy a pitcher having *tulsi* wood, black *til*, *kardhan* (red thread), a bundle of *dasang*. The cost of the pitcher with *dasang* is not more than 50 paise.

Kardhan is tied by a person who performs the ritual of *agni* giving to the dead or else the *kardhan* is thrown on the pyre.

The fire-giver, first of all gets his head shaved, then takes bath in the Ganges and wears a new white cloth. If he has worn a *janeo* (sacred thread) he puts it off and wears a new one. After that he ties *kardhan*, otherwise he throws it on the pyre. Then the fire-giver goes to the Choudhury to take fire from him. When the pyre is burnt to ashes, the relics of the dead are thrown into the Ganges. The pyre is then cooled by pouring water a few times with a pitcher.

After that the pitcher is filled with water and the figure '90' is written on the cooled ashes of the pyre. This signifies the belief that the dead person lived on the earth for 90 years. The pitcher is then carried by the fire-giver on his left shoulder and is thrown backside. The pitcher gets broken and the person says :

"Ghara phuta nata tuta."

Then the *shava yatris* and the fire-giver go to other *ghat*. First of all, the fire-giver takes bath and then the rest of the persons follow him. After taking bath each person offers black *til* and water five times to the Ganges. This ritual is done to abandon the dead for ever. When the ritual performers visit their respective homes, they eat a little black-pepper to purify themselves.

I pay Rs. 2.50 per month as rent and my income is Rs. 10 per day.

Secondary Profession

My secondary profession is brokerage of gold and silver which I do with my brother-in-law.

Professional Association

I have neither professional interaction nor social interaction with the Dom/Tantrik/Mahapatra/Aghoris but previously we used to pay commission to them and they were in interaction. This has been stopped because these days number of shops has increased.

I do not have any idea about them so I cannot tell you anything about them.

Religious Life

I remember Bholenath and Gangamai daily early in the morning. I do not perform any puja and do not take bath in the river Ganges daily but do that only occasionally. I do not take any interest in religious activities. Rest of the time I devote in my business. I remember Ram while I go to sleep.

I pay subscription to the Ram Lila Committee of Manikarnika once a year but I am not a member of this Committee.

I have visited *tirthas* such as Vishwanath (golden), Annapurna, Vishwanath (B.H.U.), Bharat Mata Mandir, Mangleshwar Mahadeva, Sankatamochan, Sankata Mandir, Atma Vishweshwar, Santoshi Mata, Sarnath and Ramnagar and also Vindhyachal which is outside Kashi many times uptil now. But I visit the local *tirthas* occasionally.

I believe in all the *tirthas* of Kashi being a follower of the traditional outlook but mainly in Shankar that He helps me in any kind of work.

There are 33 crores Devatas in Kashi and the importance of Kashi can be cited as :

Kashi Dhundham,
Prayag Mundam,
Gaya Pindam.

I know that Kashi is situated on the *trisul* of Shankar as is mentioned in the *Shiva Puran*.

There are 162 ghats and the important *tirthas* of Kashi are—Vishwanath (golden), Kalabhairava, Sankatamochan, Assi (Tulsi ghat), Hanuman Mandir, Kashi Karvat, Nilkanthe-shwar Mahadev (Nilkanthi Mohalla), Pataleshwar (Bengali-tola), Tilbhandeshwar because they have become popular.

It is said about Kalabhairav that He is the chief of gods because once when the soldiers of Aurangzeb invaded the temple and wanted to destroy it, a number of black bees attacked his soldiers and the soldiers fled from there and could not destroy the temple.

I often go to listen to the *katha* of Gyanvapi. I visit Manikarnika Kund once a year. In my house Satyanarayan Puja is regularly performed.

The area falling within Assi to Varuna is Kashi.

I have read Gangalahari edited by Pundit Vishwanath Prasad Mishra and there you will find the description of the ghats. I have also read another religious text, *Kashika*, written by Kashi Naresh. There you will find the description of the *shmashan*.

Number of poems have also been written on Shankar by Munshi Kavi of Banaras.

World-View

Death : Death is a phase of life and a man takes birth again even if he is cremated at Manikarnika according to the deeds done in his life.

Life : I cannot tell you about life.

Pap : By *pap* I mean a bad deed.

Punya : By *punya* I mean a good deed.

Past and Present : I know that previously number of shops here were less in number than these days.

Electric Crematorium

Once the Municipal authorities decided to fit in an Electric Crematorium at Manikarnika but I feel that it is not good because our traditional method of cremation will be ended. The *pandas* of Kashi also opposed this idea.

I feel that a man after death should not be burnt in an oven like an Electric Crematorium. The dead body should not be burnt in a closed box.

Sacred Wood

The woods of *Bel*, *Aam*, *Plash* and *Chandan* are supposed to be sacred. The woods of *Pipal* are used in cremating person who belongs to the Marwari Caste.

You know that the whole of Kashi is a *shmashan* and Manikarnika is a part of that whole. Manikarnika is sacred. Previously the cremation places were at Harha Mohalla (Harkeshwar Mahadev) and Thana Chowk. The remains of dead bodies were found there when those places were dug up.

Life-history No. 13

Name :	B.S.
Age :	30
Sex :	Male
Caste :	Brahmin
Sub-caste :	Saruparidube, Mushar
Education :	High School
Primary Occupation :	Shopkeeping (of articles for mortuary-rites)
Secondary Occupation :	ghatiya of Jalasen ghat.

He has good knowledge of the Mrityu-Sanskara, as he dictated the whole process of *antyesthi* as well as the importance of each *karma* to some extent. He outlined the process of *antyesthi* of his own caste and informed that among all Hindus, the same process goes on. He also dictated the names of the valuable books for textual reference such as *Garur Puran*, *Reeveet Shraddh*, *Godan Veedhan* and *Pretmanjari* (*Pretmanjari* depicts the wandering and action of the *pret*, dead soul after life, etc.).

He also dictated that there are five types of shraddh such as (i) *Pakshik Shraddh*, (ii) *Masik Shraddh*, (iii) *Shashthamashik Shraddh*, (iv) *Trayamashik Shraddh*, and (v) *Varshik Shraddh*.

His shop is full of the articles for mortuary rites, such as sarees, both light red and red with shining wires, pitambari, earthen pots of which the upper portions were painted with red lines, and a number of boxes with the wood of *chandan*, *dhoop*, bundles of white threads, betel-nuts, white clothes, *agarbatti* and so on.

Family background

I was born in 1942. I have my personal house at Jalasenghat donated by some Maharaja to my forefathers. I passed my High School examination in First division having distinction in three subjects—Mathematics, Sanskrit and English. But after the death of my father my economic condition began ot deteriorate. So in 1960 I adopted this profession of selling the articles for mortuary rites which I learnt through observation and from contact with a person of my neighbourhood.

I do not like this profession because I wanted to be a good businessman but due to economic crisis, and unavailability of good service, I have to live on this profession because to sell the articles of mortuary-rites for a Brahmin like me is a mean work from the social point of view and it has lowered my prestige in my caste group.

My nephew who is 12 years old sits at the shop in my absence.

I bring the articles for mortuary rites from different market centres.

I pay Rs. 15 as rent to the owner of this house. My daily income is also Rs. 15.

I have no professional interaction with *mahapatras*/Doms/ Nais but I pay 10% to them if they bring any person to take the articles for mortuary rites.

The articles which are used in mortuary rites have no caste-variation but variation due to the economic factor. The names of the articles may be listed as below :

(a) *Kafan*
(b) *Dasang—jau, til, chawal, ghee, bhojpatra, panchameva.*
(c) Ashtagandh —*devdar, chandan, aguru, dhoop, ghee, kapoor, karayal* (Ral or Dhoona).
(d) Pitcher tied with red threads.

Secondary—My traditional profession is *pandagiri*. My forefathers had been donated a temple named *Kumar Bhairava* of Kashi khand attached with a building of Jalasen ghat. Jalasen ghat is under my ownership. Previously I followed this profession but I could not depend on it because of the less income insufficient to fulfil my economic need. I was constrained to adopt the profession of shopkeeping.

But I have not left my traditional profession. I earn money on my *ghat* when any person comes for *pindadan* and *godan*.

Religious Life

When I wake up in the morning I remember Ganga Mata, Laxmi, Saraswati and observe palms because :

Karagre basate Laxmi, karamadhye Saraswati.
Karamoole sthito Brahma, Prabhate Kar Darshanam.

I also do salutation to the Sun for ten or fifteen minutes every morning. After taking bath in the Ganges on the Jalasen ghat I perform the Sandhya Pooja (i.e. Devarchan) and worship Lord Shankar for 15 minutes. In the day I do my business. In the evening I take bath in the house and remember Shankar. Sometimes I visit the Vishwanath temple for the *arati-darshan*. I take bath in the evening, because to live on the Brahmanal near Manikarnika is not good. I have not constructed any temple but I take care of the temple of Kumar Bhairav donated by a Raja to my forefathers. I do Brahmin Bhoj when any *manata* (wish) is fulfilled. I have worshipped Vishwanath (golden), Durga, Sankatamochan, Shitala (Dasashwamedh), Bhairavanath (Batuk Bhairava), Kalabhairava, Latabhairava, Kumar Bhairava, Hanuman (Assi ghat) and Gopal of Gopal Mandir. I visit Sankatamochan, Durga each Tuesday and Saturday because their visions provide *punya*. I visit Sankata on each Friday and to Shaiyad Ali on Thursday (near Cantt). Besides this I visit *shmashan* daily for *darshan* of Masan baba. In the month of Chaitra, Masan baba is decorated (*shringar* of Masan). It is under the sway of a person who is Kandoo by caste. I pay subscription to the Ram Lila Samiti each year. I worship Ganga daily because

Ganga gangeti yo bruyat, Yojnanam shetaiharapi Mokshte,
Sarv Papebhyoh, Vishnu lok cha gachchati.

And

Vishnupadabja shambhute gangesh tripath gamini
Dharmah praveti vikhyato pap mehar Jahanvi.

It has been also said

Mahadevi Kashi vashonivasini
Sarvaduhkh harodevi Narayani namostotute.

I have visited Calcutta (Kalighat), Vindhyachal, Prayagraj (Allahabad), and Gaya.

I perform *yajna* irregularly on a *punya tithi* to make the gods and goddesses pleased.

The sacred geography of Kashi falls in between Varuna to Assi.

I have read the *Ramayana*, the *Gita*, the *Bhagwat*, the *Markandey Puran*, the *Shiva Puran*, the *Vishnu Puran*, the *Geetawali*, the *Dohavali*, the *Vishnu Shahasranam*, the *Manusmriti*, the *Garur Puran*, and a few portions of the *Rigveda*, the *Yajurveda*, and the *Samveda* and also *Aryasamaj ka Bhakti Darpan* written by Swami Dayananda.

This Kashi city is situated on the *trishul* of Shankar. This whole city has been 'Shankarised' (in each particle, there is the existence of the Lord Shiva). Mother Annapurna exists here and no one can remain hungry in Her grace. This city Kashi is sacred and is bow-shaped. There is not a single house within the area of Assi and Varuna where Shankar does not exist. His *lingas* cannot be counted.

It is said that '*Kashyam marnam mukti*', i.e. one who dies in Kashi achieves the supreme position (*parampada*). Previously Kashi was named as Anandvan where all the gods existed.

There are five important *tirthas* in Kashi. Those are : (*a*) Assi, (*b*) Varuna, (*c*) Panchaganga (meeting place of five rivers). (*d*) Manikarnika (the most important and the greatest *tirtha*), and (*e*) Dasashwamedh (for the performance of the ten Ashvamedh yajnas).

The chief temples of Kashi are Kashi Vishwanath, Naya Vishwanath, Bare Vishwanath (B.H.U.), Adi Vishwanath, Sarang Nath, Sanktamochan, Durga, Batuk, Kalabhairava, Latabhairava, Mrityunjaya Mahadeva, Adi Keshav, Shitala, Annapurna, Chakrapushkarni Kund (it is said that the Lord

Vishnu made it by digging it by His Chakra (Wheel), which later on was named as Manikarnika).

I know that

Na Manikarnika samotirtham
Na Kashi sadrishah puri
Na Visheshwar samo lingam
Nasti brahmand golake.

I do Satyanarayan *puja* on each *purnima* and *shankranti*, because it gives desired results as it is said :

Namovang mansatitah rupayant Shaktye
Adarmadhyant hinay nirgunayatmne.
Sarvesam ad ibhutay bhaktanam artnashne.

I have visited Laxmi Kund, Agastya Kund, Suraj Kund, Ram Kund, Laxman Kund and Bharat Kund. Besides that I have visited Gaibi Kund (near Batuk Bhairava). It is said that if one visits and takes bath in the Kund, it is good for health.

Although I am not a political worker but I support the Congress Government : because it has given us independence.

Complementary Questions

Death

It is said that every creature has a soul of its own. Neither it can be destroyed nor can it be cut. But the emergence of soul out of a body is said to be death.

Birth

After the sexual conjugation between two anti-sex the soul comes to reside in the body formed and the outcome is marked after its delivery. Thus the coming out of a body from a woman's womb is said to be birth.

It is said by Vyas in the volume XVIII of *Purana* that to help others is *punya* and to oppress others is *papa*.

Tulsidas has also cited—

Parahit saris dharma nahi bhai
Parapira sam nahi adhamai

Past and Present

Previously there were three shops at Brahmnal but now it is nine in number. In the past the Dom were paid arbitrarily by the persons who came to cremate but these days they are forced to pay the demanded amount of money.

Electric Crematorium

It is good by that the Municipal authorities wish to instal an Electric Crematorium because then the dirt will be less and less chance of disease. The Ganges will remain clear and the cremator will have to pay less.

Sacred wood

Am, *chandan*, *bel*, *tulsi* and *plash* are the sacred wood.

Manikarnika Sacred or Profane ?

The *shmashan* was made for cleanliness but it is profane.

Belief Associated with Manikarnika

In the olden days, there was a king. He used to disguise himself and roam in his kingdom to learn at first hand the true condition of his subjects. One day he saw a Dom forcing a poor person to pay exorbitantly for cremation. The king sensed the situation and asked the Dom to cremate without vexing the poor. Then the Dom told the king that if you are wealthy you make another *ghat* for cremation. The king came back and asked the pundits where another cremation place should be built. He bought the land from the land-owner at Manikarnika. Since then it has become a cremation ground.

Kapal Kriya

To throw a pitcher filled with water on the burnt portion of a dead in the last is said to be *kapal kriya*.

Samskara Before Death

A person who is to die, first gets performed the Chhaur Karma (gets his hair cut). Then to be able to cross the Vaitami river (as said in the *puranas*), he performs Godan to the Pandas so that his sins are washed. For it is said :

Dharmen hanyate vyadhi
Dharmen hanyate graham,
Dharmen hanyate shatru,
Yato dharmastato jayah.

The dying person is offered *charnodak* of Kashi Vishwanath, Mahamrityunjay and Kalabhairava for his purification and salvation.

The dying person is given place on the *asan* (mat) of *kusha* (in the sitting position) and he is given *Gangajal, tulsi* and *swarna*, etc. (It is believed that gold is the best of all the metals and the person having gold teeth does not tell lie.)

The *Gita* and *Ramcharit Manas* are recited before the dying persons because :

Jasunam bal Shankar Kashi
Det sabahin sab gatiavinashi.

Method of Performance of Jeevit Shraddh

Jeevit Shraddh means the Shraddh done for a living person to benefit him after death. The flour of *jau, til* are used on this occasion. This *shraddh* is performed on the Vedi of soil and spreading Kush on it. For details you must go through *Garur Puran* for the importance of *til* and "*Jeevit Shraddh*" and for its method.

Shraddh After Death

For cremation the following articles are required:

For Male—*Bans* (bamboo), *kari* (stick), rope, *nara* (red thread), 5 yards cloth, etc.

Shringar of the Dead

When an old person dies, he is shrouded with white cloth (kafan), 5 yards in length. Besides this he is also covered with coloured cloth, of red, yellow and blue colours. In case of an old lady, she is enveloped with white cloth, 5 yards in length but *pitambari* is also offered to her. Some time each relative of the house offer clothes from his own side. Even if she is a widow, she is also offered *pitambari*.

If any young person dies, he is offered a piece of white

cloth only. If he is a lad, he is shrouded with a piece of white cloth, 2½ yards in length. If he is a child he is offered a white piece of cloth 1 or 1½ yards in length.

If a married lady expires, she is offered a red-coloured *chunri* with yellow border, worked with golden or silver *gota*, bangles, vermilion, powder, soot (*kajal*), ornaments and *alta* (to colour nails of hands and feet), i.e. she is offered all the articles required for the shringar and make-up of a living married lady. If she is a widow but young, she is offered white cloth only. If she is a girl she is offered either white or red cloth.

Those persons who are not cremated but are thrown in the Ganges are as follows : (*a*) Babies of 8 or 10 years are tied with a stone, (*b*) *Sadhu* or *sannyasi* is tied with a pitcher, (*c*) Persons died due to leprosy and pox.

A *Sannyasi* is enveloped in a piece of cloth of geru or jogiya (ochre) colour, with *Ram-Ram* printed on it.

Those persons, who die due to pox, are not enveloped with new cloth and '*Ram-nam satya hai*' is not recited on way because *Shakti devi*, i.e. Mata Bhagvati is supposed to be more powerful than Ram (i.e. God). The persons who follow the dead keep silence on their way.

Pinda-dan

Pinda-dan is performed by a person who offers fire to the dead. Pinda dan is performed at these places : (*a*) where the person died, (*b*) where the dead is kept (on way or ghat), (*c*) on pyre, (*d*) on the 10th day of the death i.e. *Daskarma.*

Shraddh

This custom of *shraddh* is of the varieties as listed below : (a) *Pakshik Shraddh*, (b) *Masik Shraddh*, (c) *Shashth-masik Shraddh*, (d) *Varshik Shraddh*, (e) *Trayomasik Shraddh.*

As far as the *pinda dan* is concerned, it is performed yearly but when any dead-soul is given place in Gaya, his yearly *pinda dan* ends.

When a person dies, he is daubed with *ghee* and scent and is carried on an *arthi* to the *ghat*. There dead is dipped in the Ganges and then placed on the ground. The family members offer water five times (*Panch-panch anjalis*) to the dead for *shraddhanjali*. The fire-giver gets his head shaved off and takes bath in the Ganges. After that he covers his body with two pieces of cloth 5 yards and 2½ yards in length separately, i.e. one piece to cover the waist portion and the second piece to cover the upper part of his body. Sometimes *pinda dan* is performed three times on the funeral pyre by the fire-giver. *Pind* is made of the following things : (a) *jau-flour*, (b) *khova*, (c) *sand*, (d) *cooked rice*, (e) *kheer*, (f) *pancha meva*, (g) *Curd*.

Besides these things, black *til*, *kush*, *jau* and honey are also used on the occasion of *pinda dan*. Pind is prepared sometimes in an earthen pot, sometimes in a pot of silver, gold or brass.

Mrityu Sanskar

Among the Hindus, the dead is mostly cremated, but sometime, the dead is also consigned to the Ganges (*Sannyasi*) or burried (in the case of a child) where there is no source of water. The details can be sought in a book *Pret-manjari*.

The *parikrama* or, *pradakshina* of the dead is done because :

> *Yanikani cha papani janmantar kritanicha,*
> *Tani tani cha pran shyanti pradakshina pade-pade.*

To perform *pradakshina* for the reverence of the dead is essential.

After that the Brahmin recites mantras and offer *ghee*, *chandan*, *jau*, *til*, *chawal*, *dhup*, i.e. *ashtagandh* (or *dasang)* i.e. *devdar*, *chandan*, *aguru*, *guggul*, *bhojpatra*, *panchameva*, *jau*, *til ghee*, *chaval*, *kapoor*, *karayal* (*ral* or *dhoona*) etc. to the dead.

Those persons who do not know *mantras*, offer *dasang* or ashtagandh without any *mantra*, to the dead.

The pyre is lighted and adjusted with the help of the bamboo which is used for *arthi*. (The Brahmin cannot take *dan* on the *shmashan* as it is textually prohibited). For details you see *Nirnaya Sindhu* and *Dharma Sindhu*.

Tax to the Dom

Traditionally, to pay tax to the Dom is essential. A piece of cloth (*kafan*) and some portion of wood are given in the form of tax but besides this they are also given *Swarna-mudra*, *villages*, *land* and *buildings* by the rich.

When the dead body is fully burnt, the funeral pyre is

quenched with water or milky water kept in an earthen pot. After that the fire-giver takes an earthen pot filled with water on his left shoulder, facing south, throws it backward over his head on the pyre. It is done traditionally. It is also believed that *yama* or the God of the death resides in the south direction.

After that the fire-giver and others go to another *ghat*, stand in the Ganges facing south, offer *til* and water to the Ganges, remembering the name of the dead and uttering *svaha* for the last *shraddhanjali*.

Then they all take bath and change their dress. The relatives and other persons who accompany the fire-giver eat a little black-pepper or molasses or sweets. All of them then return to the dead person's house, remember God and then go to their respective houses where they change their *janeou* (sacred thread).

Next day the fire-giver visits the *ghat* with *nai*, takes bath and lays Ghanta under a *pipal* tree and lights an earthen lamp.

Articles for Ghanta

(*a*) Two earthen pots, (*b*) two *parai* (big lamp), (*c*) *kusha*, (*d*) Rope, (*e*) an earthen lamp containing *ghee*, (*f*) *til*, (*g*) match.

Making a hole in the pot, the fire-giver places *kusha* in it and lights it. Then he offers one *pinda* and one *chullu* water to the dead on the first day, two *pindas* and two *chullus* water on the second day, and so on in an increasing number with every passing day till the tenth day from the death, when he gives ten *pindas* and ten *chullus* of water.

The fire-giver is given to eat those things which the dead liked. It is believed that the shadow of the dead remains on the fire-giver. The fire-giver is supposed to be untouchable.

On the tenth day all the family members shave heads. The fire-giver wears new clothes. The shaving of head is for the purification of all.

The *mahapatra* is paid for the performance of *pinda dan*. He is paid according to the income and for the satisfaction of the dead.

On the thirteenth day, the *chauchak bhoj* is completed and this ends the *antyeshthi*.

Life-history No. 14

Name :	K.C.
Age :	52
Sex :	Male
Caste :	Dom
Place :	Chota Mirzapur
Profession :	Cremation work.

Personal Observation

He is from Baraipur of Chota Mirzapur. He is well behaved, cultured and a good natured person. He was eager to respond me. Though other persons of his locality including his wife were apprehensive about my questions, he was not at all afraid and boldly replied, "If anything happens I'll face it without any complaint as I have always done in my life." He replied to my questions with patience and enthusiasm, and when he forgot, he asked his wife.

His house was built of mud and the roof was covered with tiles. As he also cremates bodies at his own *ghat* of Chota Mirzapur, I found maunds of woods lying outside his house. There were bamboos burnt at the corners which signified their use during cremation. The campus of his house was fenced with bamboos.

His as well as his wife's and son's dresses were made of the cloth used as shroud for the dead bodies.

Family background

I am a son of late Sri R.C. of Banaras. I was born in Banaras city 52 years ago. I have three younger brothers who live in the city of Banaras at the Manikarnika ghat. I have no sister. All of us have separate economic establishments.

I am at Baraiyapur for the last 30 years. But my father lived in Banaras although my grandfather resided here. When my father went to live in Banaras, my grandmother handed over our landed property to my cousin-sisters. When I became young I claimed through a court and won the suit.

I live here because I want that my son should get educated. If he lives in Banaras, he will deviate from his path. He might fall into the trap of evil persons.

Education

I have studied only up to the second class. I can read Hindi fluently. In fact, more than studies, I was interested in wrestling (*pahalvani*). I started wrestling before I was 16 and continued upto the age of 40 years. I have also trained four persons in the art of wrestling.

Marriage

I was married at the age of 18 years with Mahadei, the eldest daughter of Shamlal of village Chandravati near Chaubepur thana of Banaras. Unfortunately she died after three years. Next time i.e. after a year I married Sukhdei, a younger sister of Mahadei. She gave birth to four daughters.

The eldest is Nagina devi (30 years old) who has been married with Bengali Choudhury of Mirghat, who cremates dead bodies at Manikarnika.

The next one is Narmada devi (25 years old) who has been married with Ramnath of Rameshwar ghat. Ramnath also cremates dead bodies at Manikarnika.

The third one is Sarbda devi (22 years old) who has been married with Ratan Choudhury, who too cremates dead bodies at Manikarnika.

The last daughter expired at the age of 10 years.

By my cruel fate, the second wife also expired while giving birth to the fourth daughter.

After three years of her death I was married with the 30 year-old Roshan devi, who is cousin-sister (*mauseri* sister) of my second wife, and the daughter of Kedar Choudhury. Roshan devi has given birth to a son Mithai Lal who is 14 years old. One child expired after two months of her birth. Mithai Lal is a student of sixth class in a school of Rajghat.

There are 100 houses of the Doms in this area. All of us are related and marry within the group. All our relatives reside in Mirzapur, Ghazipur and Jaunpur. We the Doms of Uttar Pradesh cannot marry with the Dom whose occupation is basketry because they are ranked lower in sub-caste status (sub-caste hierarchy). There are seven categories of the Dom caste. We the Dom, whose occupation is to cremate dead bodies, are ranked high.

Profession

Primary profession

I engaged myself in the profession of cremation at Manikarnika at the age of 16 years and am doing that uptil now. It is the primary source of my income and livelihood.

I am paid four annas per dead body for cremation plus two rupees as daily wages by Kailash Choudhury who is the major owner of Manikarnika. The amount of money four annas per dead body is shared by the 20 persons engaged in cremation for 24 hours.

'Paree' system

We work on the basis of a *Paree*-system as our owner has his own share at Manikarnika based on the *Paree*-system.

Altogether the owner takes at least Rs. 7.62 for each body such as :

Articles	*Rs.*
Sarhat (Straw used in touching fire with mouth and in igniting the funeral pyre)	2.00
Pyre decoration	2.00
Labour charge	1.25
Milk	0.25
Aghori (ascetics)	0.25
Municipality tax	0.50
Fire	1.25
Miscellaneous	0.12
Gross amount	7.62

This much is taken from the person who has himself pucrhased wood for the funeral.

I work for 8 or 10 days approximately in a month at Manikarnika and rest at my own *ghat* of Chota Mirzapur. Out of 365 days in a year I work for 200 days and cremate here. I have learnt this profession only by observing my relatives.

This work of cremation is a sacred one but I do not like this profession. Why have I to do it ? It makes me sad to think that.

Rituals Performed at the Shmashan

While cremating the dead body, the *fire-giver* moves five

times (*panchaparikrama*) around the funeral pyre. Sometime, the persons coming with dead bodies bring fire from their own houses and get it touched to the mouth of the dead. At that time they do not take fire from us and we cannot claim money for fire, although they pay it without any hesitation.

In case of the Marwari and the Khatri, they do not touch the mouth of the dead with ordinary fire but with the flames of Camphor (kapoor) and the pyre is also lighted with it.

The Arya Samaji cremate the body at Manikarnika but the ashes of the body are preserved for three days and the Doms are paid for it as we take care of the ashes. They also offer 56 varieties of edibles to the dead.

But no ritual regarding the collection of the relics of the dead is performed. The outsiders cannot collect the relics from the *ghat*; we hand it over to them and pay for it.

Sacred Wood

The wood supplied for cremation such as of *aam* (mango), *bel* and *chandan* (sandal), is considered sacred.

Electric Crematorium

Once the Municipal authorities decided to equip the *shmashan* with an electric crematorium but we the people of Varanasi opposed this idea of the municipal authorities.

First of all, if they could be successful in fitting in the electric crematorium, Doms would remain idle without earning any income. It would become difficult to perform cremation rituals. It would not be possible to purify the mouth of the dead with fire or to move five times around the funeral pyre (*panchaparikrama*). It would also not be possible to get the relics of the dead.

Beliefs Associated with the shmashan/aghoris/Ghosts

As far as the beliefs associated with *shmashan* are concerned, I believe that Masan Baba resides at Manikarnika. He is worshipped daily at midnight by us and we donate two annas per person for it.

As far as the *aghoris* (ascetics) are concerned we are superior to them. They also consider us superior but both of us are the disciples of the same guru, Baba *shmashan*. Really speaking, the *aghoris* are vagabonds and live on others.

I worship Baba to be freed from worries and distresses. I believe that ghosts live everywhere and even at Manikarnika. It is only a state of our mind.

Secondary Profession

My secondary source of income is from my landed property but it is negligible. Recently I got 2 *Bisa* land from Kailash (Major share holder of Manikarnika) and in return I gave a chain of pearls to him which I was presented by the King of Nepal. Besides this I receive income from the Mirzapur ghat as I have already mentioned about it.

Important Events

Now I am relating before you certain unforgettable accidents which took place before my eyes during my life time at the Manikarnika ghat as below

(*a*) There were two Brahmin brothers, Hazari and Parmeshwari. Parmeshwari was a *gunda* (ruffian) so he used to take enough money from the persons who used to cremate dead bodies at the *ghat*. Parmeshwari had a number of *chamar* attendants. These attendants worked as servants to cremate the dead. This reduced the income of the Dom Raja, and as a result the Dom Raja fought with Parmeshwari's attendants. In the fight Parmeshwari was injured with lathi and died after 20 days in the hospital. For this, Shadeo Choudhury Kashinath, Chimman, Chandar and Batuk were jailed for a few years. This accident is of 30 years back.

(*b*) The second important event which I saw was that a lady of Lakshmanpura once came to cremate herself with her dead husband on the funeral pyre. But she was forced not to do so by the Government authorities. She after coming to her house, burnt herself and expired. This happened 20 years ago.

(*c*) The third accident as I remember is of a mad man who jumped in the funeral pyre and died there.

Religious Activities

I take bath in the river Ganges daily and perform *puja* of Masan, Phulvati Devi (Bhagvati) for 25 minutes and I also go

9. Pilgrims taking Holy bath

10. A pilgrim performing Gangapujan at the bank of Ganges

(Between Pages 248-249)

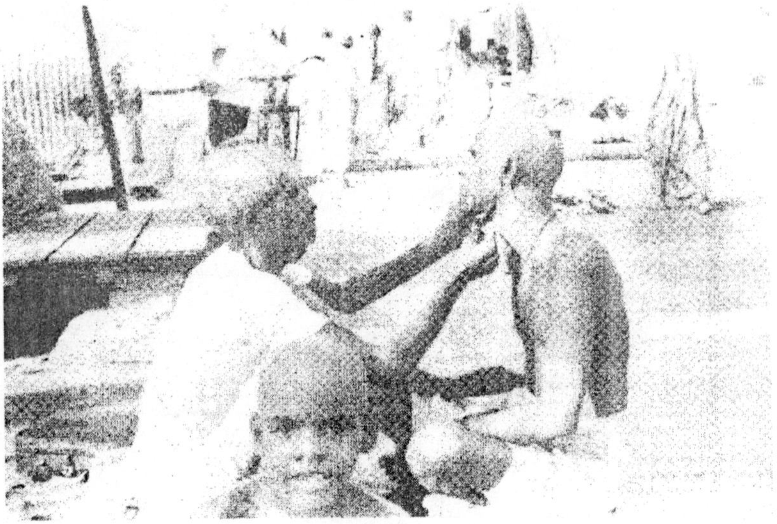

11. A Barber in Action

12. An Ascetic Pilgrim at Kashi

13. A Ghatia sitting on his Sacred *Takhat*

14. A view of Tulsimanas Mandir

15. A Ghat at Kashi

16. Another view of Tulsimanas Mandir

to Shitala devi from time to time.

I have also visited Sarnath many times and have gone to Vindhyachal approximately ten times uptil now. I have also visited the place of Markandey Mahadev (in Kaithi a place 14 miles away from Banaras).

I also do Satyanarayan *puja* once a year. The *puja* is performed by the purohit (Vikram Maharaj). He does not take meal in my house but we offer *sidha* and cooked meterials purchased from the market.

I perform the *puja* for Phulvati Devi for atleastonce in three years, on the day of *Naga panchmi* or *Panchahinyan*. She is also offered goats, sheep if any one has any kind of *manata* (after fulfilment). On that day Phulvati devi is decorated. I have also got the facial portion of Phulvati devi of silver worth of Rs. 200. On the occasion of the *puja*, villagers who are Gwala and Harijan by caste also worship the goddess Phulvati. She is the goddess of Dihbar.

As far as I know that the area falling within the *Panchakosi* is the sacred geography of Kashi. I have read *Ramayan*, *Sukhsagar*, *Hanuman Chalisa* and *Arjun Gita* in Hindi.

There are five important *tirthas*, *viz*., (*a*) *Assi*, (*b*) *Dasashvamedh*, (*c*) *Manikarnika*, (*d*) *Panch Ganga* and (*e*) *Varuna Sangam*.

I have visited Vishwanath temple (golden) from outside. I believe in Masan, Satyanarayan and Phulvati that they give me happiness. Sometime I visit Dasashvamedh to listen to *katha*. I have also visited the Lahurabir and Deoriabir (Deokinand ki haveli mein) for *darshan*.

Kashi is the very place where a king like Harishchandra was bought by a *Dom* and he used to fetch water in the house of a *Dom*.

World View Life

I know that life is nothing and a day comes when everyman is burnt to ashes. Life is like air and it vanishes into the sky but the body remains on this earth and has got no significance.

In our Hindu society three systems such as cremation, burial and flowing are incorporated. Three processes *Phukantu*, *Gerantu* and *Bahantu* are applied at the same time.

Re-birth

I believe in re-birth : that a man is reborn after three days of his death. I believe that even after the cremation at Manikarnika, man has to cross *Chaurasi lakh yoni* according to his deeds.

Pap-Punya

By *pap* and *punya* I mean that both of them are our left and right limbs respectively. By *pap* I mean 'bad deed' and 'bad behaviour' and by *punya* I mean just 'good deed' and 'good behaviour'. To cremate the dead body on the *ghat* is *punya.*

Past and Present

This world has changed now because previously things were cheaper than now. The people of that time used to donate liberally but these days we receive meagre donations. The number of dead bodies brought to be cremated has no doubt increased. This may be because of the easy transportation and the extension of Mahatmya of Kashi.

Entertainment

For entertainment, I see a movie film once a week. The films such as 'Kangan', 'Bandhan', 'Nagin', 'Putlibai' and 'Pakeeza' were good. My favourite heroes are Ashok Kumar, Dilip Kumar and heroines are such as late Meena Kumari and Sulochana. I like those films which are instructive, suggestive and religious.

Life-history No. 15

Name :	G.C.
Age :	27
Sex :	Male
Caste :	Dom
Occupation :	Cremation

Family Background

I, G.C., am a son of S.C. I was born in 1946. I have two brothers Safedi and Punnan, and five sisters, namely, Pavittar,

Bapni, Jaitra, Shaila and Kamla. All of them are married. Pavittar has been married to Ghanna who cremates dead bodies at Harishchandra ghat. Jaitra is married to Bikanu of Mir ghat, and Kamla is married to Achhelal. Both of these brothers-in-law work at Manikarnika ghat. My fifth sister is married to Dharmo who does metal work. My brother Safedi, who works at Manikarnika, is married to Urmila and the other brother, to Pusa.

My father cremated dead bodies at Sherpur ghat and also did agricultural work.

Educational Life

When I was six years old, I was admitted in Sherpur Middle School where I studied upto seventh class. I read there History, Geography, Hindi, Social Study. I was not interested in my studies, because its expenses only added to the financial problems facing my father burdened with a large family. So I left school at the age of 14.

I was interested in *pahalvani* (wrestling) and wrestled at two places : Sarnath, where I got a certificate, and Saspuran where I was given a *lungi* and two napkins in prize. At Saspuran I fought with a Gareri. I had mastered the *dhobiapat*, *kalajang*, *kamartega* and *gardaniya* tackles in wrestling.

I got my professional training at my own *ghat* of Sherpur. Besides that I used to visit my *nanihal* (mother's parents) at Banaras where I used to see the methods of cremation.

Married Life

I was married in the year 1970 in village Shadibhadi (near Auriya station of Ghazipur). I am leading a happy married life. A year ago I had a son who died after 6 months.

Professional Life

Primary :

My primary source of Income is the *shmashan* (cremation ground) at Manikarnika ghat where I work under the paree of Kailash Choudhury. We are paid Rs. 2 for every cremation. Besides that I also get some *dan* money from the cremation party. We work in shifts and there are about 20 persons working in a single shift. I started my profession of cremation in 1965. Before that I was a gate keeper in State Bank near Chitra Cinema.

We doms do not cremate dead bodies from every class and caste of the people. Khatris, Marwaris and Punjabis are cremated by a person named Mangal Guru. He is Brahmin by caste but I do not know to which category of Brahmins he belongs. This is his traditional profession but the tax is taken by the Dom Raja and he is given his labour charge. Bengalis are cremated by a Harijan named Kallu who has been appointed by the municipal authorities.

If we contact the wood-seller, we are paid 10 per cent commission, the cloth merchant gives 15 per cent and the florist, 20 per cent. Besides this we also have interaction with Nai (barber). Thus, from Manikarnika I earn approximately Rs. 15 daily.

Secondary :

My secondary source of income is the local *shmashan* ghat of Sherpur where the poor persons come to cremate their dead. Those persons come from the following villages : Sherpur, Visesarpur, Lollong, Bhormar, Bari-Jiwanpur, Bekpur, Katiyan, Rupauna, Kamalpur, Bhoktin, Ramrapur, Parasiyan, Pasaulpur, Maraipur, Pahari, Gharvaspur, Purkapur, Bangla, Devariyan, Mahripur, Naipurvan, Amolapur, Rampur, Dayalpur, Shirajpur, Pirsipur, Kailhat-Nakuhra, Jalalpur, Pachaura, Dikshitpur, Mararipur, Belvari Jorkan, Milki, Jagarnathpur, Shivshankari dham, Bela, Saspuran, Parsodha (Purushottampur), Phatehpur, Partappur, Kashipur, Niyamatpur, Baghera, Bagheri, Mahua barsi, Darran.

The performers have to pay tax for the *agni* they take for cremation. The poor people give Rs. 5, the *grihastha* give 20 kg. rice and the rich more than a thousand or 3 or 4 acres of land. Thus one has to pay at least Rs. 5 for fire, Rs. 5 for cremation, Rs. 2 for pyre decoration.

Other Sources :

Another source of my income is from agriculture. I have our acres of land which I cultivate. Besides this I take land of others by paying either Rs. 200 per acre or 6 maunds grain for a year and also on *tihai*, i.e. one third of the harvest.

In addition to these sources I also get income from *jajmanika pavaniya*, i.e. I visit the places of the Yajmans to collect the *pavana* for a month. I start for this on the next day of the *khichri* (Paush-Magh). For this the Dom Raja pays Rs. 2 per day. I visit Ghazipur, Mirzapur, Monghyr, Arrah, Patna, etc.

Social Interaction

I freely interact with all the members of my village such as with the castes like kahar, kurmi, dhobi and Yadav and so on. (The researcher personally observed the dom sitting with a kurmi in his house and gossiping.) I have also observed the interaction on the *sumashan ghat* with the article sellers, florists, wood-sellers, *mahapatras*, *aghoris*.

Religious Life

Daily Routine :

I remember of Ram, Vishwanath and Bajrangbali in the morning because I live happily with their grace. I do *Ganga-snan* daily and do the *puja of Bajrangbali.*

During the day I remain engaged in my profession.

Visit :

I have visited the Golden Vishwanath temple. (The informant says that he has entered into the main sanctum of Vishwanath and touched the *Shiva linga.*) *Annapurna*, Satyanarayan, Bajrangbali (Manmandir) Sankatmochan, Durga mandir, Manas mandir, Vishwanath (B.H.U.), Sankatadevi, Kalabhairava and Shitala mandir.

Besides this I have also visited Sarnath, and Ramnagar (to visit Ramlila). I have also visited *Durgakhoh* Chunar, Prayag (to visit the mela of Kumbh) and Vindhyachal. I visit Vindhyachal yearly for *manata*. When I visit the Kashi city, I touch the ground because Kashi is a sacred place.

I also do *Satyanarayan puja* which is performed by a Brahmin. I also recite the *mantra* at the time of *yajna* performed during the Satyanarayan *puja*. The name of my family priest is Bachchan Maharaj.

The Brahmin priest takes only fruits in my house.

I also visit Dasashwamedh and Satyanarayan mandir to listen to *Katha*.

Important Events of Life

Once it happened that a dead body was brought to the Manikarnika ghat. The elder brother as well as the uncle of the dead person, both wanted to offer fire to the dead, which led to a dispute between them. There was a fight and both of them were jailed. This happened in 1967-68.

Miscellaneous question

Life and Death :

Life is air. It is like a running clock. When the spring is unwound, the clock stops. Similarly life stops when the body stops working. The life air goes to the place of Bhagwan (God). This is death for the body.

Life-history No. 16

Name :	K.L.T.
Age :	52
Sex :	Male
Caste :	Saryuparin Brahmin
Linguistic group :	Banarasi
Profession :	*Ghatia*

The informant is a leader-type man and always wears khadi dress. He is quite politically conscious.

I was born perhaps in 1920 or 1921. I remember that being the youngest child of my parents they were very much fond of me. My eldest sister was married in the village Laddupura in the Varanasi circle. Other sisters were also married in the nearby villages and I always spent my early days with them because they loved me and I was out of guardianship. Once I had been to Laddupura with my eldest sister. It was summer. So whole day long I used to remain in the mango grove with a few boys. There was a ripe mango on the top of a tree; all the boys tried to get it but could not. It was a challenge to one group. In my turn I also tried and aimed at it with a stone. But unfortunately it got deflected back and hit my forehead. I became unconscious. I was taken to Varanasi and admitted in Kabir Chaura hospital. I remained in the hospital for about a fortnight and the injury left my eyesight permanently affected. Now father put a restriction on my flying visits to my sisters' villages and I was admitted in the Municipal School where I studied upto the fourth class.

After passing my primary school I joined High School at Sigra but could not complete the education mainly because of my engagement in a family. We were very much money-minded. Once I along with my elder brother Pyarelal Tiwari were sent to one neighbouring village to realise money from the sale of our paddy fields. We went to Pandypur. The purchaser gave us the amount of Rs. 100. On the way to home, my brother hatched a scheme to cheat our father of the money we were carrying. He bought a pair of scissors and with it cut his pocket. As we reached home and saw father, Pyare started weeping and told father that his pocket was picked on the Bus and the money stolen. Father believed him and the matter ended there. I got Rs. 25 as my share out of this. Hence, however, he sensed that he was duped by Pyarelal and me. He was very much concerned on account of our idle habits and loaferism. For this reason, ultimately, he sold all his land at a low price during his life time.

While I was a student of class sixth I was very much loved by the family of my maternal uncle who had no issue. I spent hours with my uncle (M.B.) who is a *ghatia* at Ahilyabai ghat. These were the days when Sardar Bhagat Singh was hanged and the Salt Movement was led by Gandhiji. The Congressmen and other freedom-loving persons decided to break the salt law. In my mohalla in Aurangabad also, salt was made. I was taking interest in running it. We would prepare salt and when police came, we all disappeared. I heard about the cruelty of the British rulers and felt rebellion against the white tyrants. I went to listen to the speeches of our leaders in our Town Hall. Though all the things were not clear to me, but I understood clearly that the whites were outsiders and Gandhiji wanted them to leave India. For these efforts he was imprisoned and

Bhagat Singh was hanged. This greatly angered me and I decided that I should also do something for the country. So I took a vow not to wear mill clothes but only *Khadi*.

At the age of 15 years I came in contact with the Rashtriya Swayam Sewak Sangh. My political interests were the gifts of the Ahilya Bai ghat which was the venue for the meetings of all political parties. As my uncle used to sit on this *ghat* as a *ghatia*, I got the chance to come into their contact.

One day I and my friend Bishun Mukherjee decided to meet Bakshi Sachindra Nath (now a Jana Sangh M.L.A.) then the organizer of Congress party. We went to him and expressed our desire to work actively with him. He was very happy at our offer, and told us that he was soon going to start a new campaign in which he would like us to take part. The Jana Sangh Party men came to know of my ties with Bakshi Sachindra Nath and put pressure on me against the proposal. They also warned me that if I joined Congress I shall have to go to jail. These threats by Jana Sangh partymen very much irked me and I left Jana Sangh completely. The other factor which disappointed me was their attitude towards the Mohammedans. Thus, at the age of 16 years I was a full-fledged Congressman.

In a meeting held at Ahilya Bai ghat I met Shri Shiopujan Tripathi of Congress. He was a very energetic person and he appreciated our interests. Henceforth we met him several times at his residence at Assi ghat. But on an issue of favoured appointment by him of one of his family member as the secretary of a local committee, we developed serious differences with him and resigned from Congress. We then joined Rustam Satin's group (Communist). Rustam Satin took daily coaching classes which we attended regularly. After this had continued for a long period I got the sympathiser membership in 1941. After one year, I got the full membership and became a card-holder. Till now I am a card holder member of C.P.I.

I just do not remember the year but it was perhaps the year 1944 when a general strike of the Water Works Employees' Union was announced. We had a plan to hold a meeting in the Town Hall but police and administration were alert and they locked the Town Hall and imposed Section 144 in Varanasi city. I and three other party members were arrested at about 4 p.m.

For four days I remained in jail and then came out on bail. The case went to the court which I won. In 1945, Varanasi was disturbed with students' unrest. The students had several clashes with the police. One day they burnt the patrolling car of the *kotwal*. Though this was completely a students' movement, the police arrested me and four other members of the Communist Party. I was in the jail for seven days. The court case continued for years but in the end we won in this case too.

In 1950 my father expired. Soon thereafter in the same year, my mother also died and now I was faced with the problem of supporting myself. As long as my parents were alive I had never bothered to earn. I lived on my parents and did the party work. So I joined a jewellery shop as a runner. But after six months I left the shop and came to this *ghat* for my traditional profession. In the profession of a *ghatia* I have never felt any difficulty as I had often been sitting on the *ghat* with my uncle (MB) and assisted him many times. I had learnt the technique by seeing my uncle and since then I have been engaged in this profession in my spare time. I lead a simple life. Since I became a Congressman, I have never used mill cloth and always wore *khadi* with a notion that through this measure I am helping the village handicraftsmen.

I was married in the year 1954 at the age of 24. Before the marriage I had dreamed of a beautiful wife, but I was shocked to see the ugly, illiterate, village girl. I became very much frustrated and started to neglect the wife from that first night. This gap in my life never filled up. Of course I used her for sexual satisfaction but never extended love to her. An year after my marriage I contacted *phthisis* and suffered from it for two years. Doctors had forbidden me sexual intercourse, so my wife was sent to her father's house. Even after being cured I could never give her affection. At last, after six years of marriage her father remarried her in a distant village. In later years when I learnt that she had expired, I felt a little guilty. I never married again and avoided women. I engaged myself in party work.

As my interest lay in social and political service, I could never adjust myself in the *ghat* business. I work as a *ghatia* as it is the only source of livelihood I have. I sit on the *ghat* but my consciousness is not reconciled to it. The *ghat* business is of cheating and humiliation. Whenever any *ghatia* commits a mistake I condemn him publicly and this has made all of them annoyed with me. My association is always with cultured and learned persons; they all come to me and this makes other *ghatias* jealous of me.

I have deep reverence for Ganga because for us *ghatias* Ganga is like a mother. Ganga is our source of income. I do not understand the concepts of sacred, secular and profane. But just following the traditional way. I can say it is actually one's feelings towards a particular object at particular time that make it sacred, secular or profane.

Life-history No. 17

Name :	R.T.
Age :	42
Sex :	Male
Caste :	Kanyakubja Brahmin
Profession :	*Ghatia*

I come from a respectable family. I have seen good days, good in the sense that I was properly cared for in my childhood. I was born in the year 1930. I remember that when my father planned to send me to school he brought a new pair of half-pants and a shirt for me. At that time such a dress was worn by the wards of well-to-do modern families. Though my father was not much educated, he was rich. He was the *pujari* of Kedar temple which was visited by the Hindu pilgrims from all over. I was not different from my colleagues of my locality. I made friendship with Bengali boys and spent most of my time with them. This influenced my language and my personality. I learnt to speak Bangla fluently and became aggressive as the Bengalis generally are.

Once when I was studying in the third class I had a clash with my class-fellow, Tapan Banerjee. He was the son of a Post Master and was very proud. Being the only son of his parents he had so many sets of good dresses. He always tried to show off his riches. Once after showing a new pair of *chappals* he jeered at me and touched the *chappals* to my nose. I was very much annoyed since I am a Brahmin. I started beating him and he began to cry. The class monitor Bipin Mukherjee tried to intervene but unfortunately he also got some slaps. The matter was reported to the teacher who called both of us. I was very much afraid of my teacher who usually carried a stick to beat mischievous boys. I at once left the class and ran to my house and never returned to that school. The teacher did complain to my father but my father did not care even to ask me about it. From that time I hated Bengalis because they are aggressive by nature and, if any body touches them, they start quarrelling.

After that I was admitted in the Sanskrit Pathashala. I developed interest in learning Sanskrit and proved a good student. But I was not obedient to my teachers. One day when the teacher was teaching us I was drawing his caricature. By a chance he saw this and became so angry that he threw the duster at me. The duster hit my head and my head started bleeding. A boy reported the incident at my house. My mother came to the school and took me away saying that she did not want me to study there. Although my father was not in favour of my leaving the school but he did not have the courage to oppose my mother. So I left that school.

Next year I was admitted in another school at the Harishchandra ghat. By this time I was 15 years old and was still only in the sixth class. Somehow I passed that class and got into the seventh class. But that year I sustained a fracture in my hand and remained under plaster for about four months. Thereafter I discontinued my studies for ever.

When I was a student of fourth class I started taking interest in wrestling. My house was very close to Ganga so I daily bathed in the holy river before going for exercise. I joined the *akhara* of Sri Bhanu Guru and got a good training in wrestling and stick playing. By the age of 17 I had become a proficient stick player and wrestler but my fracture also disrupted this. But as soon as I regained my strength I started exercising and wrestling again and became a proficient wrestler. I travelled throughout India with Bhanu Guru as his assistant and personal secretary. This way I got chance to see different places and came to know many techniques of wrestling.

From the very beginning I had been in close contact with Bengalis, who are free mixers. Thus I had an opportunity to meet Bengali girls. I had matured early and by the age of 22, I was married. I loved my wife. Our first issue was a girl.

After marriage I began to sit with my father in the temple and assisted him in temple performances. This was when I got proper training by seeing him. After *puja* we used to sit together for hours in the small, dark and damp sanctum of Kedareshwar. I hated this dreary dungeon and became quite frustrated after four or five years. In fact the income from the temple was not sufficient for our needs. I was the eldest son, so it was necessary for me to look after the home affairs and father was not in a mood to leave the temple. So I left the temple of Baba Kedareshwar after a long continuous service of 10 years and got the contract of the Vijayanagaram ghat on the monthly rent of Rs. 3.

Here on the *ghat* though my income is very small I feel myself free. On festival days I assist my father in the temple besides the *ghat* work. On the *ghat* the youth of the neighbouring areas come for exercise. Talking with them reminds me of my past.

In the beginning I did not believe in *Dharma* and *Karma*. But gradually with advancing age I started developing faith in these matters. When I was serving in the temple I saw pilgrims from far off places, showing great devotion towards the deities. It inspired me to think that at least there was something which attracted all sorts of persons. But now I myself feel the same attraction and devotion.

I cannot define 'sacred' and 'profane'. My sense of the sacred developed with my age.

Nothing was new for me when I joined the *ghat* because most of the sacred performances were the same as done in the temple. In the temple one worships the Shiva *linga* and here one worships the Ganga. A simple training is sufficient for the *ghatia's* profession.

Life-history No. 18

Name :	R.M.
Age :	33
Sex :	Male
Caste :	Saryuparin Brahmin

Linguistic group : Banarasi
Profession : *Ghatia*

I was born in the year 1942 and, being the eldest son of my parents, I was loved by all. Mother went to her father's place, Rameshwar after three months of my birth. There I was cared by my *nani* (grandmother) and *mausi* (mother's sister). One morning when I was crawling near the kitchen garden a snake came near me and people say that I started playing with it. The snake did not harm me. When my aunt came she began to cry at which the snake quietly went away. When my father came to know about it he rushed to Rameshwar and was angry at my mother and he brought us to Varanasi next day. An astrologer was consulted who forecast that my star is closely associated with snakes so I should have a snake of silver hung around my neck which is still with me. Even today I am very much afraid of the snakes.

I was a dull student and usually went to sleep in the class room. The teacher warned me and one day when I was sleeping he gave a stroke of the wooden duster on my head. From that day I was very careful and always remained attentive to him. He complained about my dullness to father who appointed a private tutor. With the help of this private tutor I developed interest in studies. By the time I was of 10 years, I was a student of the fourth class. I remember that I was preparing for the final examination when unfortunately I was ill with pneumonia. This illness continued for two months and I wasted my one study year. But by way of compensation I made myself strong in the class. The teacher as well as my guardians were surprised at my good result when I stood second in my class. But it was all due to the labour of my private tutor. From that time I was always a good student in the class.

When I reached the tenth class, an unfortunate incident happened to me. As the final examination approached I injured my right hand in a wrestling bout. I had to drop the examination. I therefore started sitting with my father regularly on the *ghat*. Next year I appeared in the examination and passed in the second division. By this time I was fully engaged in the *ghat* business and had also started earning a little. So I gave up my studies. I tried many times to get a regular job but could not. As I remained on the *ghat* and was out of touch with reading and writing I had forgotten what I had learnt at the school. In one interview in D.L.W. I was given to copy a paragraph of 10 lines in English. I became so nervous that the interviewers doubted my matriculation certificate and called it false. After that incident I never tried for any other job. Also I was earning a good amount on the *ghat* without much effort and got proper regards from my clients.

From my very childhood I used to come on the *ghat* but not from any professional point of view. I was very naughty, so my mother always sent me with my father. It became my routine to come to the *ghat* with father, particularly on Sundays and holidays. I was very inquisitive to know the process of the *karmakanda* of the *ghat*. In my childhood I used to think that the pilgrims were fools that they gave paise instead of a little *roli* and *chandan*. But as I attained maturity and learnt the *mantras* and the meanings of the *mantras*, I understood the significance. From the age of 15 years when I was student of the ninth class I started to conduct *sankalpa*, Ganga *puja* and *tarpan*. Though I had no formal training of *karmakanda*, I learnt every thing from my father, by seeing him practise the rites. That is why I faced no problem when I dropped my studies and came to practise the profession of *ghat*.

My sex consciousness started at the *ghat*. Frome the very beginning when I saw the girls bathing or a female dressing herself, I always tried to look at their private parts. This curiosity aroused a great sexual urge in me. The first time I cohabited with a woman when a sister-in-law of mine, whose husband was out of station, told me about the sex act and showed me how to do it. I cohabited with her. This training helped me a lot when I was married in 1961. My wife was an illiterate village girl. I was romantic having seen many films. I tried to make her romantic but in vain. However with the passage of time I have become more realistic.

I do not believe in 'sacred' and 'profane'. I only know that I have to survive in this economic world so I survive at any costs if one pays paise on hearing the importance of Ganga, I praise Ganga. Since Ganga is the source of my livelihood, it is certainly sacred for me but if, for instance, I lost a son in this Ganga, it will at once become profane for me. It is for business interests that I always perpetuate the myths that by worshipping Ganga one gets this and that.

Life-history No. 19

Name :	R.M.S.
Age :	47
Sex :	Male
Caste :	Brahmin
Linguistic group :	Banarasi
Profession :	*Ghatia*

I do not have any record of my birth. However, perhaps I was born in the year 1925. It is said that during my childhood I frequently remained ill. My father's income was not much so he could not take me to any doctor. So instead he took me to an *ojha* (witch-doctor) of Mirzapur. The *ojha* told my mother not to worry about me as I was a *murti* (image) of Ram (God), and therefore no one could harm me. It is said that I was named Ram Murti because of that *ojha*. The *ojha* gave me charmed ash (*bibhooti*) and I was cured within a month. My parents had taken the vow that if I were cured, they would pay their obeissance to goddess Vindhyachal. Accordingly, they went to this temple. Thus my early days started with deep religious impression.

I was very much interested in books from the very beginning.

After my sixth year, I was admitted in the Primary Pathashala of Baluwa Bazar. At first I was not ready to go to school but when the teacher told me that I will be given a new slate, pencil and a book I became ready and became so much interested in school that I got the first prize in attendance.

After passing my fourth class from Baluwa Bazar Primary Pathashala I got admission in the Mokalpur Middle School. Here the students were also given physical training. I became interested in body culture and started taking exercises. During a sports-week in this school, I won a prize in tug-of-war, and was awarded a *safa* and a brass plate. At another time I also won the first prize for acting in *Abhijnan Shakuntalam* play. After passing Madhyama examination from this school I got admitted in Queen's College and did my Shashtri in the year 1941. In the year 1945 I got the degree of Acharya from the Sanskrit University.

I had also studied in the Arjuna Ayurveda Vidyalaya, Kashi. After getting the diploma from there, I was registered as an Ayurvedic practitioner. But I never practised, though in the practical training programme, I distributed free medicine to the needy in the Kabirchaura Hospital.

From the very beginning I had a soft heart for the poor. In response to Gandhiji's appeal for *achhootoddhar* I started a night school in 1938 and gave free education to the Harijans. The Arya Samaj organization bore all the expenses of books, slates, pencils, light, etc. I came in contact with Arya Samaj for the first time when I was student of Madhyama and thus came in the field of social service.

After passing Madhyama I came to Shastri class. Then I came in contact with the Hindu Mahasabha, run at that time under the presidentship of Shri Madan Mohan Malaviya and secretaryship of Swami Sarwadanand. I became an active member of the Hindu Mahasabha and attended the Mahasabha conference held at Habibudaula Park in Lucknow. In this conference 750 Mohammedans were converted to Hinduism. This impressed me very much. After that I attended many functions for Gau Hatya Nirodh, at Delhi, Mathura, Balia and Lucknow. I also led many demonstrations and was even imprisoned many times.

Once I along with Bhagwat Datta Mishra, Deenbhatta Vyas, Kamalnath Pathak, Durga Prasad Sharma and Sukhdeo Muni had gone to Lucknow to participate in a demonstration. We reached the place and organized a meeting. Then in the form of demonstration with flag and posters, we marched to the commission house but were challenged by police and were arrested. We were released after 20 days' rigorous imprisonment and only when we had signed a bond of assurance that we shall not join the Hindu Mahasabha again. But we all joined it again after returning to Kashi.

On 30 January 1948, I was attending my convocation

function. Chief Minister Sampurnanand was the chief guest and I was offering him orange squash. Suddenly the loud-speaker announced that Gandhiji was no more, he had been shot dead by a mad man Nathu Ram. We were all stunned and shocked. Immediately the principal called me and instructed me to leave the campus because he was certain that police would arrest the members of Hindu Mahasabha. He also instructed me not to disclose that I was associated with that college. I fled away and, crossing the provincial boundries, reached Bengal. There I got a job as a teacher in Sri Ramkrishna Vidyamandir of Burdwan (W.B.). Again I re-established my contact with Arya Samaj and travelled to Chatgaon, Tripura and Komilla and preached about the *Vedas* and Arya Samaj. Once I attended the meeting at Bahu Bazar (Calcutta) and gave a highly emotional speech. The moment I sat down on the dais I was arrested and was sent back to Kashi. In my absence, the police had confiscated my household goods, harassed my family members and arrested my friends. After four months in jail I was released on the bail of Sri Jhingan Saha, the then president of Hindu Mahasabha. For a long time thereafter I was continuously harassed by the C.I.D. men.

Being an active member of the Arya Samaj I always tried my best to spread my message of the Arya Samaj throughout India and in this connection travelled as an Arya Samaj *upadeshak* (preacher) in Bihar, U.P., M.P., Punjab, Rajasthan and Hyderabad. Once a *shastrartha* (debate) between Sanatanis and Arya Samajis was organised in Ram Nagar Fort. I participated in this *shastrartha* which continued for seven days. The Sanatanis feared me and were angry with me. While I was returning from Ram Nagar Fort a stone boulder was thrown towards me from the roof of Kali Matta, Visheshwarganj. I was injured and hospitalized. But these instances never deterred me. In the year 1956 I participated in another *shastrartha* with Swami Karpatriji at the Town Hall, Varanasi.

During the period of Harijan entrance in Golden Vishwanath Temple I was the supporter of the entrance and so had many clashes with the orthodox Brahmins. At that time I was working with Baikuntha Nath Upadhyaya. When Harijan entry became successful we were greeted with garlands.

In the year 1962 during the time of Chinese aggression I was elected the Secretary of the Varanasi Youngmen Association. I worked hard to collect money and blood for the Jawans fighting for the country. In this campaign along with doctors and medical students of Banaras Hindu University I travelled in many villages and collected a good amount of blood.

In the year 1963 in a function of Savarkar Library Foundation I came in contact with Shri Munulal Ragul. By his inspiration I became a member of Ganga Mahasabha. By this time I was in financial difficulties and was in need of a source of maintenance. Ragul introduced me to Kishori Lal Mishra who appointed me as a tutor for his sons. After two years Shri Kishori Lal advised me to choose any of his *ghats* and start in *ghatia* profession. I at once agreed and came to this *ghat*.

Once when I was sitting on my takhta near the last steps on the *ghat*, a boy of 12 years was swept away by the current of the water. His relative women started wailing and crying for help. I rushed into the water and saved him at the risk to my life.

For the definition of the 'sacred', the 'secular' and the 'profane', I depend upon my conscience. Of course my conscience is guided by the philosophy of Hindu Dharma and religious books I have gone through.

Life-history No. 20

Name :	R.J.
Age :	28
Sex :	Male
Caste :	Joshi Brahmin
Linguistic group :	Banarasi
Profession :	Ghatia (at Dasashamedh ghat)

I was born in the year 1944 as the first son of my parents. My parents were very happy at my birth and spent a lot of money on that occasion. After three years of my birth one day my mother gave birth to a girl but unfortunately both the child and my mother died within a week. After the death of my mother many relatives came to my house to perform the *shraddh* rite. After this an aunt stayed with us to look after me and my father. After two years, one day my father went to Vindhyachal and returned the next day with a woman. He introduced her as my new mother. I remembered my mother very well and was shocked at this. But no one paid heed to my sentiments. So I kept quiet but never accepted her as my mother. However I had to live with her.

My father admitted me in a school of Bari Piyari. My teacher was related to me through my late mother. He was very sympathetic to me and he taught me with great affection. This sympathy resulted in my interest in study and I tried my best to remain most of my time at the school. After sometime, my stepmother turned harsh and started teasing me. I complained to my father and he checked my mother many times but my step-mother did not desist and my father felt himself helpless. She was a wilful woman. She started my father on drinking. The habit took hold on my father so much that ultimately to get money for his drinks, he sold all his property. Drinking also affected my father's business as in a drunken state he could not attend to clients (he was a *bhaddar*). So he then started to send me in his place. I was then only 12 years and was studying in the fourth class.

I was a good student so my teacher met my father and pressed him not to send me on business and distract me from my studies. But this did not really work and gradually I started attending to clients.

One day I could not earn a single paisa and returned home empty handed. When my step-mother heard it she was very angry with me and did not prepare meals and ordered me to eat elsewhere. I kept quiet and patiently waited for my father. My father came in the evening and as usual he was drunk. When he learnt that the meals were not prepared because I had not brought any money, he took a bamboo stick and started beating me. Our neighbours saved me. This news reached my aunt. She came and took me to her house where at last I found some peace. She had no issue of her own and treated me like her son.

I am now very happy because my income is considerably good and the expenditure is limited. My aunt does not ask for much. I want to give her account of all my income and expenditure. Many times it has happened that my father and myself came face to face but none of us accosted the other and we passed like strangers. One day I came to know that my father had sold the only house left with him and shifted with my step-mother to her parents' place at Vindhyachal.

Owing to the tough competition in the profession of *bhaddar* and less regard paid to the *bhaddar*, I became frustrated. I hated running after clients. My frustration reached its peak when one day I met a typical group. The group of five members of a family was from Bardwan district of West Bengal. I escorted them to different places as they desired. When we reached Manas Mandir one of them suddenly said that her purse was stolen. All of them blamed me. I was concerned about her loss and was puzzled how this had happened. But the expression of concern on my face was interpreted by them as guilt. They started beating me and handed me over to Bhelupur police. For two days I remained in the lock-up at the police station. I felt much ashamed of myself. Many of my friends came to the police station and with their efforts a compromise was made and I had to pay Rs. 250 as the price. The amount was paid by my aunt. Thus I faced much trouble and also lost income of several months. With such an experience I decided to leave the profession and stopped attending to pilgrims for some time. My friends and relatives persuaded me to forget what had happened as it was nothing very uncommon for the persons engaged in this profession. But my conscience never permitted me to rejoin this line. After some time I got an engagement in a tailoring shop, of fixing buttons and acting as a runner from laundry to the tailoring shop. This job was quite peaceful but brought very little income. Even then I was satisfied and tried my best to acquire skill in sewing techniques. I gradually learnt more in tailoring art and became proficient in different types of sewing. I now started doing other jobs also besides just stitching buttons and was paid comparatively better though it was still not a comfortable income. Unfortunately the business of the shop deteriorated on account of the death of their chief tailor and so the owner of the shop shifted it to Kanpur. So after working for two years in that shop, I was once again out of job.

While I was serving in the tailoring shop I got married with a girl Piyari. I was trying to establish my house but I was unlucky that I lost my job. I took up work with another street tailor as his assistant but this job brought very poor returns. I also did not have sufficient money to purchase a sewing machine to start independent business.

Baboo, the son of Shri Kishori Lal Mishra was known to me from the time I was engaged in the tailoring company. He was one of our clients. I established a good friendship with him. One day after leaving the shop I met him and told him of my helplessness. He promised to do something for me and said that his father had a number of ghats at Dasashwamedh ghat. So if it will be possible he would try to get one *ghat* (takhta) for me. After a week he took me to his father Shri Kishori Lal Mishra, who allowed me to sit on one of his *ghats*. It was something quite new for the *ghatias* that some one who was originally a *bhaddar* had become a *ghatia*. They opposed it with all their best but Shri Lal did not change his mind. Till today I am grateful to him for his kindness.

For the last three years I am serving as a *ghatia* and enjoying some peace. Initially I felt uncertain of the *mantras* needed to be cited on different performances, but after a week or two I realised that the clients were not at all concerned with the utterances of *mantras* rather it was the gestures and action that satisfied them. In course of time I learnt a few different *mantras* and tried my best to learn whatever was utmost necessary. Again here the profession is full of cheating but now I have learnt how to survive so whatever comes I welcome them but never try to harm anybody. When I see that a client can pay well I try to get maximum out of him and when it seems that he is poor, I accept whatever he gives happily. I never insist for anything more.

Whatever cultural knowledge I have acquired had been through my friends. I do not know any texts. Myth perpetuation is the normal technique of a professional priest. So we perpetuate the myth of the *mahatmya* of not only of Vishwanath, but also the *dakshina*, given in the name of Vishwanath and Ganga. Sometimes I tell some concocted legends about the *mahatmya* of *dakshina*. For instance I would relate how some one got kingship by giving good *dakshina* to the Brahmin on the bank of the Ganga, or that some one lost his whole property by cheating a Brahmin. To make the *ghatias* specific we correlate the Ganga. But these stories impress women and the illterate folks more than the educated class.

Life-history No. 21

Name :	M.M.
Age :	54
Sex :	Male
Caste :	Saryuparin Brahmin
Linguistic group :	Banarasi
Profession :	Ghatia

I do not remember my childhood. It flashes in my memory that I was fond of bathing in the Ganga. So I always tried to go along with my father to the *ghat* and find there the chance to take a bath in the river. There was another temptation for me to accompany my father. My father, who was a *ghatia*, used to keep all the change under his mat. Whenever he left his seat for any performance on the river bed I quickly stole a few paise from under the mat. He could never detect the loss of a few coins from that mound of coins.

One day my father had gone with a group of pilgrims to perform a *puja* on the bank. Taking advantage of my father's absence I pinched a four-anna piece from the stock under the mat. Unfortunately, a girl of 5 years, sitting on the *takhta*, saw me doing this, without my knowledge. She reported the matter to her mother and her mother communicated it to my father. My father checked his money and discovered a four-anna piece short. I was caught and the coin was recovered from me. I got a severe beating that day, and from that day, father decided not to bring me with him. He took me to a neighbouring private school of Andha Guruji (blind teacher) and put me as a disciple in his class. This teacher taught us *paharas* (tables) which I hated. One day he asked me to recite the table of elevens and onwards. When I could not, he gave me a good thrashing with his cane. I could not restrain my anger and I snatched the cane from him and struck him with it three or four times. Then I threw the cane at him and ran away.

I fled to my aunt's village about 13 miles from Varanasi. I covered the distance by motor and on foot and reached there in the evening. My aunt was very glad to see me but as soon as she came to know that I had come without informing my father, she became anxious and the next morning she sent her son to inform my father that I was there safe and sound. At my house all were worried due to my sudden absence. They were relieved to get the news.

I remained with my aunt for about six months. There I joined the village school, but I never attended any classes there and mostly remained absent. My joining the school satisfied my father that at least, I was pursuing my education. But in reality I was not at all interested in my books. So when I failed in the examination, my aunt sent me back to Kashi. There I started working at my uncle's betel shop but due to the wicked nature of aunt, I could not continue there. By this time I was in my tenth year. My father took me to the Chausathi Devi temple and entrusted me the task of cleaning the temple and ringing the bell at the time of *arati*. For this job I was to be paid Rs. 10 p.m. The temple priest Manda Guru also taught me some *mantras*. This created in me the interest also to learn the *mantras* necessary for the *ghatia* profession. Whenever in the night I sat with my father I tried to learn the *mantras* of Ganga *puja* and in this way got an informal training.

After two years of temple service I returned to *ghat* again. There I remained with my father for about one year. During this period I learnt all the techniques required for a *ghatia*.

I was married at the age of 14 to a girl of a distant village. For sometime it was a new and pleasant experience for me but as the days passed, the parents started demanding money from me to put my share towards the expenses of the joint family. At this I had a clash with my father and so from the next day my kitchen was separated. I took a new *ghat* on rent and started my own business separately. It is now 40 years from that incident and since then I am sitting on the same *ghat*.

Nothing important has happened to me in this *ghat* life, rather it has become a machine like routine. I come here every day early in the morning, spend the day, earn whatever I can and go back. I am an illiterate man and do not have any other source of my livelihood except the Ganga bank. So I have submitted myself before the Ganga.

I am giving proper education to my sons and daughters because I have learnt that without education a man suffers much. Education teaches one proper conduct, proper behaviour and prepares one for professional training.

A *ghatia* can learn a lot even in his professional life because after coming in contact with persons of different linguistic regions, a *ghatia* learns different languages and cultural norms. I myself am multi-lingual, and know Bengali, Marathi, Telugu and Hindi apart from my mother tongue, the Banarasi dialect.

The tradition of a Brahmin is not clear to me because there are so many different customs. The Brahmin, for instance, should not ask for any amount in *dakshina* and should let the *jajman* give according to his own will. But, as it is, unless you demand you are not paid anything. Modern values can be adopted only if they do not harm our own values of life.

Life-history No. 22

Name :	R.M.M.
Age :	37
Caste :	Saryuparin Brahmin
Profession :	Ghatia

I do not know when I was born. All I remember of my early childhood is that my father was a *ghatia* and he used to bring me sweets when he returned in the evening. Then one day my father escorted me to the neighbouring school and admitted me there. The Bhutani guru was actually the teacher of my father and would many a time told me of my father's childhood. At the age of 6, I started going with my father and sit on the *ghat*. He gave me training of the *karmakanda*. Soon I learnt from him a few *mantras* necessary for the *ghatia* profession. Whenever any known client came, father would depute me to perform the rituals. Thus along with my school education, I was getting practical training of the profession of my father.

When I was of 9 years, my father expired, leaving behind my younger sister and a younger brother besides myself. This misfortune completely upset my life. I left my studies and started sitting on the *ghat*. I faced no problem in taking up profession but I could earn only a meagre amount in spite of sitting on the *ghat* for whole day long. Then I got a service in a *biri* (Indian Cheerut) shop. I worked there after 12 a.m. and before that I sat on the *ghat*. The shopkeeper paid me Rs. 2 for every thousand *biris* made by me. At that time my age was 14 years and I used to make about 2,000 *biris* daily. This gave me a good income. Whatever the income was, about 70% of that was spent on household affairs and the remaining 30% was kept for future.

Seeing the profit in the *biri* business I thought of settling my own business and opened a *biri* shop. But only after a year I had to vacate it because the housemaster himself opened a Medical store in that shop. Now I faced very difficult days because I was nowhere. I had left the shop where I learnt *biri* making and had no shop of my own. It was also very difficult to work efficiently in the home. I remained jobless for about two or three months and only had the *ghat* business in the morning. Then I took up a job in silk shop of a Gujarati businessman at Doodhavinayak and I was assigned to polish the Banarasi sarees. Although I was not happy there on account of rough behaviour of the proprietor but was interested in learning the work so I continued to work for about one and half years.

Here I learnt that the world is based on capital. A man with capital just invests his money and gets handsome returns without any hard work. The labourers work their hardest yet they only get meagre salaries while the capitalist gets major profits on their investment. Anyhow I passed days.

One day I had a clash with the manager of the firm and was fired from the job. But I was fortunate enough to get another assignment with another Saree factory. The job was the same, i.e., to polish sarees. Here I stayed for about two years and was quite satisfied with the service conditions. My daily income was four to five rupees a day apart from the income of the *ghat* where I used to sit in the morning hours till 10 a.m. I was very sincere in my work and gained appreciation and confidence of my proprietor. So much so that when he went outside he left the cash with me. The proprietor was without a child and he gave me affection of a father. I myself paid my best regards as is due to a father. Though I was Brahmin and he was Khatri, we never felt any caste difference. Once he fell ill and after all sorts of service done by me, spending a lot of money on the treatment by his old wife he left this world, leaving me in the midway. After his death the business went into the hands of his brother-in-law, who sold it and shifted to Punjab. At the time of departure the widow gave me one hundred rupees. I did not wish to accept the sum but with tears she said that I should spend it for my sister's marriage. She was like a mother who gave affection not only to me but to the whole of my family.

By this time I had attained 21 years of age. After one month I got a job in a Soap factory at Assi. The job was to cut soap-bars into pieces and pack them. I earned Rs. 4 to 5 daily and my financial condition bettered. By this time my younger brother Moti had also started sitting on the other *ghat* (*takhta*) of Jalasen ghat.

We negotiated for the marriage of our sister and finally the marriage was performed in the year 1955. In all, we spent about Rs. 1200. After the marriage of my sister I left the soap factory because it was quite far away from my residence. After my sister's marriage we ourselves cooked our food. I now joined Lucky Tea Co. of Rajghat where both I and my brother filled up tea packets. This job continued for about one year. Though the income was not so good but we were managing.

After one year I started my own tea stall and earned a good amount in seven months. Now I was in need of some one to look after the household work, and also for company at home. So my marriage was settled with a girl of my own *mohalla* and I was married in the year 1957. Though the girl was quite known to me but as a bride she proved to be a quite new experience. I became so much attached to her that I started neglecting my business, which naturally deteriorated till finally I was compelled to close it. I then opened a betel stall in the Shiotola Mohalla and since then I am running it in my spare time after the *ghat* duty.

By the grace of Lord Shiva I was earning sufficient to run

the family. In the year 1966 the marriage of my younger brother was also performed. This marriage finally separated us, brothers. Our wives quarrelled so much that we were left with no other choice.

I also act as the domestic priest of the *Ahirs* of my *mohalla.* Yet now I have never worked for the untouchables. This *ghatia* profession is a sacred profession because Ganga is the mother and Lord Shiva is the father of the Kashivasi. I am proud of my profession that I am associated rather, directly connected with mother Ganga. Whatever the things may be if it is attached with the name of God it will be sacred and rest are secular. But the secular is not secular for ever. When it is against the *shastras* and when it gives trouble to others, it is called profane.

The only bad man I experienced ever was a jeweller. He was a friend of my father. He used to come to my house. We were then quite young. He established illegal contact with my mother and now it appears that my father did not have a natural death. After the death of my father he took away all our money. After one year of this happening he also expired in a taxi accident.

I have had sexual relations with atleast five or six girls and women before my marriage. The first one was an unmarried Nepali girl who was living in the same building where I lived. It was she who excited and provoked me to have sexual contact. She taught me all the techniques of making love. I often used to give her rupees and clothes. When her parents came to know our relations, they shifted to another *mohalla.* Even after my marriage I had extra-marital sexual relations. The last one of these was with a married Brahmin woman. But now I feel that these relations hampered my social status, my business and money too. I was not giving proper care to my children, so I have given up all these habits.

Now I am simply a *ghatia* and sit on the *ghat* and serve the people who want to be served. I do not have more cultural knowledge of the performances so I do whatever I can. I have learnt by heart a few *mantras* necessary for the Ganga *puja, sankalpa* and *pindadan* and conduct rituals related to the Ganga. The clients are mostly from the backward castes among which most are the *Ahirs.*

The profession I like because it is a peaceful life. As this *ghat* is not so busy, most of my time is spent in leisure. In leisure time I recite *bhajans* or the *Ramayana* or reflect about the Ganga. When I see the calm-flowing Ganga I feel happy and it gives me a type of satisfaction. Though the income from the *ghat* is so little that I have to add to it by doing *biri* business in the evening, but I am satisfied with my easy life.

I start my day with a *pranam* to mother Ganga who is my source of livelihood. Then I come to the *ghat* and sit there till 11 a.m. and after that I return home to take lunch. After taking meals I get busy in making *biris*. In the evening I sit in the betel stall. At night I take meals with my children because now I consider them as my *dharohar* (capital). Before going to sleep I remember lord Shiva and beg his pardon for all the sins done in the day. Sometimes when I am upset, I take *bhang* which brings sound sleep.

I myself do not know what should be the definition of sacred but apparently Ganga is sacred for me because my pious feelings are attached with it. Also Ganga is the source of livelihood. All the things or activities which give trouble or harm to any one are profane.

This *ghutia* profession is losing in income as well as popularity and respect so I do not want my children to take up this profession.

Life-history No. 23

Name :	C.L.P.
Age :	35
Sex :	Male
Caste :	Saryuparin Brahmin
Linguistic group :	Banarasi
General Education :	Non-matric
Profession :	Ghatia.

I was born in the year 1935. Though my father kept no written record but he remembered that at the time of the earthquake in Bihar I was of 13 months and a refugee from Bihar was engaged for my care because my mother was keeping indifferent health. She never regained her health and expired when I was of three and half years. She left behind her two sons and a married daughter who afterwards cared for me as a mother. I was brought up by my elder sister and a maid servant.

At the age of five years, I was sent to study under a *guru.* I was given a new slate and a full stick of pencil. The Guru loved me and gave me sweets. On instruction of *Didi* (sister) I touched the feet of the Guru and he blessed me. It was my first experience of school. The Guru never beat me because I was an intelligent student and a good singer too. I passed class three from that school.

For my further education I was sent to Sanatan Dharma School because the teachers in that school were known to my father. One day my father took me to the school and handed me to the teachers, saying, "The boy is naughty. So you please handle him carefully." Actually I was not so naughty but the first word of introduction stuck in the minds of the teachers and they got a firm impression that I was naughty and treated me harshly. One day the boys were playing with a ball in the playground of the school and I was sitting on the edge of the ground and watching the game. Suddenly one of the boys was hit by a stone flying off the ground. Though I was out of play and was sitting on the wall but the boys and later the teachers blamed me. I was beaten. This beating angered me and made me stubborn. I did not forget the beating and one day when I was sitting on the roof of my friend's house, the teacher seemed to me to be coming through the lane. I poured water upon him as he was passing by the way. On another occasion he came to Dasashwamedh ghat, I myself served him, but on my instigation, my friends pulled him into deep water as he was in the river. He was saved after he had desperately shouted for help for some time.

I took revenge from all the students and the teachers but was never caught or blamed. When I was of 13 years I started sitting on the *ghat* with my father and Munnu. But more than earning I was interested in the activities of the *ghat*. Besides helping my father in bringing *puja* materials and in other miscellaneous activities, I was getting interested in the opposite sex.

I was now of 15 years and was very much excited by seeing

the semi-nude bathing women at the *ghat*. The thin wet sarees stuck to their bodies almost completely exposed their bodies. I never tired of looking at the bathing scene. Then I had my first sexual experience.

Among the regular bathers at the ghat, there was an unmarried Bengali young woman of about 25. Whenever she found me alone, she tried to talk with me. She would often praise my healthy body. I too liked to talk with her. She used to change her dress in the dressing room in front of me. She undressed herself and stood completely naked there in a manner that I could see her. This excited me very much. One day she came to me and said that she had dropped her ear-ring somewhere in the room, and asked me to help her in searching for it. I went with her in the room to look for the lost ear-ring. But there instead of letting me search she embraced me and started kissing me. I too hugged her forcefully. After necking for some minutes we came out. She was very happy and praised me before the bathers for finding her ear-ring. The young lady went away leaving me in highly passionate state. So I went to my place and masturbated to pacify myself.

The young lady was however not to leave me alone. One day she invited me to her residence. At her home there was no one except her old father as her brothers were serving outside Varanasi. She introduced me to her father who was very glad to meet me. She took me to her room and there for the first time she gave me the taste and excitement of sex with a woman. This continued for about a year. After one year she left Varanasi and shifted to Kanpur with her brother and was later on married there.

Now I was always in search of girls to satisfy my sexual urge. I could get some through my friends. Particularly on festival days it was very easy because the village women came from distant places and they would need shelter to stay. I offered my house and other sacred places for their comfort and thus got the young girls away from the others. These innocent village belles liked to be loved by a townsman. I was endowed with good health and also good looks. So I came across not much obstruction in making love to them.

This excessive indulgence of mine affected my health and I fell ill. I remained in bed for about a month. My doctor clearly said that I was indulging in bad habits. So my activities were now watched by my family members. I myself was afraid for my health. So I gradually controlled my urges and gave up sexual adventuring. To divert my interest I joined the Ramsahay Sangeet Mahavidyalaya and started learning *tabala.* Here Ram Babu was my inspiration and after a keen interest and regular practice I learned to play reasonably well. I also learned flute and since then I am associated with some musical societies.

When I was the student of tenth class I was married to a girl of Prayag. She is a fashionable girl. So she inspired me to give up our orthodox way of life. Her influence made me a little modernised; I now wore pants. But when I went in pants for the first time to the *ghat,* I was made the target of severe criticism. However, I did not care for all that. Then I failed in Matric.

Other *ghatias* made fun of me for my being 'fashionable' and also when I could not pass my matriculation examination. Gradually they had to quieten and give me due regard. I do not have to pay rent for the *ghat* and my livelihood does not depend solely upon this *ghat*. I have my own buildings and paddy fields which give me income. If any one comes to my *ghat* I welcome him but do not try to solicit as others do. During the slack hours of the day I keep myself engaged in reading stories and novels at the *takhta*.

During working hours on the *ghat* I see various characters. Generally the ladies are more talkative and misinformed than the males.

To increase my income I have acquired shares in Ganga Silk Factory. These days I devote my maximum attention to that shop and if I am able to run that business properly I shall leave the *ghat*, because the *ghat* business commands no respect. The *Yatris* treat us like their purchased slaves.

Daily I attend the *ghat* at about 6 a.m. and offer *pranam* to mother Ganga. Though I am not interested much in the *ghat* business, even then I am associated with mother Ganga. Though I do not believe in this aspect of *dharma* (*dhonga*) but as I have to be on the *ghat*, I wear a *chandan* print on my forehead, so as to be easily identified as a *ghatia*. It has become a form of identification to show the *yatris* that I am a priest. Any time in between 5 to 10 a.m. I take bath and after 10 a.m. go home for breakfast. Then after my lunch I rest upto about 2 p.m. and then go to Ganga Silk Factory and sit there till 7 p.m. After that I practise music. At night before going to bed I pray to Lord Shiva to pardon me for my sins which I might have committed during the day. Usually like others in my trade I have to conduct rituals without requisite knowledge. I hate this sort of cheating but have to do it just to maintain my family.

Though I believe in the existence of one God and consider Him the Supreme Power but I do not believe in idol worship because I think that idol worship is just a medium to show one's devotion and one can do without it. The *pap* and *punya* are nothing and it is impossible to define the *pap* and *punya* because the concepts of *pap* and *punya* change according to the context. Fishing is *pap* for a Brahmin, but for a *mallaha* it is not *pap* because it is the source of his livelihood. Actually this theme is guided by the traditional thought.

The sacred or profane only signify the feeling of a particular person attached with a particular subject which may also change according to time and space. Snakes are worshipped on the eve of *Nag panchami*; they are secular on other days; but if a snake bites somebody, causing thereby his death, the family of the dead person should consider the *nag* to be profane and try to kill it.

The future of the *ghat* business is dark because the income is by and by declining. Now only the unemployed persons having no knowledge of performance, and having no other alternative employment sit on the *ghat*. The competition is stiff and the greedy attitude of the *ghatias* have made this profession unpopular.

Life-history No. 24

Name :	R.P.
Age :	29
Sex :	Male
Caste :	Joshi Brahmin
Linguistic group :	Banarasi
Primary profession :	*Bhaddar*
Secondary profession :	Betel shop.

I was born in the year 1944 and, being a very weak child, I was nursed with great care. Till the age of 8, I did not attend any school and wasted time in playing. I was admitted to a primary school at the age of 6, but I went there for only a week or so, then I discontinued. The teacher made several complaints but my guardian did not pay any attention.

When I was of 8 years my *phoopha* (uncle) expired and his son Dinesh came to live with us. He was admitted in fifth class in the same school. I liked him and just to be with him I started going to school. Ultimately I took interest in studies and passed my fifth class from that school.

After passing the school examination of fifth class I gave up my education and became interested in my father's profession as it provided good income. By this time Dinesh was the student of class tenth. He tried his best to make me change my mind about taking up the profession of *bhaddar*. But as it was writ in my fate, I entered this profession. Dinesh passed Matriculation and took up a job as a clerk in D.L.W. and I run around in search of pilgrims.

First day I accompanied my uncle, who was a professional *bhaddar*. He took me to Vishwanath Gali. A rickshaw carrying two women and a man was coming. Uncle looked at them and guessed that these passengers were country folk. He approached them to accept our service and they agreed. Uncle instructed me to escort them to Vishwanath temple where I had to assist them in offering flowers. I was then to come back to Dasashwamedh ghat. I did accordingly. While I was returning to Dasashwamedh ghat, my uncle met me on the way and I handed over the charge of the pilgrims to him. He escorted them to different places and I accompanied them. For this I was given Re. 0.50. This was my first professional experience. My feelings at that time were of shame at seeing my uncle running at the command of the pilgrims.

This was repeated several times. I saw and gradually learnt professional tacts and a few sacred *mantras* required for *puja* and offerings, though many of them were just memorised by me without knowing the actual meaning.

There are times when even after a lot of service and spending a lot of time, the clients do not agree to pay the customary amount, rather they start bargaining and at times it even leads to conflict. Once I had a group of five pilgrims from Kanpur. I escorted them to different sacred centres, like Durga temple, Sankatamochan and B.H.U. Vishwanath. They hired a taxi and I was also with them. After I had been with them for about four hours they offered me only one rupee. I requested them to give me at least two rupees. But they were so rough that they refused straightway. When I insisted they said that one rupee has been deducted as the fare of the taxi in which I had a ride with them. We reached Godaulia Chowk where most of *bhaddars* sit. I called them. When they had gathered around me I told them of the unfair payment by the *jajmans*. The *bhaddars* started abusing the pilgrims till the police came and settled the matter by getting me two rupees. This was the bitterest experience of my life. But from that day I avoid asking the help of the *bhaddars* in such an event because they only make the matters more complicated.

Daily I leave bed at about 4.30 a.m. and take bath at the house tap. At about 5.00 or 5.30 I go to either Godaulia Chowk or Vishwanath Gali. Here I offer *pranam* to Lord Vishwanath and pray for a prosperous day. Only after this I take my breakfast. The whole day passes in search of clients and many a time I even miss my lunch or have to take it as late as at about 3 or 4 p.m. Sometimes lunch is provided by the *jajman*. Wherever I go with the *jajman* I perform the *puja* of the deity concerned. It is with two motives. One, it gives me an opportunity to increase my goodwill with the gods, and secondly it impresses the *jajman*. I also tell the mythological background of each temple to the *jajmans*. Ladies, particularly the Rajasthani women are very keen to listen to the mythological tales. At night when I go to the bed I sit on the bed and pray to Lord Shiva at least for five minutes and seek His pardon for the mistakes done by me in the day.

For me all the temples, the *tirthas* as well as Ganga are sacred, because our forefathers have said so and also because they provide us with our livelihood. I think the objects related with any supernatural power or the unknown are sacred. The worldly things that are not associated with any other worldly beliefs are sacred, and the things or activities condemned by the society and social laws are profane.

Bhaddars do not have any specific ceremonial dress or

food. They traditionally wear *dhoti-kurta* and red *angochha* (towel), and go barefoot. They all the time chew the betels.

A *bhaddar's* secular life is not very distinctive. They usually drink *bhang* and even country wine. Few of them are vegetarian but they all are influenced by western civilization. They wear wrist-watches and attend movies. In short we can say that the secular life of a *bhaddar* is not different from that of others.

Life-history No. 25

Name :	N.R.B.
Age :	51
Sex :	Male
Caste :	Maharashttian Brahmin
Profession :	*Karmakandi.*

I was born in the year 1921 in this sacred city of Varanasi. At that time we were living in Ram Ghat Mohalla in a rented building. My family had come to Kashi three generations ago. My great grandfather had come here to learn Sanskrit and settled here. I do not remember my childhood but I remember that my father always insisted that I should attend school. I was very much afraid of school and would often run away from classes. In this I was helped by my mother who was illiterate. When I was of 10 years, one day my father told me to come with him. I followed him to the Golden Vishwanath temple where he performed one *abhisheka*. After the performance he was given some money and a *dhoti* and *chadar*. I was also given a *dhoti* and two rupees. I was very much pleased at that and was interested in this profession which was paid so handsomely. I now lost all my interest in education and was always seeking an opportunity to accompany my father. But my father had different ideas. He had dreams of seeing me educated and learned. Of course he wanted to keep me in his profession but only after I had got proper education.

I was then in the eighth class of Sanskrit and was studying in Sang Veda Vidyalaya. Then my family purchased a house (Agasta Kunda) and that provided me with a chance to escape school. Every-day my father sent me to school but instead I would play on the way and return home in evening. Later I also started stealing money from my mother's box to meet my daily expenses. One day my teacher met my father and told him of my long absence from school. My father was quite surprised. He asked me and learnt that I had been deceiving him. He gave me a heavy beating. I was then of 17 years. My father was very much upset by my conduct. He contacted one of his friends who agreed to teach me and I started going to Chatgaon. It continued for six months till one day my teacher informed us that he did not have time to teach me. Now I told my father that I was interested in learning Sanskrit and was sent to learn *karmakanda*. By that time my father understood well that I was not going to be a learned *karmakandi* so he started taking me along with him on some of his visits. This way I learnt the profession of *karmakanda*.

In the year 1961 once two client groups came from Maharashtra and we had to assist them in *karmakanda (abhisheka)*. One group which reached a day earlier than the other, got my father to perform for it while the other group was entrusted to me. I was very happy to act independently for the first time and conducted the *abhisheka* at Vishwanath temple so carefully that the clients were very much pleased. But when they were to give *dakshina*, my father came and took the amount. The clients praised me before my father but I was unhappy that the total amount earned by me had gone in the hands of my father. After that my father often deputed me with various groups and I also started getting money. By this time I had also become sex conscious and had started looking for contacts with opposite sex. Of course I did get chances with the girls of neighbouring families and so the affair always became known. In 1963 at the age of 23 years I was married. Nothing was new for me except that my wife had started living in my house. In fact I had been having sexual contact with her even before our marriage. Now I was a husband and I felt responsibility of my own family.

One day I had been to Dasashwamedh Sabzi Mandi and there I came to know that one of my client groups was caught by the *bhaddars* and the *bhaddars* were going to conduct *karmakanda*. Immediately I rushed towards Vishwanath temple (golden) and found them going with three *bhaddars*. I checked them and introduced myself as their hereditary *karmakandi*. The *bhaddars* also claimed over them and the dispute took a form of clash and a number of *bhaddars* came on the spot and began to abuse me. I thought it better to escape from them without being beaten. This was nothing new for me, rather it is a common occurrence because *bhaddars* are more in number and are aggressive by nature. I never faced any trouble with *ghatias* because they have fixed the rate according to the rituals of *karmakanda*.

Once I settled with a temple priest of Durga Mandir for the *puja* of a group at Rs. 5 but when he saw 23 persons in the group he refused to abide and asked for 75% of the total *dakshina* although usually his share should not exceed more than 50%. He became very rigid on his point and lastly to keep the prestige of the group I agreed on the point and he started the *puja*. In the mean time I signalled to the chief of the group that they should not give *dakshina*. He instructed all of them accordingly and after the *puja* the total *dakshina* given to the priest was only Rs. 3.88. The same incident was repeated once again. Thereafter the priest made a compromise with me and we established a good professional relationship and never had any conflict.

I have come across a number of different characters in my professional life and all gave me a new experience. The client, if he is rich, always treats his *karmakandi* haughtily. He does not care for the *karmakandi's* difficulties rather wants to get the work done on the sound of the bell, by any means. Once a group from Poona visited Vishwanath temple for *abhisheka* and I was to perform for them. At Vishwanath temple the place where the *abhisheka* was to be done was crowded. So I suggested to them to return from the temple and come after an hour. But he did not agree and directly approached the priest of the temple. He offered him extra money and got them to allow to do the *abhisheka* in the eastern corner. This upset me very much because the eastern corner of the temple was not used for *puja*. Though I conducted the *abhisheka* but could not concentrate on the performance, rather I was thinking that the priests must be laughing at my performance being done in the eastern corner of the temple. God knows how far the Lord Shiva became pleased on my client when I was so disturbed. Of course I would have refused to perform but it was a question of the *dakshina* money which I did not want to lose.

The poor pilgrim always show great enthusiasm and respect for me and the priests. They always try to please the priest so that they can do the *karmakanda* within their (client's) limited resources. For such a client we always have a soft corner because we know that these poor pilgrims come from far off places, managing within their meagre means, not spending much even on themselves, and saving the necessary amount for return fare and other expenses.

I have deep faith in Vishwanath and the Ganga because, whatever be the different opinions, it is clear that it is only lord Vishwanath who is the centre of everything in Kashi. In his name all the business is done and thus He is instrumental in feeding lakhs of persons living in Kashi. Ganga is always associated with Kashi and it is only Kashi where the Ganga flows down from south to north. With the *uttaravahini* Ganga and Lord Vishwanath at one place, this city has become most sacred. I feel proud of living here.

I daily leave the bed at about 5 a.m. and pronounce the name of Lord Vishwanath. After leaving the bed I answer the call of nature and then go to Dasashwamedhghat to take bath. During my bath I utter Ganga *mantra* and perform Ganga *puja*. Taking one *lota* (pot) of *Gangajal* I go to Vishwanath temple and pour the water upon the main Shiva *linga* with a offering of *pranam*. Then I return to my house. This is the only performance I do in the morning. During the whole day my performances depend upon the clients. At night before going to bed I read the *Vedas* for at least one and a half hours and then with the name of Lord Shiva go to sleep.

Life-history No. 26

Name :	R.N.V
Age :	73
Sex :	Male
Caste :	Saraswati Brahmin
Sect :	Shaiva
Profession :	Vedapath (*karmakandi*)

I was born in a Saraswat Brahmin family. My father Pt. Bhabhu Mishra at that time was one of the prominent *karma-kandis* (*Vedapathi*) of Kashi. Because of his scholastic genius he was well known among the Sanskritists all over India.

My mother died when I was only eight months old. Being the eldest issue of my parents I was very much loved by all the family members. In the absence of mother, my grandmother brought me up with great care and love. I became so much attached to her that I began to call her *Amma* (term used for own mother). Two years after the death of my mother my father remarried and my step-mother started taking care of me. At that time I was only three years old and do not now remember much of the period.

At the age of 5 years my *yajnopavit* (sacred thread) ceremony was performed at our residence. My father became the Acharya of *yajnopavit* and my maternal uncle, maternal grandfather and other relatives were invited on this occasion. They brought new clothes, sweets and even ornaments for me. *Shehnai* was played during the ceremony.

As soon as the *yajnopavit* performance was over my father began to teach me to recite the Gayatri *mantra* and *sandhya vandana*.

I was admitted in a primary school at Sati Chautara (Varanasi) under the guidance of Pt. Bageshwari Prasad, a local pundit. He taught me the Hindi letters and *pahara* (tables) only for a year. On the day of my admission I was offered new clothes and Ganesh Puja was performed at my home.

At the age of six I was transfered from Sati Chautara school to Nilakanth Vidyalaya near our house. For three years I studied in this school and learnt simple mathematics as well as to read Hindi fluently. During this period I had three close friends with whom I used to play and read. They were Hari Narayanjee Saraswat, belonging to a Saraswat Brahmin family, Samarti Ramjee belonging to Nagar Brahmin family and Shivaram Pandey, a Saryuparin Brahmin.

Swimming in the Ganges and walking along the riverside were my favourite pastime in my childhood. Sometimes I used to play football in the lane in front of my School. But I never practised any game very seriously owing to my Sanskrit studies at home. When I was off from my school my father used to teach me *Sabha Rupavali* in Sanskrit. I had to daily learn by heart two new stanzas of Sanskrit and narrate these from memory to my father. My father was very strict about this and if I ever failed or forgot in my recitation, he would beat me. My father also taught me sentences from the *Shukla Yajuraveda* and *Rudra Samhita*. Whenever my father had to go away from Kashi, his friend, Pt. Narottamji of Nirmal Mohalla (Kashi) came in his place to teach me the Vedas.

When I attained the age of eight, my grandmother died. My father was away from Kashi on engagement for a *Yajna* in the state of Kota (Rajasthan). I bitterly cried—not due to the death of my grandmother, but on account of the absence of my father at such a time. I felt absolutely helpless. So along with my younger step-brother Govardhan, I went to my *guru* Pt. Narottam to seek his advice. My neighbours advised me to perform the funeral ceremony and I became the chief performer of the *antyeshthi sanskar*. Eight days after her death my father came and then he took up from me.

At the age of nine I was placed under the guardianship of Pt. Ganeshram Bhatt 'Nirmal' and Pt. Atmaram, for training in *karmakanda*. Both the teachers were South Indian Brahmins and they gave me a rigorous training of *karmakanda* for a year.

As I attained the age of 10 I was asked by my father to assist one of his *jajamans* in performing Rudrabhisheka. One night before the performance of Rudrabhisheka I had to wake whole of the night, reciting the sacred *mantras* of the *Vedas* in order to rehearse my performance.

I now started *karmakanda* profession as a part-time occupation because I was a student at that time. After passing the Nilakanth Vidyalaya I got myself admitted in Rambir Sanskrit Mahavidyalaya, Kamachha (Varanasi).

I remember very clearly the first day of my starting the *karmakanda* profession. It was the month of Kartik. There was a businessman (Marwari Vaishya) from Madhya Pradesh who was my *jajaman*. He had to perform the Rudrabhisheka. I along with my father went to the Golden temple of Vishwanath. There were several *karmakandis* of Kashi there. I was a newcomer, so I was asked to recite the last *shlokas* (verses) of the *Rudrastotra* so that I might not commit mistake. I lacked confidence in my capability to declaim the *shlokas* properly. So I became nervous and could not pronounce the assigned *shlokas* very loudly. My father shouted at me when we reached home. It hurt me very much and I made up my mind to do it boldly in the next performance. Since then I have always recited the verses boldly.

I was married at the age of 18 in a Saraswat Brahmin family at Muzaffarpur in Bihar. My wife at that time was only 13 years old. My father-in-law was engaged in *Jajamani* profession at Muzaffarpur. The main hand in negotiating the marriage was an inhabitant of Kashi. I got some dowry but I do not now remember the correct amount. The marriage day was happy one but my heart became heavy when I remembered of my own mother who had left me at the age of eight months only. My marriage was performed strictly following the Vedic customs.

I could not spend a happy married life for a long period for just after three years of my marriage, my wife fell seriously ill. She was pregnant and owing to some complication, she died giving birth to a son. Days became painful for me and I decided not to remarry. But after a year of her death, my father negotiated my marriage with the daughter of a landlord of Gaya district in Bihar. I had refused the proposal but due to the keen desire of my father, I had to agree for the second marriage.

After two years of my second marriage, my wife got a son. My family members and relatives were very happy. In the meantime I also attained proficiency in my profession (*karma-kanda*) and I began my career as an Acharya of *Yajna* and other sacred performances.

Two more sons and three daughters were born from my second wife. At the birth of my last daughter, the second wife also died. I had to perform her *antyeshti sanskar* (death rites) according to the vedic *paddhati* (way) and spent nearly 5,000 rupees in feeding Brahmins and performing other sacred death rites.

Now I was faced with the problem of bringing up my children. My sisters occasionally assisted me in looking after the domestic work. But mostly I had to manage on my own.

Though I felt the need of a wife, but I had six children and so dared not take a third wife for fear of creating more problems. To suppress my sexual urges, I practised yoga and read books on spiritualism. During this period I got the sacred thread ceremony of my sons performed and also started to teach them *karmakanda*. Till then the eldest son was grown up and I got him married in a village of District Lucknow (U.P.). His father-in-law was an agriculturist.

Since my childhood I had no interest in politics. I was more attracted towards our scriptures, because my father inculcated in me a religious outlook by telling me mythological tales.

As regards my profession, I feel that there has not been much change in the sacred performances. Major change has taken place in the behaviour pattern, way of feeling for the religious matter, in dress, etc. The orthodox priestly community still gets respect from the people but the honour and respect given by the Rajas and Maharajas has decreased due to the abolition of princely states. About forty years ago I was invited by the Maharaja of Bikaner, Maharaja of Panna, Maharaja of Chhattarpur, Maharaja of Hathua, Maharaja of Indore, Raja Shakti and others to assist them in performing various sacred performances. From such honourable invitations I got prestige as well as money. And it is due to this fact that I have become one of the prominent *karmakandis* of India.

Even nowadays I have often been invited by the big people like Birla, Tata, Singhaniya, Jalan, Jaipuria and other businessmen of India to assist them in performing various sacred performances.

I was not an active freedom fighter. I know it very clearly that the Britishers did not interfere in our religious matters. Everybody at that time was free to choose his own religion.

The Harijan entry in the Golden temple of Vishwanath did a serious harm to Hinduism and the Hindu culture. About 65% citizens (Hindu) of Kashi in the beginning were against it but it was enforced against their will.

Whenever I go on my *Jajamanika* tour for performing *yajna* and other sacred performances, specially among the business communities (generally the Marwaris) I find that they pay more respect than the others. They gladly provide all the essential ingredients of *puja path.* I have experienced that the Marwaris do everything according to our advice and do not hesitate to provide a costly thing essential for the performance of *yajna,* etc. But other communities always try to explore for a less costly alternative whenever they are asked to present an expensive thing like land, building, etc.

There has been a great change in the management of the Golden temple of Vishwanath. A few years back, the *mahantas* themselves were the chief priests of the temple but now they do not take any interest in *puja path.* They now waste their energies in quarrelling among themselves for the distribution of money offered to Lord Vishwanath.

As regards the conception of 'sacred' and 'profane', I believe that anything so admissible by our Dharma Shastras is 'sacred', and which is not so admissible is 'profane'. For instance, cow's urine according to the Shastras is 'sacred', so I too believe it is 'sacred', but onions or human urine are 'profane' according to the Shastras and I too consider them profane.

'Moksha' is unseen but I believe that our Dharma Shastras have defined this concept. Therefore I must believe in it and should try to attain it to get out of the cycle of births.

I feel that our traditional way of life, codes, customs, rituals, rites, etc., are losing popularity very fast because these days our children are not taught Sanskrit. The western mode of education has certainly brought changes in the whole social structure.

Life-history No. 27

Name :	V.M.
Age :	25
Sex :	Male
Caste :	Mallaha
Linguistic group :	Banarasi.

(The informant is very jolly, and he could be interviewed only in two meetings of three hours each. He was very friendly to us. He freely gave information on all matters).

I was born in the year 1948. The month and date is not recorded, but my mother says that it was in the rainy season. We were then living at Allahabad. My father was a boatman at Allahabad and, as the sacred centre of *triveni sangam* attracted a large pilgrimage, his income was quite good. It is said that at my birth, my father had come to Varanasi and visited the temple of Lord Vishwanath. Because of this fact, I was also named as Vishwanath. In fact similar had been the case with my brother who was named as Kashi. He was a very religious man and had travelled widely to different sacred places.

When I was three years old my father fell ill and remained so far a long time. During his long illness, my mother spent all our savings, but the condition of my father went on slowly deteriorating. After one and half years of illness he was brought to Varanasi, the place of my maternal grandfather. My maternal uncle (M.B.) was a magicman. He supported the family as well as the expense of my ill father. My mother had already sold all her ornaments and we were penniless. My elder brother Kashi, who was a boy of 15 years, was by now a trained boatman. So he started ferrying a boat and began to earn a little.

Within six months of coming to Varanasi, my father expired, leaving behind two sons, two daughters and my mother. Only my brother was the earning member. So my mother and sisters also started working as maidservants with some families. We somehow passed our days.

For about three years we lived with our maternal uncle. Thereafter we took another house in the same mohalla (Manmandir). Another reason for our separation was the marriage of my sister which was settled with the help of maternal uncle. We felt the need of a separate room at least for the married couple as well as for my brother, who was also now marriageable.

At the age of six years I was sent to Primary School, Panchopandava, Meerghat. I was not at all interested in studies. But I was very much afraid of my maternal uncle, so I just continued to attend classes. My lack of interest in studies resulted in my lagging back in all the subjects. I was often beaten for not doing my home task. I started to flee from my classes and used to hang here or there upto 4 p.m. when I returned home as if I were coming directly from school. After my continued absence from the school, my teacher started sending boys to find me and bring back to school. At school I was beaten blue and black. This made me loath the school and I finally gave up my studies just after passing fourth class in 6 years.

I left school at the age of 12 years. During my school days I used to ply the boat along with my elder brother. He trained me in swimming and boating. Now I started working as the helper boatman with my brother. After three months of my professional training, one day I was independently given a boat. I was to carry four persons. They were carrying big cameras and taking photographs of the *ghat*. I rowed them to the other side but coming back I got much tired. Though I was trying to row but it was very hard against the fast current. I called another boatman who was passing nearby. He helped me and brought my boat out of the current. Anyhow I came back to Dasashwamedh ghat and handed over the boat to the master. He gave me three annas. I had not the strength to move even a step. I sat on the bank for half an hour. After I was rested a little I went to home. There I bought *ghee* (butter oil) for two annas and ate it with *dal*. I wanted to spend my first earning on something which gave me energy. The remaining anna I spent the next day. Though I had offered it to my mother but she let me keep it for buying something for me to eat.

When I entered this profession of ferrying a boat I attended to it in morning and evening which are the two service periods for boats. Rest of the day I learnt sewing and stitching from Bhagchu master of Tripura Bhairavi ghat. This side profession helped me to earn a little more for my family. This tailoring job continued for about foui years. But being a boy of 14 or 15 years, I was always interested in festivals. In this tailoring job the pressure of job comes specially during the festive days. This made me dislike the job. So at the age of 16 years, I gave up tailoring and wholly gave myself to the profession of boatman.

One day the General Manager of D.L.W. was enjoing boating. He became very glad of my behaviour and on my request he assured me to give a job in his factory. I met him twice at his residence and finally I was appointed as a Khalasi on a consolidated pay of Rs. 45 per month which was increased up to Rs. 60 p.m. next year. The duty hours were from 6.30 a.m.

to 3 p.m. and rest of the time I engaged myself in boat service as my side business, from which I was now earning from 1½ to 2 rupees which was sufficient for my pocket and other expenses. This continued only for two and half years. The completion of the project and the transfer of the General Manager made me again unemployed and compelled me to solely depend upon my boat. Since then the life has become like a machine.

At the age of 22, I was married to a girl of Ghazipur. She was beautiful but very proud. So there was always trouble between us. She is now with her parents. I had known sex even before marriage. In fact boatmen are generally considered by wealthy women to be sexually strong and satisfying men. For instance, when I was of 18 years, two rich women one day came late in the evening and hired my boat. When I rowed them to far north, they started making obvious sexual overtures. I was aroused and finally I cohabited with both of them for which they gave me ten rupees in addition to the boat fare. Thereafter they became my regular clients for both the purposes.

As we lived on the *ghat*, I frequently saw women showing almost nude in their wet clothes sticking to their bodies. Again in another instance, a fashionable girl of 19 or 20 hired my boat. She was all alone. My experienced eyes told me that she wanted something else than the boating pleasure. I started talking to her on those line and she was at once ready. I cohabited with her in the mid-water of the Ganga. After she had had her satisfaction, she put a five rupee note in my pocket. This is nothing unusual for a boatman, so I do not think much about it.

For me the Ganga is the only sacred place in this world, apparently because the life of the boatman depends upon the mercy of Goddess Ganga. The mind is the controlling station and it decides about sacred or profane. A thing which is against the will is profane. Money is everything for me and I think that all the relations are based on money. Nothing can be done without money. The quality of a sacred performance, for instance, also depends upon the amount you are expending on it. The decoration of a boat attracts passengers, devotees, pilgrims and tourists all alike. And the decoration needs money.

A man having money owns a number of boats and lets them to boatsmen at a royalty of 50% of the income.

Nowadays although my income has increased because people are also interested in boating for fun, the dearness has gone comparatively much higher than that. Then rainy season is the dull season when there is hardly any income. Thus our income is dependent on the vagaries of the skies and is called *akash vritti.* I shall therefore gladly leave it for a regular job of even Rs. 90 or Rs. 100 a month.

A relative of Nepal Maharaj, who lives here at Varanasi, is my best passenger. He is a very good patron of mine; whenever he comes to the *ghat*, he calls me and even waits for me. He also takes with me *bhang-buti* and *thandhai.*

We do not consider ourselves even a bit less than the Brahmin priests. The difference between us is only that they are Brahmins by caste and we are mallaha. We both depend upon the mercy of mother Ganga. They are not entitled for Ganga *puja* because it is only the Mallaha who are entitled to perform *jal-puja*. We are also pujari because we conduct ritual at the other bank of the Ganga. By force the *ghatias* have acquired this profession. On the city side of the river, Brahmins have recently started conducting rituals but on the other side we do the *puja*. Thus we both have got equal status.

The magah starts after the Vyasa temple which is about three miles away from that bank of the Ganga so we conduct *puja* in Kashi.

My day starts at 5.30 a.m. I take a bath in the house and come to *ghat*. Here I first offer my *pranama* to goddess Kali then to Shitala and Ganga. Then I take a glass of tea and a betel. Then whenever a farer is available I touch the boat and offer *pranam* to the boat. Again here I pray to mother Ganga for security and prosperity.

A dead body is always lodged in a boat from its aft side and after the body is taken away, the boat is washed by *Gangajal*. This practice is not observed if the boat is to carry the ashes for immersion. On the eve of *Dhamterash*, we offer flowers, garland to our boats, light *agarbatti* in it and worship it and distribute sweets. No other priestly assistance is needed on that occasion and we conduct the *puja* solely ourselves.

Appendix VI

SACRED MYTHS RELATED TO VARIOUS TIRTHAS AT KASHI

SACRED MYTHS RELATED TO GOLDEN VISHWANATH TEMPLE

There are two myths related to the Mahatmya of the Vishwanath temple in connection with the destruction of the temple by the Muslims.

It is said that when Aurangzeb came to ransack and loot the Vishwanath temple of Kashi, the Lord could not be touched by the Muslims and jumped into the Gyanvapi well. Because of that the Sacred well of Gyanvapi is still worshipped.

According to another belief it is said that Aurangzeb became blind after destroying the temple of Vishwanath. Then he sent a messenger to call the priest of that temple. The priest came and Aurangzeb expressed regret to him and promised to return the articles of Vishwanath temple. Only then he regained his eye-sight.

There is an oral myth that the iron chain attached to the door of the temple is so powerful that all the diseases of the body are cured if they are touched by the chain. It is told that a person in Kashi was suffering from fever and on the day of Shivaratri he reached the temple although the members of his family forbade him to go out in his sick condition, but he disobeyed them. After reaching Vishwanath temple he heard a forecast that he would be cured if he touched the chain of the door with his body. He did accordingly and was at once cured. Since then has started the practice of touching the iron chain by all devotees coming to the temple, particularly sick ones.

It is true that violation of the sanctity of the temple has

caused misery to many offenders and there are a large number of myths regarding it. It is said that once by mistake a local devotee, who was in her period, entered the precincts of Vishwanath temple. She became seriously ill as soon as she reached home.

AGASTESHWAR TEMPLE

The shrine of Agasteshwar was originally made as believed by the people, by Agastya muni who used to do *tapa* here. It is believed that eating of offered *belapatra* cures diseases and fulfils the cherished desire.

ANNAPURNA TEMPLE

(*i*) Sacred oral myth known among the Sanskrit knowing Brahmins :

Initially the name of Annapurna was Parvati, the daughter of Himalaya. Himalaya had several other daughters also but Parvati was the most beautiful and gentle among all. She was married to Lord Shiva, and was living in her parents' house. But other sisters were married in wealthy families and they were living in their husbands' houses. So whenever the sisters met together they felt envious of Parvati and Shiva. Regarding Shiva they would say, "Shiva is poor, and has nothing to wear. So he wears the skin of a tiger. He has a *basaha* (bull) to ride. He has neither house to live nor wealth." They also passed remarks about Parvati.

Parvati could not bear their taunting comments and she told her parents, "Now I cannot live here." On this her parents advised her not to leave the parents' house, as Shiva had no house to live and nothing to spend. But Parvati did not agree to live there.

She requested Lord Shiva to leave that place and finally both left for Ka ilash in the Himalayas.

Lord Shiva ordered Vishwakarma to construct a city. He constructed Kashi on Lord Shiva's *trisul* (trident).

As soon as Parvati reached near Kashi with Shiva, she was amazed to see this Kashi, made of gold. She asked Shiva, "If you could build so wealthy a city, your house must be full of riches. Why did you not bring me here earlier?" Shiva told to Parvati that they did not need it previously, but they could now live there. "You will be Devi of grain here", Lord Shiva said to Parvati, "You will distribute grain to the inhabitants of Kashi. In your kindness none will be hungry here. You will feed every person of Kashi and I will give *moksha* to those who die here." From that very day Parvati was known as Annapurna and she and Lord Shiva reside there in Kashi. Even Lord Shiva has to beg in his Khappar for grain from Annapurna.

(*ii*) Myth known among Brahmins not knowing Sanskrit (men/women/old-young)

No one knows about the origin of the temple, except a few old women who used to keep the Annapurna Vrata. Such old women are also seen visiting and worshipping Annapurna frequently. They know the origin of the shrine (Ref. *Bhavishyotan Puran*).

The young and old Brahmins do not know about the origin of the shrine. They simply know the Mahatamya of the temple as for example (*i*) Annapurna is the giver of food, (*ii*) Shiva used to do *tandawa* dance before Annapurna, (*iii*) Shiva begs alms of grain from Annapurna.

SHITALA TEMPLE

In the temple there are three main deities, (*i*) Shitala, (*ii*) Dasashwamedheshwar, and (*iii*) Dashareshwar along with other deities. Different myths are known related to different deities.

Shitala is said to be a manifestation of Parvati; she is the deity of curing disease like pox.

Regarding Dasashwamedheshwar, it is said that when Brahma was doing his Dasashwamedha yajna here, He enshrined this Shiva *linga*, which began to be known as Dasashwamedheshwar.

No myth related to Dashareshwar could be told by any informant. This Shiva *linga* is not so popular by its name.

KASHI KARWAT (BHIMESHWAR)

The Shiva *linga* Bhimeshwar is manifestation of Jyotirlingam.

This Shiva *linga* is said to be *Putrada Mahadeva* (the diety which bestows offspring). From ancient time, devotees (both pilgrim and local) used to come here to be blessed with child by hearing *katha* (story) of Ganesh Khanda and Raghuvansha.

GYANVAPI KOOP

(*i*) Gyanvapi Koop is older than the Ganga. Long ago when Shiva came in Kashi, it was full of forest. There was no source of drinking water. Hence Shiva dug this *koop* with His trident.

(*ii*) When Gyanvapi Vishwanath Temple (presently Gyanvapi Mosque) was attacked by Aurangzeb, Lord Vishwanath jumped into the Gyanvapi Koop.

(*iii*) Sometimes it is narrated that the priest of the said temple, along with the *linga* jumped in the *koop* when Aurangzeb attacked the place.

BARE-GANESH TEMPLE

Kashi was previously full of jungles. Later on Shiva and other Devatas arrived in Kashi. But the period of their arrival in Kashi is not known. So anything definite regarding the origin of the shrine can not be said. However it is most ancient.

(*i*) Sankatha Mai is manifestation of Durga.

(*ii*) She fulfils *Manauti* of her devotees.

PISACHMOCHAN KUNDA

There was a Muni named Balmiki. He was doing *tapa* near the Kapardishwar-Shiva *linga*. One day a *pishach* (evil spirit) came to him and requested help for being granted *moksha*. The muni gave him sacred *bhasma* to paste over the body and advised to take bath in the Vimalodak Kunda (previous name of Pishach Mochan Kunda). The *Pishach* did accordingly. He was freed from *Pishach Yoni*. He then became a smart Brahmin and went to the *swarga* (heaven). Since that very day the Kunda has been named as Pishach Mochan Kunda.

KEDAR TEMPLE

I. At Kashi, Raja Mandhata was doing *tapa*. He daily used to go for *darsan* of Kedarnath at Himalaya. And after doing *darsan* he gave half of his *khichari* meal to any *atithi* (visitor). Only after that he ate the remaining portion.

One day he prepared his *khichari* and waited for an *atithi* for several hours but none came. At last he decided to go on fast because he did not like to break his rule of sharing his bread. Then came a person. Mandhata divided his *khichari* into two equal halves and offered his guest one half. But he saw that his own *khichari* was still as much as before. Raja wondered and looked towards the visitor, who now revealed himself as Lord Shiva. Shiva told him, "Now I will live here in the form of Shiva *linga.*" Since that day the Shiva *linga* is worshipped here.

II. The idol of Gauri, at Gauri Kunda in the precincts of Kedar-ghat is said to have been installed in the *treta yuga.* It is believed that in *treta-yuga* when Gauri left Himalaya she came here and did *tapa.*

SANKATAMOCHAN

I. The great sage Tulsi Das prepared the Sankatamochan Hanuman, with cow-dung, and enshrined it.

II. Tulsi Das used to go for the call of nature everyday with a pot full of water and when he returned, he threw the left over water in his pot under a certain *pipal* tree.

On that *Pipal* tree there lived a *pishach.* The *pishach* was very pleased with Tulsi Das for watering his tree every day and offered to grant him *Vardan* (boon). Tulsi Das requested him for his help in getting *darsan* of Ram. The *pishach* advised Tulsi Das to approach Hanuman who used to come as an old Brahmin, suffering from leprosy, to hear Satyanarayan Katha at Karnaghanta.

Tulsi Das began to approach the same Brahmin daily, at the end of the *katha.* One day at Sankatamochan Tulsi Das caught the leg of the old Brahmin and requested him to show his real manifestation as Hanuman. At first the Brahmin tried to avoid him with the saying "I am not Hanuman but a poor Brahmin suffering from leprosy." But Tulsi Das did not leave his leg and continued his entreaties. At last the Brahmin turned into Hanuman and told him to enshrine his idol there.

Since that day Tulsi Das began to worship him at that very place (Sankatmochan).

DURGA TEMPLE

After the self-immolation of Sati in the Yajna performed by her father, Shiva came and took away her dead body. In great grief He began to wander like a mad person round the earth. Seeing that all the *Devatas* became anxious that if Shiva went on like that, the universe will not continue. So to make Shiva get over his grief, His *moha-maya*, Brahma created an insect *deemak* and left it to destroy the dead body of Sati. It began to destroy it organ by organ and as Shiva was wandering hither and thither different organs of the dead body fell at different places which were since then accordingly named. The name of some important places, where the organs of Sati fell, are given below:

Place	*Organ*
Kamakhya	Sex Organ
Calcutta	Mouth
Kashi Durga Temple	Right thigh (*jangha*)

All these places became *Siddhapitha* (for detail, see *Kamakhya dham*, a book in Hindi, where list of 51 *tirthas* has been given).

2a (13) No myth.

2a (14) As the name Chatpati Devi, she fulfills *manauti* (boon asked for) immediately.

2a (15) No myth.

2a (16) No myth.

THE SACRED MYTH RELATED TO SHMASHAN

I. Sacred myth about *shmashan* as the giver of mystic 'power' held by ascetics/tantrics/*Karan Pishachis*/*mahapatra*, etc.

(a) The *shmashan* is a giver of mystic 'powers' where many *aughars* like Keena Ram, Vijoy Ram, Bhagvan Ram, etc. have acquired spiritual and mystic powers. Thus it is called the 'Siddhpitha' as well as the Shaivapitha and the Shaktapitha. The characteristic of this *shmashan* is that the *samadhi* is achieved easily. Once it happened that Swami Ramkrishna with his disciple Mathur passed by boat through Manikarnika. He said that one could easily achieve *samadhi* there. He saw with his insight that Lord Shankar (Mahakala) recites tarak *mantra* in the case of the dead and that was why the dead got *moksha* after being cremated there. The *aughar* (R.N.S.) said that the *shmashan* is the *abadikhana* and this external world is the Barbadikhana. By Barbadikhana he meant this world where men are engaged in fulfilling worldly desires, struggling, deceiving, *plundering* and so on. They suffer from worries, diseases, temptation. Actually they are being destroyed. They are not engaged in searching the ultimate reality. The *shmashan* is the Abadikhana which provides the true picture of life and where the souls are sleeping peacefully.

The *aghoris* want to keep aloof from worldly desires and the *shmashan* is the place where they cannot think of it as well as feel the reality and truth of life. This *shmashan* provides mystic 'knowledge'. For example, whenever you come with a dead body to cremate, you feel yourself *shunya* (vacuumized) i.e. every worldly thing seems useless and meaningless to you. Thus to retain this feeling of meaninglessness of the world the *aghoris* come to *shmashan* for acquiring *siddhi.*

The *aughar* (R.N.S.) said that ghosts live in the *shmashan.* Those souls which do not get *gati* (movement to the other world) continue to hang about in the aery-world for getting a proper place and they disturb the human beings. These ghosts are formless and are regarded as *upadevatas.* The Lord of those ghosts is Bhootnath who resides on the *shmashanghat.*

The *aughar* (R.N.S.) cited the examples of those *aughars* who have acquired mystic powers at Manikarnika and Harishchandra. Those are Kharab Das and Keena Ram.

Kharab Das

Kharab Das Lala was a *siddh purush* (man of mystic powers) of Varanasi. He used to meditate in water where he had built a stand of wood for the purpose. Once a British man came and asked him to come out of the water. But instead of coming out he abused him. The secretary of the man understood his abuses and jailed the *aughar.*

In the jail, the prisoners had to grind a *chakki* (hand mill). Kharab Das asked the prisoners not to do so. The prisoners stopped: the wheels of the *chakkis* now started moving on their own. This miraculous news reached the jailor's ears and also that of the Secretary. Coming to Kharab Das, both of them bowed before him and expressed regret. The *samadhi* (monument) of Kharab Das is at Ramnagar near Bare Vyas.

Keena Ram

Baba Keena Ram was a famous *aughar* of Varanasi. He

was a Ramabhakt. For 20 years he served but he could not find him. Once he thought of taking wine. As soon as he raised his arm to drink, the Lord held his hand. Keena Ram said to the Lord, "I can't leave it now as it has brought me in contact with you and thus this wine is my Guru."

Phakkar Baba

Aughar Phakkar Baba dictated as follows: Soon after this earth was created, Lord Shankar and goddess Parvati built here a house of mud. Both of them wanted to perform a *yajna*. A Brahmin was called. As his fee, for helping to complete the *yajna*, the Brahmin demanded the Lord's house. Having gifted the house after the yajna was over, Shankar and Parvati went away. On their way, Shankar saw a dead man on a stretcher carried by four persons. They were saying "*Ram nam satya hai*" (the name of the Lord is the only truth). When Shankar heard "*Ram nam satya hai*", he followed the truth, i.e. the death. The dead was brought to the cremation ground and was cremated. When the cremation was over, the relatives of the dead man left the place. At this Lord Shankar observed 'How foolish are they that they have left behind the truth' i.e. ashes of the dead. So He began to smear His body with the ashes of the dead, saying, "*Chita bhasma-snasam Om namah shivay.*"

Therefore, for the *aughar shmashan* is the place where the truth is present. He also accepted that he had seen Masan Baba. He is very dreadful and has a terrible figure. An ordinary man cannot stay before Him. He has also seen ghosts having large teeth at Manikarnika. For him *shmashan* is a place where he can get *siddhi*.

Tantrics

Not even a single tantric has been interviewed. The *aughar* (R.N.S.) informed that the tantrics have no special use for the *shmashan* because they belong to the *Vampanthi* group of saints and sects.

Karan Pishachi

No such person who belongs to this group has been found by the interviewer.

Ghatia

Actually the mystic power of *shmashan* cannot be perceived and acquired by a man who is not a *siddh* person. It is beyond our reach. The *shamshan* has mystic power that is why it has become the *siddha pitha* of *aughar*, tantric and *ojha*. All of them have acquired mystic powers on the cremation *ghat* through proper penance. The examples may be cited as below.

(a) Near Saraswati Phatak, there lived an *aughar* (follower of *aghori* cult). He brought one measured *Dharan* from the jungle. When he began to attach it, the height of the *Dharan* was short. The *aughar* was surprised and kicked the *Dharan*, at once it became of original height. Even these days every one goes to visit that *Dharan*.

(b) One who is cremated here, i.e. on the *shmashan* of Kashi, gets Moksha. By *moksha* is meant 'getting the release' from rebirth.

(c) There is a miraculous story of Keena Ram, a *siddh purush* of Varanasi. Once he saw a dead body flowing. He called on the dead and lo! the dead became alive and came to him.

(d) This is a story of Lota Baba, who was also a *siddh purush*. Once Lota Baba organized a *bhandara*. All saints were invited. Keena Ram also came and wanted to enter but the darban, who knew Keena Ram as a meat-eater *aughar* did not allow him to attend the *bhandara*. Varieties of things had been cooked. When the eatables were served, it was found that all cereals had turned into meat and the water, into wine.

Lota Baba was surprised to see that and came to know that Keena Ram was not allowed to attend the *bhandara* and he is thus angry. Lota Baba went to meet Keena Ram who was sitting at a short distance at Hartirtha and invited him. It is said that as Keena Ram sat in the *bhandara*, the meat again turned into cereals and wine became pure water.

The *gaddi* of Keena Ram is at Bhadaiyani, at Kabir Chawra and of Lota Baba at Hartirath.

Boatman

(a) V. said that the ashes from *shmashan* have mystic 'power'. If the ashes of a *teli* caste are sprinkled over a person slept at night after uttering *mantras*, he will not wake up till the spell-caster has completed his work, such as 'theft'. Thus the ashes from *shmashan* are considered a spell by thiefs.

(b) L.M. said that the ashes from *shmashan* has a mystic power to cure such diseases as stomach pain, blood vomitting, etc. This is done by an *ojha* who recites *mantras* and offers ashes to the victim or patient.

Mahapatra

No myth regarding the mystic power about the *mahapatra* has been reported.

Dom

(a) The Doms believe that the *shmashan* has such a mystic power that if, after reciting three times the *mantra* "*Om namah Shivay*", you keep the ashes from Manikarnika *shmashan* into your treasure, the articles in your treasure will fast increase.

(b) If you smear your forehead with the ashes from *shmashan*, your face will become brighter.

Karmakandi

The *shmashan* is the giver of mystic power and it can be proved by citing the example of Baba Keena Ram who was an *aughar* of Varanasi. It is said that a person went to meet Tulsi Das and expressed desire for a son. Tulsi Das said that he will ask God. God told Tulsi Das that the person cannot be blessed with a son.

The disappointed man then went to Keena Ram (near Lolarak Kund) and started serving him. After some time Keena Ram asked him why he was there. The man begged for a son. At this Keena Ram beat him four times with a stick. The person was blessed with four sons from his wife.

When Tulsi Das learnt of it he was surprised and asked God. God said that Keena Ram has given four sons due to *punya* acquired by him at the *shmashan ghat*.

THE SACRED MYTH

2. The performers believe that after performing the *antyeshthi kriya* at the Manikarnika and Harishchandra, the

performers get the *punya* of sending their ancestors to the Vaikunth or Shankardham.

3. (a) It is said that the fire-giver who is always with a Lota and a Bamboo fitted with a nail in his hand is relieved by the *mahapatra* from *chootka* (pollution) when he performs the *shraddh* on the tenth day of the death. That is why the *mahapatra* is given gifts.

(b) It is believed that making of gifts to the *mahapatra* leads the dead to rebirth.

(c) It is believed that the gifts made to the *mahapatra* are received by the dead who are in heaven. Thus, the *mahapatra* is the medium through whom the dead receives.

THE SACRED MYTH

4. (a) The *mahapatra* claims that if the *mahapatra* is not given gifts, the performer cannot be cleansed of impurity. Therefore, his (*mahapatra's*) help is compulsory on the tenth day of the death. That day his *dan* cannot be shared by other Brahmins. Thus they are called the *mahabrahmin*. If he is not gifted, the dead cannot attain *moksha*, nor peace in the heaven, and also the dead cannot receive the gifts made to them. The dead cannot get *uddhar* (uplifted).

(b) (*i*) The persons come from outside U.P. to cremate the dead at Manikarnika for the 'upliftment' (*uddhar*) of the dead with the help of the choudhrys in lieu of gifts.

(*ii*) We are bound to take the tax from the persons who use to cremate the dead here. Even Harishchandra who was bought by Kallu Dom and who was serving under him had to collect the tax from his wife Shaivya. It is said that when Shaivya came to cremate his son Rohitashva, Raja Harishchandra did not allow her to cremate him. At last she had to pay tax by tearing a part of her saree. Since then we also take clothes and ornaments in the form of tax.

(*iii*) Only Doms can give fire to the person who has come for cremation. Any person who comes with a dead body, has to give tax to the Dom Raja. If he will not give the dead person will not get proper cremation and consequently will not attain *moksha*.

THE SACRED MYTH

5. (a) The *shmashan* is pure. It is the *tirtha* which existed even prior to descent of the river Ganges. The place from Manikarnika to Scindia is pure.

(b) *Non-Brahmins:* (*i*) All *shmashans* are impure except the *shmashana* of Kashi which is very pure because Lord Shankar lives here. The dead body becomes sacred at the Manikarnika ghat.

(*ii*) The *shmashan* is an impure place because any one cannot take bath in the area of *shmashan.*

(c) The *shmashan* of Manikarnika is supposed to be pure and sacred because it falls between the *tirthas* like Dasashwamedh and Manikarnika. Thus it is also a *tirtha.* Kashi is sacred and thus its *shmashan* is also sacred because Lord Shankar is the owner of this place and resides there.

THE SACRED MYTH

6. Both the boatman and rickshaw-puller ply their vehicles carrying the dead. They hold that if their vessel or vehicles were not washed in the water of the Ganges, other passengers will not sit in it, because carrying dead bodies is regarded as inauspicious.

SACRED MYTH RELATED TO GANGA

MYTHS RELATED TO PANCHATIRTHA GHATS

Panchatirtha ghats are those five *ghats* which have been given more importance than the other ghats of Varanasi. These *ghats* are Assi, Dasashwamedha, Manikarnika, Panchaganga and Varuna. The first two are the protectors. After the names of Assi and Varuna the nomenclature of Varanasi has been given. Assi ghat or Assi *sangam* is termed because here river Assi meets Ganga and forms a junction. Same is the case with Varuna ghat; it is also known as Varuna *sangam* where river varuna meets Ganga and they form a junction. Thus these two *ghats* do not have any myth related to them. Rest three *ghats* of the Panchatirtha have some association with their origin and nomenclature.

It is a popular myth among the specialists of *ghats* and the persons of Kashi that in the *Satya yuga* when Raja Sagar started his Ashwamedh yajna, he had performed his

Dasashwamedh yajna at this place. Before arrival of Ganga this place was known as Dasashwamedh tirth and now the ghat has been termed as Dasashwamedh ghat.

The third *ghat*, Manikarnika has an interesting myth. It is said that once upon a time both Lord Shiva and Parvati were going in the sky over this place. They saw a tank on the earth. The water of this tank was quite fresh and clear and the pool appeared beautiful to Parvati. She expressed desire to take bath in this tank. Lord Shiva and she came down and she took bath in this tank. But while taking bath she lost her ear-ring (*kundal*) in the water and could not find it. She told Shiva but after several attempts Lord Shiva also failed to find it. Finally Shiva became angry but at that time Lord Vishnu appeared and said that this is earth and every bather has to pay something as *dakshina*. So your *kundal* (ear-ring) has gone as *dakshina*. They were satisfied and left the place. As the *kundal* (ear-ring) was bedecked with a *mani* (diamond), the *kunda* has come to be known as Manikarnika, which means the diamond ear. When Ganga descended upon the earth, it attached to this *kunda*, known as Manikarnika ghat.

The fourth *ghat* Panchaganga has one myth related to it. Regarding Panchaganga it is said that this is the place where five underground rivers meet. These five rivers are Ganga, Yamuna, Saraswati, Karuna and Dhootpara. All these five rivers are called Ganga here so this is the junction of five Ganges constituting the term *Panchaganga*. Two peripheral springs Kạrza and Dhootpara, are also said to be there.

Thus out of five, the above mentioned three *ghats* have got some deep-rooted mythological association.

Appendix VII

CHRONOLOGY OF MAJOR EVENTS AT KASHI

With a view to provide a glimpse of the various cultural phases and the historical events which the city of Kashi has passed through, we record here briefly some of the important events in chronological order :

Ancient period : 1000 B.C.

Suparasanath, the seventh Jain Tirthankar, was born in Kashi.

8th century B.C. : Paraswanath, the 23rd Jain Tirthankar was born in Kashi.

6th century B.C. : The first preaching of the Buddha of Sarnath.

7th to 1st century B.C. : Annexation of Kashi to Kosala, Magadha and Kausambi.

240 B.C. : Emperor Asoka visited Kashi.

4th century A.D. : Gupta rule.

490 A.D. : Building of the Vishwanath temple, perhaps, for the first time.

5th century A.D. : Fa-Hien visited Kashi.

6th century A.D. : The Beersaivism was established and the foundation of the Jungambari Matha.

7th century A.D. : Huien-Tsang, a famous Chinese traveller, visited Kashi.

8th century A.D. : Sankaracharya stayed in Kashi and composed his celebrated commentary on the Brahmasutra; perhaps visited the city twice.

8th century A.D. : The rule o˜ the palas.

9th century A.D. : The rule of the Pratiharas.

10th century A.D. : The rule of the Chedis.

MEDIAEVAL PERIOD : 1000 A.D. TO 1750 A.D.

1013 A.D. : Ahmad Nialtgin plundered the city and demolished Hindu temples.

12th century A.D. : The rule of the Gahadwal.

12th century A.D. : Ramanujacharya visited Kashi.

1194 A.D. : Qutb-Uddin-Aibak demolished the Vishwanath temple.

1294 A.D. : Sant Jnaneshwar visited Kashi.

13th century A.D. : Ala-Uddin demolished one thousand Hindu temples.

13th-14th century A.D. : Turko-Afgan domination.

14th-15th century A.D. : Ramanand settled in Kashi, founded a sub-sect in Vaishnavism.

15th century A.D. : Raidas became the disciple of Ramananda.

1469-1539 A.D. : Guru Nanak visited the city and had Sastrartha with the Pundits of Kashi.

1494 A.D. : Sikandar Lodi demolished one thousand temples.

15th century A.D. : Sharque's rule.

1478-1530 A.D. : Vallabhacharya settled here in the later part of his life, and died in Kashi.

1485-1533 A.D. : Chaitanyadeva lived here for many years.

1532-1623 A.D. : Tulsidas composed the famous *Ramacharitmanas* between 1574-84, and died here in 1623 A.D.

1567 A.D. : Akbar defeated Jaichanda, the King of Kashi, and established a mint.

1575 A.D. : Restoration of the Vishwanath temple by Todarmal.

1600 A.D. : Construction of Man-Mandir ghat and nearby one thousand temples by Raja Man Singh of Ajmer.

1628 A.D. : Renovation of Gyanvapi by Baija Bai, the Queen of Gwalior.

17th century A.D. : Shahjahan demolished 76 Hindu temples.

1655-56 A.D. : Dara Shikoha translated *Upanishads* in Persian with the help of 150 pundits of Kashi.

1664 A.D. : Battle of Gyanvapi between the Dasnami Naga Sannyasi and the army of Aurangzeb.

1666 A.D. : Shivaji found a refuge with the Brahmins of Kashi on his flight from the imperial court of Aurangzeb.

1697 A.D. : Raja Jai Singh Swai of Jaipur built an observatory.

17th century A.D. : Shri Guru Tegh Bahadur visited Kashi.

1722 A.D. : The rule of the Nawab of Oudh.

1725 A.D. : The establishment of Kashi Raj.

MODERN PERIOD : 1750-1947

1752 : The Ramanagar fort was constructed.

1757 : The control of the East India Company.

1773 : Warren Hastings visited Kashi.

1777 : Ahilyabai, the queen of Indore, constructed the Vishwanath temple.

1791 : The Manikarnika ghat was constructed.

1794 : The Municipal Board was formed.

1810 : Protest against the ghor-chari tax.

1817 : Maharaja Jainarayan Ghosal opened the first English School.

1839 : The Vishwanath temple was gilded by Maharaja Ranjit Singh of Punjab.

1845 : Marwari Hindu Hospital was established.

1851 : *Kali andhi* or Black Storm.

1852 : Gorashahi movement.

1852 : Demolition of barah phatak (twelve gates) in Madanpura.

1855 : Wajid Ali Shah visited Kashi.

1857 : Mutiny.

1860 : Fire in Purani Chawk.

1862 : Rail link between Moghulsarai and Varanasi.

1866 : Organization of the Mahapalika.

1868 : Shri Ramakrishna Paramhansa visited Kashi.

1869 : Swami Dayanand visited Kashi.

1866-1885 : Bhartendu Harishchandra lived in Kashi.

1887 : Opening of rail-cum-road bridge on the Ganges (Duffrin Bridge), which is now known as Malaviya Bridge.

1888 : Establishment of the Church Missionary Society.

1893 : Nagari Pracharini Sabha was founded.

1897 : The Hindu College was founded by Mrs. Annie Besant.

1902 : The Bharat Dharma Maha Mandal was established by Swami Gyanananda.

1909 : Banaras Hindu Society was founded.

1917 : Mahatma Gandhi's first political speech in the B.H.U.
1918 : First aeroplane was seen.
1920 : The Kashi Vidyapith was founded by Mahatma Gandhi.
1928 : Electrification.
1934 : Earthquake on 15th January at 2.30 P.M.
1937 : Bharat Mata Mandir was opened by Mahatma Gandhi.
1941 : The Dharma Sangh was established by Swami Karpatrijee.
1947 : Independence.

It becomes obvious after going through these historical events arranged in a chronological order, that Kashi truly represents the important landmarks is the social and cultural history of India. It is to be noted here that although Kashi has been the prime-mover of social revolution as well as cultural reform movements, from the time of the Buddha to Ramanand and Kabir, it has not minimized the orthodox Brahminism at any time in its history and this trend still continues to a great extent.

INDEX

APPROXIMATE HEIGHT OF TEMPLES

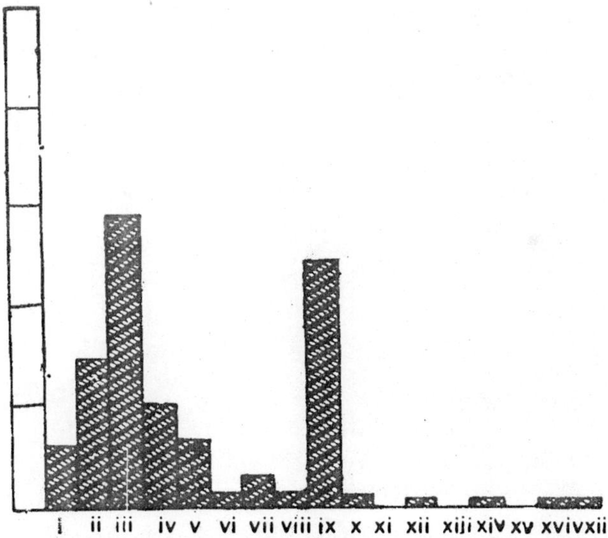

INDEX

i	1 Ft. TO 5 Ft. 5.8%
ii	6 Ft. TO 10 Ft. 15.4%
iii	11 Ft. TO 15 Ft. 29.4%
iv	16 Ft. TO 20 Ft. 9.5%
v	21 Ft. TO 25 Ft. 4.8%
vi	26 Ft. TO 30 Ft. 1.6%
vii	31 Ft. TO 35 Ft. 2.4%
viii	36 Ft. TO 40 Ft. 1.6%
ix	41 Ft. TO 45 Ft. 2.6%
x	46 Ft. TO 50 Ft. 1.3%
xi	51 Ft. TO 55 Ft. 0%
xii	56 Ft TO 60 Ft. 0.2%
xiii	61 Ft. TO 65 Ft. 0%
xiv	66 Ft. TO 70 Ft. 0.2%
xv	71 Ft. TO 75 Ft. 0%
xvi	76 Ft. TO 80 Ft. 0.2%
xvii	81 Ft. TO 85 Ft. 0.2%

THE COMPOSITION OF THE PILGRIM'S PARTY

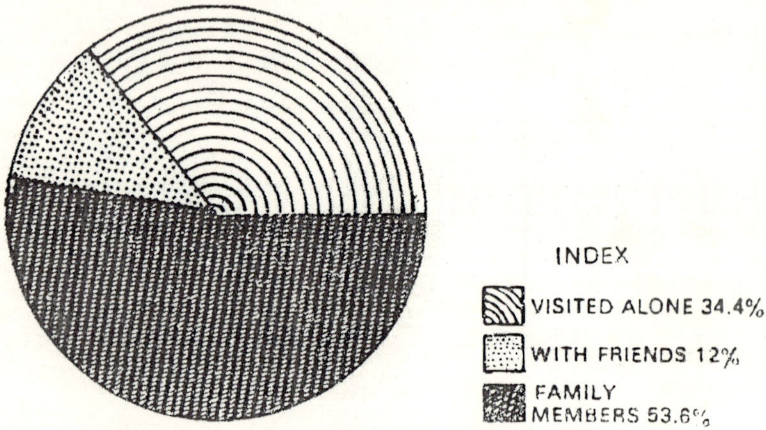

VARNA-COMPOSITION OF PILGRIMS

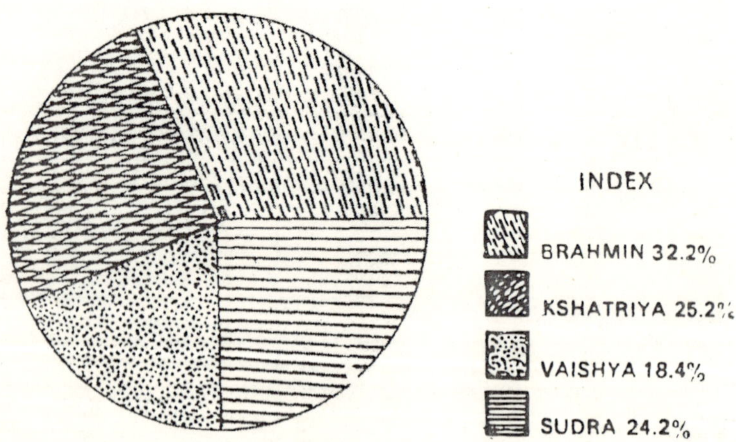

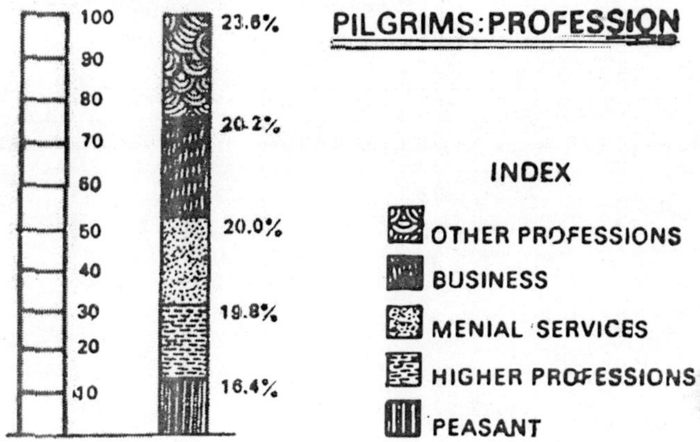
PILGRIMS:PROFESSION
100
90
80
70
60
50
40
30
20
10
23.6%
20.2%
20.0%
19.8%
16.4%
INDEX
OTHER PROFESSIONS
BUSINESS
MENIAL SERVICES
HIGHER PROFESSIONS
PEASANT

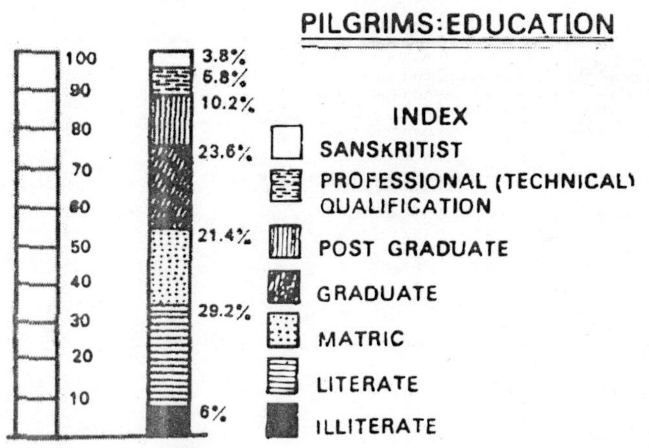
PILGRIMS:EDUCATION
100
90
80
70
60
50
40
30
20
10
3.8%
6.8%
10.2%
23.6%
21.4%
29.2%
6%
INDEX
SANSKRITIST
PROFESSIONAL (TECHNICAL)
QUALIFICATION
POST GRADUATE
GRADUATE
MATRIC
LITERATE
ILLITERATE

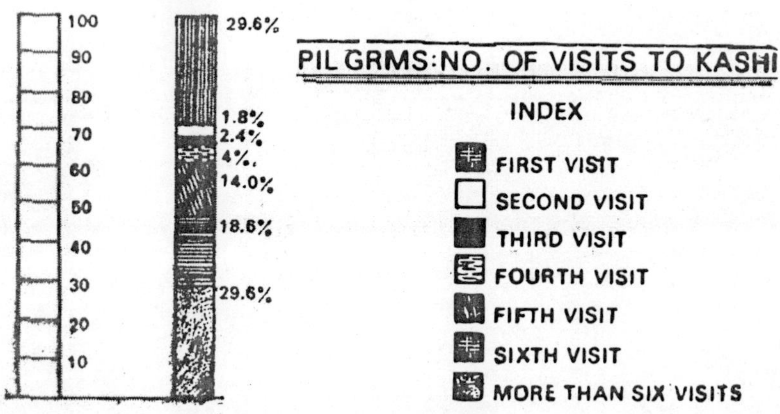
PILGRMS:NO. OF VISITS TO KASHI
100
90
80
70
60
50
40
30
20
10
29.6%
1.8%
2.4%
4%.
14.0%
18.6%
29.6%
INDEX
FIRST VISIT
SECOND VISIT
THIRD VISIT
FOURTH VISIT
FIFTH VISIT
SIXTH VISIT
MORE THAN SIX VISITS